MENTAL HEALTH AND LAW:
A SYSTEM IN TRANSITION

MENTAL HEALTH AND LAW: A SYSTEM IN TRANSITION

by
Alan A. Stone, M.D.
Professor of Law and Psychiatry
Harvard University

With the assistance of
Clifford D. Stromberg, J.D.

JASON ARONSON, INC.
New York, N.Y.

ISBN: 0-87668-288-3

Library of Congress
Catalog Number: 76-51937

Manufactured in the United States of America

CONTENTS

iv

ILLUSTRATIONS

TABLE

Foreword

Psychiatry and the law has come out of the academic closet and into the public limelight. The legal issues, no longer narrow and limited, are broad and expanding so that they now touch every aspect of mental health practice. Standard treatment activities of the past decade have created a variety of legal liabilities and still more lie ahead. Every mental health professional, if for no other reason than self-interest, must begin to understand the basic legal issues and their relevance to practice. However, most of the considerable literature either has been produced by lawyers and addressed to law students and lawyers or else takes a polemical stand against the mental health professions. Such titles as "Prisoners of Psychiatry" by Ennis (1) and "The Right to Be Different" by Kittrie (2) exemplify this bias and the tendentious tone in which it is expressed. This book in contrast is written by a psychiatrist who has attempted to find his way through the labyrinth of law and leave a trail that can be followed by other nonlawyers. Readers wary of pseudolawyers can take some assurance from the fact that several of my colleagues, professors at Harvard Law School, have read the manuscript and found no serious lapses in its explication of the law.

Some readers may still find aspects of the legal discussion alien and arcane, and they may also note that it has not always been possible for me to avoid raising my own voice in polemic. I can only say that the issues are both complex and challenging, and I have tried as best I can to present these issues in understandable language and to present the conflicting currents of the law and the provision of mental health care as I see them.

As one surveys the recent mental health litigation, one discovers a variety of interests at work. The reform-oriented litigating attorneys and legislators for their part see mental health law as the last frontier of the great civil rights struggle. The mental health professions suddenly find their authority challenged, their efforts to treat resisted, their control over difficult patients vitiated, the basic moral character of their professional endeavor cast into doubt— all this in the name of civil rights. Psychiatrists have been the particular target of litigation for a variety of reasons, and they have had to cope with this legal onslaught at the same time that their traditional leadership of the mental health professions has been challenged by psychologists, social workers, and other professions and paraprofessions engaged in mental health care. At times these status and dominance squabbles have spilled over into mental health litigation, and in the name of patients' rights, the various mental health professions have taken sides to advance their own self-interests rather than the patients'. The nonmedical mental health professions have championed legal restraints on somatic therapies without adequate consideration of their therapeutic value, the resulting management problems, or safety of other patients (3). Obviously somatic therapies can be abused, but without them the mental hospital will once again become a Bedlam. Psychiatrists, on the other hand, have pushed for total control of institutional treatment with no real consideration of the limitations both in numbers and, in some cases, the quality of available psychiatrists (4).

Ironically, some of this effort to advance self-interest has been counterproductive to those self-interests. The constraints on somatic treatment supported by psychologists has included strict limitations on behavior modification, which is a major treatment modality favored by many psychologists (5). The psychiatrists, by insisting that they alone are in charge, have made themselves inviting targets as they have been forced to defend institutional practices that are indefensible (6). Thus they are consistently in opposition to the patient advocates, and they have damaged their own public image in the legal forum. The legal advocates, for their part, have contributed to a process of precipitous deinstitutionalization in which their supposed clients have been set free in a hostile environment with rights, but without the necessary support systems to make those rights meaningful. Lawyers who have had the professional satisfaction of winning landmark decisions have also had the profound frustration of trying to implement those decisions in the face of resistant legislatures and passive bureaucracies (7).

A good way to give some sense of the conflicting currents in mental health law is to describe a case pending before the Supreme Court of the United States. The case, *Bartley v. Kremens (8)*, is a class action brought by a public interest lawyer. The class action as the court puts it, is on behalf of all "persons eighteen years or under who have been, are, or may be voluntarily admitted to mental health facilities in Pennsylvania (9). Since there were existing regulations that allowed children aged thirteen and older to contest such admissions (10), the narrower issue the court might appropriately have confronted was whether children twelve or under could be voluntarily admitted to a mental health facility by a decision of their parents and an admitting doctor.

The court concluded that all such parental decisions were not to be trusted because, as they put it in legal terms, there is a conflict of interest between parents and child whenever a child, no matter how young, is placed in any public or private mental health facility.

One example of conflict of interest cited by the court will provide some sense of how far the court went in defining this notion of conflict of interests. The institutions for the mentally retarded in Pennsylvania as in other states have what most mental health professionals consider an enlightened program that allows the parents of a retarded child to place the child in a retardation facility for two week periods so that the family can have an occasional opportunity to be free of the enormous burden of care. This is as far as you can get from dumping a child, but the court cites this as a paradigm of conflict of interest and parental abuse:

> Patient #13212, an educable, mongoloid boy with the capacity to participate in many educable [sic] and trainable [sic] activities, and who can be helped by an active special elementary program in public schools, was institutionalized for a one to two week period so that the other members of his family could go on a family vacation *(11)*.

The court's analysis of why the admitting doctor's decision to admit a child is not to be trusted is equally significant and says something about the current credibility of the mental health professions in the courtroom. The court cites at length an article by D. L. Rosenhan called, "On Being Sane in Insane Places" *(12)*. Rosenhan's article is filled with methodological error and in my view proves nothing *(13)*. The article was summarized by the court as follows:

> The article describes an experiment in which eight sane persons gained admission to twelve different hospitals and behaved normally. Their sanity was never discovered. Rosenhan suggests that the initial labelings color others' perception of the patient and eventually the patient himself accepts the diagnosis, with all its connotations and expectations and behaves accordingly *(14)*.

Even someone who has grown hardened to quotation out of context would find it incredible that nowhere does this court indicate how these "eight sane persons gained admission" to the hospitals. Nowhere do they describe that Rosenhan had his eight sane subjects practice the following deception. Quoting from Rosenhan:

> After calling the hospital for an appointment, the pseudopatient arrived at the Admissions Office complaining that he had been hearing voices. Asked what the voices said, he replied that they were often unclear, but as far as he could tell they said empty, hollow, and thud (15).

Rosenhan, of course, never tells the readers of his article that auditory hallucinations are among the most commonly experienced symptoms of serious mental illness and would therefore be a red flag to any experienced mental health practitioner. Rosenhan's pseudopatient in fact sought admission to mental hospitals while pretending to be suffering from auditory hallucinations. These facts the court simply ignores or, worse, conceals. Readers of the opinion learn only that eight sane persons gained admission to twelve different hospitals. Thus, clinical decision-making is egregiously maligned, and the court places a biased finger on the scales of justice.

Having thus defined the factual context of the legal situation to be corrected, the court offers the following remedies (16). Every child, including those under twelve, who is admitted to a mental health facility must be assigned his or her own lawyer within twenty-four hours of admission. Within seventy-two hours a hearing must be held to determine whether there is probable cause for believing the child needs institutionalization. The child is to be represented at this hearing by his or her independent attorney, and the child must be present unless his or her presence is waived by child or counsel.

Although the court emphasizes the need for an adversarial hearing, which means there must be lawyers for both sides, it makes no provision or requirement that the hospital, the doctors, the state, or the parents have a lawyer to present the other side of the case. This is typical of decisions in the mental health field all over the United States. The courts insist that lawyers be provided only for the "alleged" patient, where in fact no legal representation is ordinarily available to the other side. The remedy fashioned by the court in *Bartley v. Kremens* typifies the current state of mental health law in other respects as well.

The court failed to specify exactly what the duties of the lawyer on behalf of the child would be. But they cited with approval a case that demands that the lawyer not substitute his judgment for his client's, not be a substitute parent, but rather make a good faith effort to protect the "alleged" patient's liberty *(17)*.

Further, the court ordered that if the child were to remain in the mental health facility after the probable cause hearing; that is, beyond seventy-two hours, every single child must be provided within two weeks of initial admission a full evidentiary hearing; in fact, a trial with the one exception that there will be no jury. At this trial the child and his lawyer have a right to confront witnesses, presumably the doctor and parents, to cross-examine them, and to offer witnesses of their own. This right to offer witnesses of their own, if it is to be meaningful, may very well mean that the state will not only have to provide the child a lawyer, but also his or her own psychiatrist to give independent testimony *(18)*.

The cost of these procedures involving the time of lawyers, judges, and expert witnesses is staggering. The Chief Justice of the Supreme Court of Pennsylvania, sensitive to the existing backlog of cases and the purely legal burden of implementing this decree, took the extraordinary step of sending every member of the Supreme Court of the United States a telegram requesting a stay of the order, which was subsequently granted.

Now the irony of this procedural reform is that after all of the family tensions and conflicts have been aired, magnified, and hardened in the adversarial exchanges, the court has in law no way of compelling the parents to take their child home with them if the court rules the child cannot be admitted.

The law has always assumed parental desire to keep children. Nowhere in the law is there a principle or a doctrine that allows a court to order a family to provide a home for a child. The court can remove neglected children and they can punish parents for neglect, but they cannot prevent abandonment. Indeed, it has been argued that in America one has a constitutional right to abandon one's children. Abandonment is in fact the most significant issue in this and similar cases in which the lawyers argue about rights and the mental health professionals talk about treatment.

Bartley v. Kremens is one of a series of cases that have arisen in other jurisdictions—e.g., Georgia, Tennessee, Nebraska *(19)*. A careful factual study of the actual children involved would reveal that a significant percentage, indeed, in some jurisdictions a large majority, of the children confined in mental health facilities have already been abandoned by their families *(20)*. They are in fact the responsibility of the welfare department. It is the welfare department that functions as their legal guardian and it is the welfare department that as legal guardian has "voluntarily" admitted the children to mental health facilities. The first real issue, then, is that the American welfare system is unable to provide adequate services to unwanted children. Overwhelmed by its many burdens, it tries to dump the problem children in mental health facilities. But the question arises: Will something better happen to these problem children after decisions like *Bartley* bar their admission to such facilities?

A second real problem is that the quality of care, treatment, and habilitation in children's facilities is in many instances grossly substandard. The Supreme Court in the famous Gault case *(21)* ten years ago reviewed the conditions under which juvenile delinquents were confined by the courts. They concluded that rehabilitation was not being implemented, that juveniles were if anything socialized into more criminal behavior, and that the conditions of confinement were often an abomination. As a remedy they provided juveniles with more procedural safeguards, thus making it somewhat harder to confine children. That logic is comparable to the public health department determining that a restaurant is serving contaminated food, and then instead of ordering that the sanitation be corrected, the public health department were to bar one of the two entrances to the restaurant.

Bartley v. Kremens follows the same pattern as the Supreme Court in *Gault*. It is one more example of the legal panacea of due process. During the past five years, courts have been doling out due process safeguards in the mental health area almost as rapidly as the medical profession has been doling out tranquillizers, and the reasons are not too different.

The due process remedy allows the court to avoid the real problems of substandard institutions and inadequate services just as the tranquillizer remedy allows the physician to avoid dealing with the real problems of the patient. The due process remedy is presumed to be legally safe and acceptable in the same sense that the tranquillizer remedy is presumed to be medically safe and acceptable. The due process remedy allows the court to maintain a pure legal model derived from the criminal law, just as the tranquillizer remedy allows the physician to maintain his medical model of treatment.

Some reform oriented lawyers have recognized that these procedural due process legal solutions do not solve the real problems of the mentally disabled, and their response has been to bring right to treatment suits that force the judges to confront the real problems of conditions, services, and quality of care in mental health facilities *(22)*. But there are many problems that have arisen out of right to treatment suits which I will catalogue here briefly.

First, conservative judges are reluctant to involve themselves in right to treatment suits. They believe that that kind of responsibility lies with the executive and legislative branches of government *(23)*. When courts impose due process safeguards, the expenses involved are all court related and relatively minor as compared to costs when courts impose right to treatment standards that mean massive improvement of facilities, better staff-patient ratios, etc. When Judge Frank Johnson in Alabama did set such requirements, Governor George Wallace objected, arguing that the cost of implementation would mean doubling the state budget exclusive of welfare. Governor Wallace argued that it was up to the state legislature to establish such massive fiscal priorities and not the federal judiciary *(24)*.

Second, once judges do get involved in ordering the state to improve conditions and treatment, they find themselves involved in the long, drawn-out process of implementing changes. Judge Johnson in Alabama now has for four years been the de facto Commissioner of Mental Health for Alabama *(25)*.

Third, once the judge sets staff-patient ratios there is a tendency, and this has been true all over the country, for the mental health system to try to meet the ratios by massive deinstitutionalization. Thus the census of Alabama hospitals has been halved, and it is clear that many of the discharged patients have simply been abandoned to the community *(26)*.

Fourth, when right to treatment suits are brought in one area— e.g., against mental retardation facilities in New York—the state, already facing severe fiscal constraints, simply did away with rehabilitative programs for alcoholics and diverted the funds to mental retardation *(27)*.

Finally, once the federal court has its nose in the tent, the legal red tape multiplies and the responsible mental health professionals find that their autonomy is constrained not only by the judge's decree, but also by a new legal bureaucracy organized to interpret and implement the decree. This has contributed to an ever increasing turnover rate in mental health professionals working in the public sector.

The new mental health litigation has become a kind of brinksmanship. All of the parties to the litigation realize that existing facilities and personnel are inadequate to the need. The states keep hoping the federal government will bail them out through new programs and augmented funding. Given their own limited resources, the states have often resisted litigation that attempts to improve the quality of care at state expense *(28)*.

Ironically, the federal government has pushed this reform litigation through the Justice Department, although at the same time funds and programs to improve the quality of institutions and care are cut back by HEW, OMB, and impoundment of funds *(29)*.

The federal judges must realize that if they push states into insolvency, their own political credibility will begin to falter. And if a court order produces no result, the judges must either begin to hold state officials in contempt or see their own authority vitiated. Some of the most important major mental health litigation has traveled this road *(30)*. Federal courts have issued right to treatment decrees that have gone unimplemented, or only partially implemented, for years. Thus even the judges who have acted with righteous and rightful indignation against execrable conditions in mental health facilities have sacrificed their own credibility as one deadline after another has passed in a trail of broken promises.

Incredible as it may seem, the states have even ignored and resisted the first major Supreme Court decision in the mental health area. Thus, almost five years ago, the Supreme Court held that many of the states' procedures for dealing with mentally incompetent criminal defendants were unconstitutional *(31)*. Yet across the country there are states in which little or nothing has been done to comply with the order of the highest court in the land.

Ideology and Mental Health Law

I believe there are two separable ideologies inspiring reform in mental health law. First, a civil-libertarian approach that insists that due process safeguards must protect the individual, even the mentally disabled individual, from government intervention *(32)*. Such an approach, when it is translated into law, will to some extent place impediments in the way of mental health care. A second ideology, which is often fused with the first or lurks behind it, holds that mental health care is itself a form of government intrusion. There are a variety of different dogmas that lead to this second ideology. First there are those whose religious ideals and practices relegate to religion the field of mental health care—e.g., the Church of Scientology. Second, there are those like Szasz who hold that mental illness has no ontological significance *(33)*, that labels are applied to disfavored groups by the majority as a form of scapegoating. Since the labeling creates the illness, the treatment must obviously be suspect. Third, there is a group for whom Ivan Illich *(34)* is the spokesman, whose ontological dubiety is even more extreme. Thus, where Szasz argues that mental illness does not exist and physical illness does, Illich has doubts about both, and claims that the vast majority of medical treatment is counterproductive. Fourth, there is a group for whom Laing is spokesman that considers mental illness an acceptable and perhaps useful alternative experience of and reaction to reality (35). Traditional mental health care is seen as the imposition of one view of reality on another equally acceptable view. Finally, there are those like Rosenhan (36) who are not obviously ideological but who claim to demonstrate that the level of incompetence in the mental health profession and the inadequacies are so great that the entire enterprise should be disavowed.

These various ideologies, and there are others as well, have figured prominently in the recent developments in mental health law. Federal courts that have struck down state civil commitment statutes have relied on Szasz's and Rosenhan's accounts of psychiatry (37). Scientologists have apparently lobbied to produce state legislation that regulates somatic therapies. Many of the litigating attorneys and legislative reformers have been influenced by Szasz and some by Laing. The vast majority of law review articles and notes look to these ideologies as justification for resolving every conflict between legal safeguards and the need for treatment in favor of more legal safeguards (38).

It is my personal view that the ideological and philosophical arguments that reduce all mental disability to an arbitrarily imposed social or medical label has been a useful propaedeutic. The mental health professions needed to be sensitized to their tendency to transform every departure from the majoritarian norm of thought and behavior into symptoms to be treated rather than differences to be accepted and even respected. However, this useful propaedeutic has become another reductionism no different in this respect than the biological, psychoanalytic, or behaviorist reductionisms that have from time to time dominated behavioral science. Each of these perspectives provides a limiting conceptual model for understanding the person. Each is a distortion, and when applied alone is a *reductio ad absurdum*.

I do not mean to suggest that all legal reform is motivated by these two ideologies. There is another human dimension that has influenced the courts, particularly in the right to treatment litigation. When judges, often for the first time in their lives, visit the back wards of our state institutions they are overwhelmed by the horrors of institutional existence. They come away convinced that something must be done and surely they are morally correct. The question then becomes: what can the law do that will not be counterproductive once it recognizes the woeful inadequacies in the institutions and services provided to the mentally disabled.

In the chapters that follow, I have attempted to present the major areas of law and psychiatry in which new and important legal developments have occurred. My goal has been to reconcile the objectives of law and the objectives of providing mental health care to those in need. I have tried to offer approaches that would reconcile rights and needs. At the same time I have tried to lay out the basic legal concepts that will be relevant to the mental health professions in the decade ahead. My own ideology, to the extent it is articulated, will be found in each of the chapters, but particularly in the Introduction.

References

1. B. Ennis, *Prisoners of Psychiatry* (New York: Harcourt Brace Jovanovich, 1972).
2. N. Kittrie, *The Right to Be Different* (Baltimore: Johns Hopkins University Press, 1971).
3. Motion of Amicus Curiae for the reconsideration of Standard 9 of the court's order of February 28, 1975, filed March 13, 1975, *Wyatt v. Hardin*, Civil Action No. 3195-N, order, judgment and decree set forth July 1, 1975 (M.D. Ala.).
4. Brief of Amicus Curiae North Texas Chapter of the Texas District Branch of the American Psychiatric Association, *Jenkins v. Cowley*, CA No. CA 3-74-394-C (U.S.D.C., N.D. Texas, Dallas Division), Filed Dec. 10, 1974.
5. *Wyatt v. Hardin, supra,* note 3.
6. *Dixon v. Weinberger,* 405 F. Supp. 974 (D.D.C. Dec. 23, 1975).
7. Lottman, Enforcement of judicial decrees: Now comes the hard part, 1 *Mental Disability Law Reporter* 69 (July-August 1976).
8. *Bartley v. Kremens,* 402 F. Supp. 1039 (E.D. Pa. 1975), prob. juris. noted No. 75-1064, 44 U.S.L.W. 3531 (March 22, 1976).
9. *Id.,* at 1041.
10. *States Regulations 3 Penn. Bulletin* 1840 (Sept. 1, 1973), Supplementing Secs. 402 and 403 of the *Penn. Mental Health and Mental Retardation Act of 1966,* paragraphs 5 and 6.
11. *Bartley v. Kremens, supra,* note 10, at 1044.
12. D. Rosenhan, On being sane in insane places. 179 *Science* 250 (1973), reprinted in 13 *Santa Clara Lawyer* 379 (1973).
13. *See generally,* Millon, Reflections on Rosenhan's 'On being sane in insane places,' 84 *J. Abnorm. Psychology* 456-461 (1975); Spitzer, On pseudoscience in science, logic in remission, and psychiatric diagnoses: A critique of Rosenhan's 'On being sane in insane places.' 84 *J. Abnorm. Psychology* 442-456 (1975); and Weiner, 'On being sane in insane places': A process (attributional) analysis and critique. 84 *J. Abnorm. Psychology* 433-441 (1975).
14. *Bartley v. Kremens, supra,* note 10, at 1050, footnote 20.
15. Rosenhan, *supra,* note 12, at 252.
16. *Bartley v. Kremens, supra,* note 10, at 1049-1054.
17. *Lessard v. Schmidt,* 349 F. Supp. 1078 (E.D. Wis. 1972), vacated on procedural grounds 414 U.S. 473 (1974), on remand 379 F. Supp. 1376 (E.D. Wis. 1974), vacated on procedural grounds 421 U.S. 957 (1975), prior judgment reinstated No. 71-C-602 (E.D. Wis. May 28, 1976).
18. *See, e.g., In re Joseph Gannon,* 301 A. 2d 493 (Somerset Co. Ct. 1973); *Anonymous No. 1 v. LaBurt,* 17 N.Y. 2d 738, 278 N.Y.S. 2d 206, 217 N.E. 2d 31 (Ct. App. 1966); *Dixon v. Attorney General of Commonwealth of Pennsylvania,* 325 F. Supp. 966, 974 (M.D. Pa. 1971); *DeMarcos v. Overholser,* 78 U.S. App. D.C. 131, 137 F. 2d 698 (D.C. Cir. 1943); Accord, *Watson v. Cameron,* 114 U.S. App. D.C. 151, 312 F. 2d 878 (D.C. Cir. 1962); and *Cooper v. United States* 119 U.S. App. D.C. 142, 337 F. 2d 538 (D.C. Cir. 1964).
19. *J.L. and J.R. v. Parham,* No. 75-163-MAC. (M.D. Ga., Feb. 26, 1976), stay granted 44 L.W. 3563; *Saville v. Treadway,* 404 F. Supp. 430 (M.D. Tenn. 1974); *Horacek*

v. Exon, CV 72-L-299 (D. Neb. Pending, Order of June 4, 1974); and *Kidd, et al., v. Schmidt, et al.,* No. 74-C-605 (E.D. Wis. Pending, Order of August 15, 1975).

20. Brief of the Amicus Curiae of the American Psychiatric Association in the Supreme Court of the United States, *Bartley v. Kremens, supra,* note 10.
21. *In re Gault,* 387 U.S. 1 (1967).
22. *Wyatt v. Stickney,* 325 F. Supp. 781 (M.D. Ala. 1971), 334 F. Supp. 1341 (M.D. Ala. 1971), enforced by 344 F. Supp. 373, 344 F. Supp. 387, Appeal docketed sub. nom.; *Wyatt v. Aderholt,* No. 72-2634 (5th Cir. filed August 1, 1973); *Dixon v. Weinberger,* op. cit., note 6; and *NYARC v. Rockefeller,* 357 F. Supp. 752 (M.D.N.Y. 1973).
23. *Burnham v. Department of Public Health,* 349 F. Supp. 1335 (N.D. Ga. 1972), appeal docketed, No. 72-3110, 5th Cir., October 4, 1972.
24. Brief of Defendant-Appellant, State of Alabama, *Wyatt v. Aderholt,* No. 72-2364 (U.S.C.A. Fifth Circuit).
25. Note, The Wyatt case: Implementation of a judicial decree ordering institutional change, 84 *Yale Law J.* 1338 (1975).
26. *Id.*
27. A.A. Stone, Overview: The right to treatment—comments on the law and its impact, 132 *Am. Jour. Psychiat.* 11 (1975).
28. *NYARC v. Rockefeller, supra,* note 22; *Wyatt v. Stickney, supra,* note 22.
29. *United States v. Solomon,* No. N-74-181 (D. Md.).
30. *Davis v. Watkins,* 384 F. Supp. 1196 (D.C. Ohio 1974).
31. *Jackson v. Indiana,* 406 U.S. 715 (1972).
32. A. Dershowitz, Psychiatry in the legal process: A knife that cuts both ways, 4 *Trial* (Feb. -Mar. 1968).
33. T. Szasz, *The Myth of Mental Illness* (New York: Dell, 1961).
34. I. Illich, *Medical Nemesis: The Expropriation of Health* (London: Calder & Boyars, 1975).
35. R.D. Laing, *The Politics of Experience* (New York: Valentine Books, 1967).
36. *Rosenhan, supra,* note 12.
37. *Lessard v. Schmidt,* 349 F. Supp. 1078 (E.D. Wis. 1972), vacated on procedural grounds 414 U.S. 473 (1974), on remand 379 F. Supp. 1376 (E.D. Wis. 1974), vacated on procedural grounds 421 U.S. 957 (1975), prior judgment reinstated No. 71-C-602 (E.D. Wis. May 28, 1976); *Bartley v. Kremens,* 402 F. Supp. 1039 (E.D. Pa. 1975), prob. juris. noted No. 75-1064, 44 U.S.L.W. 3531 (March 22, 1976).
38. *See generally,* Symposium: Mental illness, the law and civil liberties, 13 *Santa Clara Lawyer* 367-612 (Spring 1973) and Symposium: Mental disability and the law, 62 *Calif. L. Rev.* 397 (May 1974).

Acknowledgments

This monograph is in part the result of intense and sometimes heated dialogue with my colleague and coteacher at Harvard, Professor Alan M. Dershowitz. That dialogue has for the past seven years been carried on in the law school classroom and thus my thoughts have been exposed to the crucible of the socratic method. As a result, many of my ideas have been influenced by a generation of fractious but thoughtful students, primarily from Harvard Law School, but also from the Medical School, the School of Public Health, the various residency training programs in psychiatry; even an occasional business, divinity, and undergraduate student. During one summer, with support from the Grant Foundation, Professor Dershowitz and I attempted to find a compromise between our view on civil commitment, but failed. Those discussions were particularly helpful, however, in clarifying my own position, which appears in chapter 3.

I have been fortunate to have had several Harvard law students work as my research assistants over the past decade. All of them were capable of hard work. A few had the kind of orderly legal mind that could cut an editorial trail through my prolixity, imposing order on the chaos of what I produced. But only one could also read my mind and supplement my own ideas with his own. That one, Clifford Stromberg, is acknowledged on the title page because this book would never have seen the light in its current form without his creative assistance.

As she has for the past fourteen years with every other piece I have written, Florence Y. Levy saw that this work became a reality by her timely prodding, editing, punctuation, and transcribing.

MENTAL HEALTH AND LAW:
A SYSTEM IN TRANSITION

Chapter 1

Introduction

During the decade of the sixties it became apparent that the legal status of the mentally ill had taken on a new and political dimension. It had been transformed into a civil rights and civil liberties issue of the first order (*1*).

Liberal progressives over the past century had urged that the courts treat the mentally ill as patients rather than criminals. That overriding principle translated into law led to an expansion of medical power over decisionmaking affecting the lives of more and more categories of persons designated mentally ill. A complex system of civil confinement arose which purported to treat the mentally ill and relegated the courts to a supervisory role. Often statutory authority clearly remained in the courts, but under the prevailing ideology the decisions of psychiatrists were decisive and the court's imprimatur was a rubber stamp, abdicating authority.

The flaws in this medically dominated system were largely ignored for several generations. Involuntary confinement in various mental institutions grew to unprecedented proportions. The mentally ill, the aged, the young, the sexually dangerous, and the mentally retarded were literally warehoused in "megainstitutions" where living conditions were, and in many cases still are, execrable. Massive Federal programs aimed at aiding the States to remedy these conditions were conceived, but implementation fell far short of the mark.

Critics began to suggest that the entire mental health enterprise was ideologically corrupt (*2*). Mental illness was a myth, the mental health professions were the new inquisition, and the mentally ill were the scapegoats of society (*3*). Ironically this criticism took hold during a decade when the biological aspects of mental illness were being convincingly demonstrated and when psychotropic drugs were revolutionizing the treatment of the seriously mentally ill. Whatever the value of these developments may prove to be, three things are now obvious:

First, the megainstitutions presided over by the mental health professions are an acknowledged disaster. Second, the panacea of community mental health centers has not yet achieved what zealous proponents had promised. They may never be able to, because

1

community mental health services, as now defined, are an infinitely expansible market. Third, there is growing distrust of the coercive uses of psychiatry in what I shall call the law-mental health system.

Litigation recognizing the unmet needs, attacking the megainstitutions, and raising the ideological questions has begun to mount. Five years into the decade of the seventies there is enough evidence to suggest that the United States is engaged in an all out legal war over the fate of the mentally ill.

That war has changed the basic nature of forensic psychiatry, transforming it from an esoteric specialty into a pragmatic concern for all mental health professionals and the growing number of lawyers practicing in the mental health field. How will this litigation affect the provision of mental health care? How will institutional treatment be changed? What will be the nature of the new relationship between the courts and the decisionmaking process in the mental health care system? What new mental health policies and planning should be initiated to meet the emerging requirements of legal criteria set up in rejection of the medical model? That is the broad range of questions which confront the law-mental health system and which stimulated the work which follows.

The Role of the Judiciary

The future development of laws regulating mental health ultimately rests in the hands of the lawgivers: the judiciary and the legislatures. During the recent past, a judicial trend has begun to emerge which portends the policies and principles which will dominate mental health law in the decade of the seventies. The reformist trend of the courts has an antecedent historic sequence in the area of criminal law. During the last few decades a series of procedural safeguards for criminal defendants has been authored by the highest courts: right to counsel, protection against self-incrimination, etc. (4). Transcending the various narrower legal arguments in each instance is the principle that loss of liberty is the most grievous penalty in a democratic society, and therefore every procedural protection must be given to citizens at risk, even if their economic status (5) requires the State to pay the costs involved.

Once these precedents were established, the courts were asked to examine loss of liberty in other contexts. The most important of these are the many forms of involuntary civil confinement. Although, as we shall see, the statistics are misleading and difficult to interpret, it is safe to conclude that civil confinement during the past two decades may have affected more citizens than did criminal confinement. (This is true only if we include juveniles, the retarded,

2

sexual psychopaths, defective delinquents, incompetents to stand trial, etc.)

Each of the landmark decisions in this new area of judicial scrutiny speaks to the same underlying principle of freedom (6). These decisions are almost unanimous in concluding that loss of freedom in civil commitment is at least as grievous as criminal confinement. Indeed, some tribunals have decided that it is considerably more injurious in its effects. The courts thus increasingly reject the long unexamined proposition that loss of freedom for purposes of treatment, rehabilitation, or custodial care is qualitatively different in law than loss of freedom for purposes of punishment. Whether this conclusion rests on a sudden, increased judicial sensitivity to individual freedom, or to a growing dissatisfaction with psychiatry and a recognition of the inadequacy of institutional treatment remains obscure. But as I shall attempt to demonstrate, consequences of the highest order flow from this distinction. Simply put, the distinction is between those who attack involuntary civil confinement as a dangerous and potentially repressive force in a free society and those who endorse involuntary confinement and proper treatment of the mentally ill as a moral responsibility of the State.

Whatever may be the goals of the litigants and the intentions of the judiciary, the general nature of change has been to impose the procedural safeguards of the criminal law system on the various types of civil confinement. That result may be good law, but whether it is wise social policy remains to be seen. Surely no one familiar with the American criminal justice system would suggest that it deals effectively with either the problem of crime or of correction. There is, therefore, no reason to hope, ab initio, that imposing one terrible system on another will be productive.

There is a critical perspective at the conceptual level to be derived from distinguishing two social functions of the criminal courts. The first is as a forum for establishing moral blameworthiness while respecting individual rights. The second is as the most powerful decisionmaking body in a huge bureaucracy consisting of law enforcement, the courts, and the system of corrections—a bureaucracy charged with controlling crime. It is when the system is examined from this latter perspective that its failures become most obvious; indeed, many believe that as a bureaucracy it is counterproductive.

A recent study of sentencing demonstrated that the law-and-order judge and the reform oriented judge often end up giving the same long sentences, the former to punish and the latter to rehabilitate; but the result for the criminal in both instances is embitterment and recidivism (7).

Perhaps this is too cynical a view, but I have seen no empirical data that refute it and much that confirms it. It is my contention that the revulsion of the criminal justice system for its own ineffectiveness has led mainly to changes in the operation of the moral forum rather than improvements in the overall bureaucracy. It is that pattern of reform which is now being applied to the civil system.

Civil vs. Criminal Confinement

As the aforementioned paragraphs make clear, the judicial trend relies on the precedents of criminal law. And the growing body of legal literature also works toward placing the mental health system in the context of the criminal justice system.

One powerful critique in that tradition is formulated in terms of preventive confinement. An attempt will be made to summarize it here because it presents a useful framework for considering what will be a theme of this monograph; namely, the overlap between civil and criminal confinement. The major advocate of this analysis is Alan M. Dershowitz, Professor of Law at Harvard Law School. What follows, however, is my own summary of his views.

A first premise is that law has always implicitly or explicitly maintained a system of preventive confinement. That is, a system in which confinement or restriction of freedom was based not on past acts proved in a court of law, but on assumptions that the individual was dangerous or in danger. Legal devices range from the posting of peace bonds by persons expected to breach the peace, to discretionary bail, to the confinement of juveniles in need of supervision, to vagrancy arrests assumed to prevent anticipated crimes, to sexual psychopath statutes intended to confine those who are a sexual menace, to all civil commitment based on the likelihood of dangerousness, and finally, to the incarceration of more than 100,000 Japanese at the outset of the Second World War. Predictions influence even those legal judgments which rest on prior acts, e.g., sentencing, parole, and probation decisions; the use of day-to-life sentences just hands over predictive judgments to the correctional system. The unifying variable in all these legal situations is that some measure of freedom is denied to the individual based on a prediction of future events rather than a pure judgment about past acts.

Viewed from this perspective, certain precise questions emerge. If such loss of freedom is to be based on prediction, then how valid

4

are the courts' predictions? How is the seriousness of the danger calculated? How are the various possible dangerous events ranked as to their gravity? How do the courts estimate the likelihood that the dangerous event will actually occur? How lengthy a period of confinement is needed to prevent the predicted danger? The argument proceeds to demonstrate that our standards for proof of guilt for a past act in the traditional criminal court are very high—better that 10 guilty men go free than that one innocent man be confined. If we assert that a standard at least as high be set for prediction in preventive confinement, it is at once obvious that there are very few instances in which specified dangerous human events can be validly and reliably predicted at that level of confidence by judges, mental health experts, or anyone else. (See chapter 2.)

The argument becomes a tour de force when we apply it to civil commitment. First, as we shall see, psychiatrists cannot reliably predict dangerous acts. Second, when the base rates for these dangerous acts are very low, the statistical problems of prediction become intractable. The base rates for suicide, homicide, and serious assault by psychiatric patients are in fact very low, and these are the events that psychiatrists are often asked to predict. The Dershowitz argument then suggests that our system of justice currently not only allows confinement through these various forms of preventive confinement, but also allows the ultimate decision to be made with few of the procedural safeguards available in the ordinary criminal trial. The conclusion based on these premises and this reasoning is that all current forms of preventive confinement are a rank injustice, and noncriminal confinement of the mentally ill is, perhaps, the most unjust.

The logical legal alternative, of course, is a full scale trial prior to civil commitment, with all procedural safeguards—all in order to arrive at a prediction which we know in the vast majority of cases will be neither reliable nor valid. The power of the preventive confinement analysis rests in part on making dangerous events the sole relevant criteria for all forms of involuntary confinement. By implication, it rejects the position that a treatment rationale in civil commitment justifies different procedural safeguards and a different kind of prediction; e.g., treatability or likelihood of decent care. In my opinion, the virtue of the argument is that it makes clear that to the extent civil confinement is no more than an exercise of the police function of the State, it circumvents or lowers the standards and procedures the Constitution and tradition require.

There is little doubt that civil confinement has been used in that way during the past century, in what Dershowitz calls the "civil-criminal labeling game." Changing the labels to civil has permitted more and more decisions to be made on the basis of predictions of dangerousness.

Recent sociological theory supplements the Dershowitz view. Deviance theory, put forward most radically by Becker, states that:

> Deviance is not a quality of the act a person commits, but rather a consequence of the application by others of rules and sanctions to an offender; the deviant is one to whom that label has been successfully applied; deviance is behavior that people so label (8).

Becker's formulation rejects the role of mediating states of the mind, glosses over the distinction between behavioral acts and society's reaction to those acts (i.e., primary vs. secondary deviance) and implies that deviance has no ontological significance. The labels applied to deviant acts are surely ambiguous and interchangeable but they are not totally arbitrary. The following Venn diagram is meant to suggest the nature of the ambiguity in everyday application of three labels: mad, bad, and normal. This model, contrary to Becker, assumes that madness and badness do exist as real entities in all societies, although both shade off along a continuum to normal behavior. There is also between madness and badness a large gray area which, depending on cultural values and administrative practice, might be labeled as criminal or mental. The major legal difficulty, of course, is that in the gray area it may be possible to confine someone simply by changing his label to conform to whichever allows the easier route to confinement. Putting aside the troubling problem of the stigma of labels, the significance of a label in law depends on the loss of rights, particularly freedom, attendant on its application.

Most theorists are less doctrinaire than Becker, but they tend to agree that when society is choosing between labeling deviancy sick or criminal, much depends on social values and perceptions which vary from culture to culture.

One way to examine this general thesis is to look at institutional resources for the mad and the bad. If the pool of deviants is viewed as relatively constant, and the criminal justice system and the mental health system are seen as alternative institutions for dealing with deviants, one can estimate their functional reciprocity. More than 30 years ago, Penrose demonstrated a negative correlation between the proportion of people in a given nation placed in mental hospitals, and the proportion held in prison (9). Other studies are

6

Figure 1.   Labeling of deviant behavior

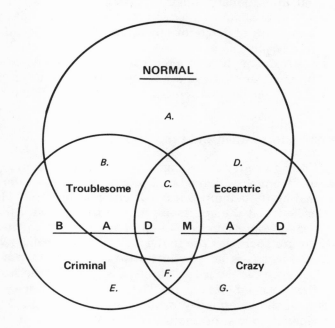

A.   Normal behavior

B.   Normal to bad (e.g., reckless driving)

C.   Normal to bad to mad (e.g., wife beating)

D.   Normal to mad (e.g., alcoholism)

E.   Bad (e.g., premeditated homicide)

F.   Bad to mad (e.g., pedophilia)

G.   Mad (e.g., process schizophrenia)

consistent with the view that these are in large measure alternative methods of dealing with two, if not identical, then largely overlapping groups (10).

Dershowitz's primary emphasis on the reliable prediction of truly dangerous events posits an objective standard which cuts through both sets of culturally defined labels. It would clearly make both routes to confinement more difficult and, if accepted as a sole standard, would make involuntary confinement of the mentally ill a practical impossibility. In the end, the preventive confinement analysis can be seen as an attack on all subjective predictions, indeed, on all discretionary judgments, whether they are made by mental health professionals or judges. At the same time, it assumes an objective standard of dangerous behavior which transcends social definitions of deviance.

The legal reform implicit in preventive confinement focuses on standards for incarceration. Another strain of reform, spurred by the social and behavioral scientists, looks to the rehabilitative process.

Institutional Reform: Civil and Criminal

Many of this country's leading authorities on criminal justice urge diversion from the criminal trial process as the most important step in upgrading the administration of criminal justice (11). They point to the fact that the courts are unable to cope with the huge number of cases coming before them. They emphasize that a jail term early in life socializes the individual into criminality. What is needed, they suggest, is an administrative model which provides a wide range of necessary social and human services for the suspected criminal rather than imprisonment. That reform, or course, has the familiar ring of the community mental health approach. Diversion from the criminal courts, no matter how benign its intent, deprives the alleged criminal of his theoretical day in court with all its procedural safeguards, a day which will now, given the developments I have described, be taken up by the alleged patient.

Thus, reform in criminal law ironically seeks to extricate that system from many of the very legal constraints now being imposed by the courts in the mental health area. In fact, if one puts narrow legal considerations to one side, it is clear that policy reform in both systems points in the same direction. Both sets of reforms were conceived as alternatives to the large "total" institutions which have developed unchecked over two centuries. There has been an accompanying rejection of the ideologies which are seen as having created these institutions; i.e., the medical model of mental health and the retributive model of correction.

Not surprisingly, both branches of reform have developed the following parallel programmatic approaches:

1. Avoid the disastrous desocializing effects of oversized, impersonal institutions.
2. Restrict confinement only to those who are dangerous.
3. Keep the person in his community; preserve freedom by substituting supervision for confinement.
4. Retain family ties.

5. Provide comprehensive social services and abandon the outmoded one-to-one model of care.

6. Define deviance (illness or crime) as a community or social problem.

7. Utilize indigenous personnel.

8. Emphasize prevention or early intervention as opposed to correction or cure.

Both new movements, if they were to reach fruition, would create monster bureaucracies expected to dispense multiple social service benefits. In a very real sense the new goals of both sets of institutions have extended beyond conventional notions of sickness and crime and aim at nothing less than rehabilitating and improving the quality of life for the disadvantaged and troubled American. Thus, both seek to become dominant change agents in the post-industrial welfare state.

The Nader Report (12) which deals with community mental health aspirations in this regard, suggests that if they were effective, they would be ideologically dangerous; but since they are not, the major problem is that they are misusing, or at least wasting, public funds. The nature of the difficulties pointed up in the Nader Report becomes apparent if we look at a still broader perspective—one which gives insight into one aspect of the politicizing of the law-mental health system.

Three Social Institutions

Thus far, emphasis has been given to two major social institutions: the criminal justice system and the mental health system. The reformist thrust of these two institutions suggests an effort to transform their goals such that they overlap with a third major social institution—the welfare system. All three social institutions are committed in principle to "processes and programs that lead toward the entry of or reentry of citizens into the productive sector of society." Romano-V. (13) has examined the extent of this task in the State of California.

On a given day in 1969 there were the following numbers of persons in these three systems in California:

Law enforcement

Adult felons:
Prisons 23,018
Parole 13,027
Probation 101,042
City and county jails 27,918

Youth authority:

Detention	5,908
Parole	14,778
Probation	94,724
Juvenile hall	4,182
Law enforcement, total	284,597

Hospitals

Mentally ill resident and on visit	16,116
Extramural care	5,406
Mentally retarded resident and on visit	12,545
Extramural care	11,591
Hospital, total	45,658

Welfare System

Cash grant	1,540,571
Certified medical assistance	212,593
General home relief	83,012
Welfare, total	1,836,176
Total, all systems	2,166,431

These figures are probably minimal; they certainly underestimate the numbers of persons in outpatient psychiatric programs, drug, and alcohol programs, etc. Yet these minimal figures comprise more than 10 percent of the population of California as of 1969 or 26 percent of the total civilian labor force of the State that year.

It is critical to recognize that the subjects of these three social institutions form a population group which is overrepresented in blacks, Chicanos, and native Americans, although the caretakers are underrepresented in those groups. The emerging self-help organizations within the subject group reflect minority ties, and this heightens the political disjunction between subjects and caretakers. In the current political context, it is easily understood how any professed goal of the caretakers, be it rehabilitation or treatment, might be experienced by the subjects as oppression. Involuntary confinement, which is quantitatively a small part of these systems, has come to be seen as the paradigm of institutional oppression present throughout.

Looking beyond the huge number of subjects, it is important to recognize the overlap and functional interrelationship between the three social institutions delegated to deal with them. The mental health system, as it empties its megainstitutions both because of new law and new administrative policy, creates a burden for the welfare system. This has happened in part because the ambitious programmatic approaches to community mental health have not become a reality. The discharged patients, for many of whom the goal of rehabilitation was an empty promise in the first instance, must now rely on the welfare system in order to survive. This functional relationship between the mental health system and the welfare system is dramatically demonstrated in New York where thousands of ex-mental patients have been discharged to the welfare dole (14). But welfare funds per se are inadequate to meet the special needs of the non-rehabilitated, and welfare services have never fulfilled the hopes of their advocates.

More than a decade ago, President John F. Kennedy spoke as follows about the public welfare approach of the New Frontier, an approach whose ideology is replicated in community mental health and correction.

> This measure embodies a new approach—stressing service in addition to support, rehabilitation instead of relief, and training for useful work instead of prolonged dependency (15).

As one commentator subsequently wrote:

> The jubilation which accompanied the adoption of a service strategy was short-lived. There simply had not been enough thought given to the benefits, costs, and limits to service programs . . . . By 1967 everyone was embarrassed by reference to the promises made in 1962 (16).

The promises, however, are still being made by all but those who advocate "radical nonintervention." Indeed, each of these systems is in the midst of redefining its role to include certain of the historic functions of the other.

Diversion from the criminal justice system relies on the administrative model to dispense various welfare services, e.g., employment counseling, job training, marital counseling, psychiatric assistance, and drug programs.

The welfare services in many jurisdictions include emergency crisis service, premarital counseling, preschool compensatory education, aftercare for patients discharged from mental hospitals, protective services for children, supervision of children who become wards of the court, etc.

The mental health system, under the banner of community mental health and preventive psychiatry, defines itself as serving public welfare goals as well. Indeed, consultation services to community agencies were prescribed by the Federal Government as an essential function of the comprehensive community mental health centers.

What has happened in the last two decades is that in the name of reform, the professionals within each of these social institutions have taken on the roles, functions, and goals of each other. The probation officer becomes a therapist, the welfare worker becomes a therapist, and the therapist becomes an advocate for welfare rights and a consultant to the criminal justice and welfare systems.

All this has happened without adequate planning or coordination and without consideration of the effectiveness of the various professionals in their new roles. The result has been homogenized professionals who no longer have defined expertise and who increasingly impinge on the fourth major social institution: the family. Is it realistic to hope that such a group of caretakers can reshape and improve the lives of their subjects? The tragedy of the current reform movements is that it has been easier to change the procedures and aggressively reduce the population of total institutions in the name of freedom and law than it has been to provide the necessary alternatives.

The Three Social Institutions and the Family

I have indicated some of the functional interrelationships between the welfare, mental health, and legal systems. Each of these systems, in its own way, also can be seen as filling a function in modern society which might once have been attributed to the family. A hypothesis will be offered here to orient the reader to a recurring theme of this monograph; namely, the provision of the State's institutional resources to deal with those who have been extruded or abandoned by the family.

The facilities in which society confines the aged, the mentally retarded, the juvenile offender, and the mentally ill, all can be understood as having assumed, wittingly or unwittingly, the responsibility of providing the kind of personal, human care that historically had been the role and duty of the family. One might immediately disagree by suggesting that the role of these institutions is not to provide that care, but, rather, to supply some more technical service, be it training of the mentally retarded, nursing care of the aged, treatment of the mentally ill, or correction of the juvenile offender. Let me answer that to the extent these more technical services are to be provided in total institutions over long periods of time, such institutions either must also provide human care, or else subject their charges to a depersonalized existence. And even short term intervention involves the State in offering technical solutions to the human problems of the family, e.g., tranquilizers as a way to remedy a domestic quarrel, or a stubborn child complaint to exact filial obedience.

The distinction between technical services and personal human care is most problematic in the mental health area. The fact is that for many of the institutionalized mentally disabled, and even for persons in crisis, enlightened human care is the most effective, or only treatment.

In this regard, a forceful argument can be made that:

1. In fact, only modest amounts of effective technical expertise exist and can be provided in the mental health area.

2. That which does exist has been exaggerated and oversold in American society.

3. The acceptance of this inflated technological posture has led to the development of a huge array of mental health technicians: psychiatrists, psychologists, social workers, correction officers, group workers, occupational therapists, recreational therapists, drug counselors, and others, few of whom in fact have significant technical skills. Rather, much of what they do is the providing of personal care, attempting to engraft a meaningful human relationship on what poses as a technical service.

4. This technical ideology has further encouraged society to define human and social problems which have moral and political dimensions, as technical problems which have scientific dimensions.

5. In this framework the family has been encouraged to evade certtain of its historic human and moral responsibilities by defining them as technical problems which require scientific solutions provided by the State.

6. The result has been the proliferation of State financed institutions, to which the nuclear as well as the extended family can legally relegate individuals who would otherwise and in other times have received their human care or neglect from their families.

In light of this argument, it can be said that a principal social function of the law-mental health system is to provide technical care for those individuals who are temporarily or permanently extruded from society's principal caretaking unit, the family. The wisdom and morality of this extrusion and the quality of this technical care are the bedrock problems of the law-mental health system. This means that in every area of State intervention, some judgment must be made both as to the morality of what is to be done and its therapeutic value. Unfortunately few, indeed, of the State's interventions have therapeutic validity because neither technical nor human care is available.

It is important to recognize that much of this State intervention is not imposed on the subject. The problems of the mentally ill, the infirm, and the disabled are not solely the product of legal compulsion. Rather, they are the product of society's institutional arrangements for the care of those who need it. Where there are no alternatives, the concept of voluntariness is a charade.

During the same period of years when the community mental health approach was devised to cope with the defects of what came to be called "total institutions" for the mentally ill, Congress was in the process of developing a whole new group of smaller sized total institutions designed for the aged. They illustrate the extent and nature of the nonlegal problems.

There is minimal technical expertise involved in the care of the aged other than that applied to their admittedly substantial chronic physical maladies. Nonetheless, there has been a spectacular expansion of total geriatric facilities whose services are paid for out of various federally funded programs such as Medicare and Medicaid. Many of these facilities are inadequate to meet either the human or medical needs of the aged. A self-fulfilling cycle is set in motion. As families increasingly reject the responsibility of keeping the aged at home, this necessitates the development of more and more nursing homes and other total geriatric facilities. The growing social acceptance of such facilities then encourages still more families to abandon the aged. Thus, the care of the aged achieves a new social definition: it is a technical care problem to be handled by specialists and paid for by government, rather than a personal moral obligation to be faced by each family.

The social isolation of the elderly and their removal from meaningful family and social participation are often the tragic result. It is a deprivation of human dignity which no degree of technical care or pseudoscientific rationalization can ever justify. But once such institutions and technological rationalizations exist, the psychological justifications of the family are seemingly intractable. To the extent that families feel guilt about consigning their elderly parents to nursing homes, the guilt is easily transformed into rage against the inadequate technical care. But this is an insoluble complaint because ultimately it is not a question of technical care; it is rather a question whether government, better than the family, can create institutional living arrangements for the elderly which are not an affront to human dignity. To preserve human dignity, a fabric of meaningful human relations must exist. That fabric has not yet been woven out of technical care or the expertise which informs it.

I do not intend to minimize the emotional or economic stresses that the aged or the mentally disabled create for the family. They are obvious and well known to all mental health professionals. Rather, the emphasis here is on the network of technology, social policy, and institutional resources, all of which combine to reduce these stresses by extruding the difficult family member.

14

Mental Health, the Law, and the Constitution

This monograph attempts to examine the important elements of the law-mental health system at a point of accelerating change both in law and in institutional practice. It will, in various contexts, suggest where change "should" take us. "Should" is an unusual—or at least uneasy—word in social and behavioral sciences, but when those disciplines are applied by mental health practitioners under color of law, the moral dimension is inescapable. The reader, therefore, has a right to ask: What are the moral premises which will give meaning to the "shoulds" they will encounter?

There are at least three "shoulds" derivable from the application of law (or the Constitution) to social policy, as in the mental health system:

1. *The Constitution should be seen as defining specific negative rights against government power.* This is familiar; indeed, it is the focus of the Bill of Rights. It is by virtue of this precept of government that, for example, a person subject to the extraordinary civil commitment power of the State has the right to various procedural safeguards required to secure a citizen against arbitrary or unnecessary government deprivation of his freedom. This "should" is deeply rooted in our jurisprudence and is seldom disputed, because in some sense it focuses only on the procedures and not on the more contentious value outcomes of the system.

The second and third "shoulds" are less familiar and more the subject of virulent debate. That is because they do explicitly deal with the policy outcomes of legislation. It is because they recognize and respond to the fact that the law is a political as well as a governmental tool. The law is not neutral—if only because the power to invoke its authority is not equally accessible to all, and because, as pluralist democratic theory has now conceded, the law favors extant or even disappearing groups over those in the process of formation.

Consider the legal rights now vested in labor unions, and those rights labor had 40 years ago. The legal rights were the result of a long history of protest, bloodshed, litigation, legislation, and voting blocs. Such power will never be obtained by the mentally ill for obvious psychological and social reasons. Thus the challenge for government is to recognize their rights and interests as a moral responsibility rather than as an urgent political reality.

The second and third moral-legal imperatives are these:

2. *Beyond negative rights, the Constitution should be seen as establishing a moral residuum for all social policy which assures all*

citizens of the modern State minimum guarantees of a decent standard of life.

3. *The law should be the watchdog of public policy. Given the ramified, dispersed power of the mega-State, the law must assure the coordination of policy systems, and insure that the legislative will is worked in the real world.*

It is worth examining each of these moral-legal propositions in some detail.

The "minimum welfare guarantees" argument is that there is a set of basic human rights which cost money, and that the prosperous American society owes to each individual the satisfaction of them (17). They include decent food, shelter, education, and medical care—or the income necessary to purchase them. This is not really a radical notion. Most of our broad national legislation includes a preamble similar to that of the National Housing Act of 1949, which said:

> The Congress hereby declares the general welfare and security of the Nation ... and the health and living standards of its people require ... the realization as soon as feasible of the goal of a decent home and a suitable living environment for every American family ... (18).

The effort to compile such a list of minimum welfare rights may be seen as a way of asserting some basic human rights in the political context without surrendering to a merely political battle over who gets how much of the social pie. Cynics may doubt that this is possible; the disparity between declaration and funding offers some ground for such sentiment. On the other hand, in "A Theory of Justice" (19), John Rawls argues forcefully that principles of distributive justice (i.e., who ought to get what) really do exist and are held consensually by the American people—if only in abstract and unrecognized form.

Rawls also recognizes that beyond "rights and liberties, opportunities and powers, income and wealth," the ultimate value that a humane society must permit to each individual is "a sense of one's own worth." Mentally ill persons, perhaps above all others, lack this "confidence in their own value and in their ability to do anything worthwhile" (20). And a society can deny people this right only at its own peril, for it is precisely this sense of worthlessness and anomie which contributes to society's ever increasing problems of delinquency, drug dependency, mental illness, and crime. And though perhaps more subtly, it also may be a major demoralizing force upon the productive sector of our society (21).

16

The minimum social rights to which I have referred may be seen as legal rights; there are a number of areas in which the Supreme Court has confirmed the existence of such social minima. It is in this context that much is said in the chapters that follow about, for example, the right of the mentally ill to decent facilities and outpatient services. Thus, the second "should" is the source of rights to rather than merely rights against. But even if one rejects the notion that the Constitution guarantees the right to anything, surely it is true that when the State interferes with the citizen's rights against, it must guarantee the rights to.

The third moral-legal imperative says that law should be seen as guaranteeing to the people of a democratic State a minimum of rationality in governance, a rational relation of means and ends. This notion finds its most obvious referent in the judicial doctrine of equal protection, which provides that when the government confers benefits or imposes burdens based on classsifications of citizens, there must be a rational relation between the classification chosen and a valid (or in some cases compelling) State purpose. There are other legal doctrines as well, such as the rule that Federal agencies must obey their own regulations. And, of course, due process implies regularity of government practice (22).

The people, therefore, have a right to know that government programs operate in a regular, reasonable way, and serve rather than defeat their stated goals. It is against this backdrop that much has been said within recent years about the arbitrary, irrational, and self-defeating policies of the law-mental health system. It has been noted by our most eminent legal scholars that one of the essential meanings of the rule or law as opposed to tyranny is that law should be known (or at least knowable), and reasonably non-contradictory (23). In a law-mental health system particularly laden with Kafkaesque conundrums, this third "should" gives individuals the right to demand that the law say what it means and do what it says. If the State claims to benefit the citizen by interfering with his life, then that benefit must be real.

Tocqueville remarked of the American system of government: "Scarcely any political question arises in the United States that is not resolved, sooner or later, into a judicial question" (24). The same might be said with some justification of moral questions. Were governing merely the political acts of the legislature, there might be little occasion to discuss the divergence of morals, law, and legislation. But the point of the three moral-legal imperatives outlined previously is that they provide a groundwork, a justification for the creative role of the judiciary in public policy.

In light of these principles, it is not usurpation of the legislative role for the courts to declare what rights are possessed by those put at risk by State power. On the contrary, since the Nation's founding, it has been thought the peculiar duty of the judiciary to serve as a counterweight on the swing of popular passion and legislative will (25). I do not deprecate the importance of the legislature; repeatedly throughout the monograph, I suggest that only the wholistic approach of coordinated legislation can truly transform the law-mental health system. But it does seem to me also that it is precisely in times when value systems are in rapid turnover, when rights long denied are being perceived, when scientific expertise and government power are expanding, that the judiciary has a special duty to remind us all of the moral-legal boundaries within which acceptable policy choices may be made.

One of the more subtle and often overlooked problems underlying these policy choices is the distinction between legal rights and social results. This point is crucial because most of the current polemics directed against the law-mental health system assume a constitutional interpretation which defines rights in the context of the criminal law and ignores the effect on the fate of the human beings who exercise them. It is the thesis of this monograph that the shoulds of the law-mental health system must realistically balance rights against social responsibility and human needs.

Justice Harlan stated this thesis in one of those decisions which applied criminal procedural safeguards to civil confinement:

> I very much fear that this Court by imposing these rigid procedural requirements may inadvertently have served to discourage those efforts to find more satisfactory solutions for the problems of juvenile crime, and may thus now hamper enlightened development of the system of juvenile courts. It is appropriate to recall that the Fourteenth Amendment does not compel the law to remain passive in the midst of change; to demand otherwise denies every quality of the law but its age (26).

Justice Harlan was suggesting, I believe, that changes in the way the moral forum of the court reaches its finding are second in importance to improvements in the lot of juvenile delinquents. And they may even be counterproductive. Whether he is correct depends on what the juvenile system in fact has to offer; the position in every section that follows is that just such an estimate has to be made in every instance.

What I shall propose has been called by my students "The Thank You Theory of Paternalistic Intervention." Its basic premise is that in the area of civil confinement the only justification for abrogating procedural safeguards is the provision of benefits which ameliorate human suffering. The details of the "Thank You Theory" and its limitations will be spelled out within the monograph.

In the public sector, the organization and quality of institutions is determined within the strictures of Federal and State legislation. Appropriations and not courts routinely decide the quality of care. Unless the right to treatment becomes both an accepted constitutional maxim and a rallying cry within the mental health professions, the quality of care will only infrequently be seen as violating the Constitution. Many States may decide that in the constellation of needs, the quality of life in facilities for the criminally insane is a low priority budget item. The result may be despicable institutions which socialize offenders to sadistic homosexuality and increased criminality. Conditions in all institutions for the mentally ill may render the distinction between civil and penal confinement itself a mockery. In many States, the "Thank You Theory" will have been made a practical impossibility. This would be, in my judgment, unwise and perilous social policy—but as a practical matter, it may not always be ruled unconstitutional. Our concern for constitutionality should not be permitted to distract us from the far higher standard of legislative wisdom.

Thus, within the law-mental health system there now exists a wide margin between the cutting line of the Constitution and the ability to establish legislative policy. The illumination of this margin and the development of sensible law and effective social policy is the task of the legislature after the smoke of the war of litigation clears away. One piece of congressional legislation seems so critical that it should be placed in this introduction as a theme for all that follows, although it was not intended to solve the problems of the law-mental health system. It provides at least a partial solution to the problem of standards which the commitment to policy reform thrusts upon us.

Professional Standards Review Organization

The standard legal approach to reform of the law-mental health system, as we have seen, is to tighten the substantive standards and legal procedures for entry into the system. The right to treatment of those confined in this more rigid system is considered a separate issue. The view advanced here is that this bifurcated approach is ill advised and counterproductive. Instead, I shall urge that the confinement and treatment decisions be made jointly in a manner that will be elucidated in subsequent chapters. Here I would like to indicate the existing Federal regulations which should and could become the structure bridging the gap between the courts and the bureaucracies they dominate.

During the passage of title XI of the Social Security Act of October 30, 1973, (27), a floor amendment was appended authorizing the Professional Standards Review Organization (PSRO). This legislation had not been the subject of public hearings, and it slipped through with little notice. Many members of the medical establishment subsequently have urged its repeal for a variety of reasons. They see it as an intrusion into their right to practice medicine by their own standards, as an infringement on the confidential physician-patient relationship, and as the creation of yet another expensive and inert bureaucracy which will propagate yet more redtape and lengthy forms which waste precious medical time. Whatever the logic of such complaints may be, they seem to have either no force or less force when applied to the law-related mental disorders.

Briefly, the 1972 amendments to title XI of the Social Security Act provide for the establishment of PSROs "to promote the effective, efficient and economical delivery of health care services of proper quality" under fully or partially federally funded programs. It will be the duty and function of each local PSRO to review the practices of physicians, other health care practitioners, institutional and noninstitutional providers of health care services which may be paid for with Federal funds, in order to determine whether:

(A) such services and items are or were medically necessary;
(B) the quality of such services meets professionally recognized standards of health care; and
(C) in case such services and items are proposed to be provided in a hospital or other health care facility on an inpatient basis, such services and items could . . . be effectively provided on an outpatient basis or more economically in an inpatient health care facility of a different type (28).

The local PSRO is intended to be, with minor qualifications, a nonprofit, voluntary, professional association of licensed physicians, and open to all. Each PSRO will investigate and compile profiles on care provided to various types of patients by each health care practitioner and facility. Moreover, it is authorized to develop "norms of care, diagnosis and treatment based upon typical patterns of care in its region." Should such standards markedly, and upon review, unjustifiably diverge from standards drafted by the National Professional Standards Review Council, such national standards may be required to be met in place of the deficient local standards—though the procedure is meant to be the rare exception.

The most powerful lever of the PSRO program, in terms of its goal of improving the average level and efficiency of care provided, is the provision that if a local PSRO "disapproves" of any health care services or items, and if after notification, hearings and an opportunity for rectifying the deficiency, the provider is found by the Secretary of Health, Education, and Welfare (if review has gone that far) to be at fault, Federal fund reimbursement to such provider may be denied. If there is sufficient cause, the provider may be rendered fully ineligible for Federal health care funds for a specific period or permanently. This enforcement action can be taken either because of a few instances in which the provider has "grossly and flagrantly" violated the accepted professional standards, or because of a general failure to "substantially" comply with such standards.

The law provides for ample opportunity to review and appeal from the local PSRO's decision, as well as precautions for insuring that those involved in the PSRO evaluation have no pecuniary interest in the services investigated or other conflicts of interest.

PSRO has two obvious goals: to insure that Federal funds are not misused and to insure the quality of care. Both goals require the development of standards of care.

The development of such standards for mental health practice is a stroke that cuts the Gordian knot. It fills a void which now exists in every instance of involuntary civil confinement to a hospital or hospital-type facility; it offers the court a tangible standard by which it can evaluate the treatment component of confinement.

It will still be necessary, however, to deal with institutions which, though designated as treatment centers, have never been considered health care facilities. Most important in this regard are the many facilities for juveniles which are called variously training schools, juvenile homes, and so on. As one considers the entire law-mental health system, its most tragic faults are to be found in what it does to the young. Treatment standards, if they do nothing else, will make it clear that our incarcerated children are prisoners.

For the institutions to which it will directly apply, PSRO offers the hope of an end of the pyrrhic battles between legal categories and medical judgment, and a beginning of progress aided by both.

A Reflection in Anticipation of What Follows

Whether or not mental illness exists in an ontological sense, it is clear that mental suffering, however it is labeled, does. The

21

law-mental health system has done less to ameliorate that suffering than it promised, and on occasion it seems to have increased it. Here, as in other areas of major social concern, there is a growing sense of dashed hopes and distrust. The mental health establishment is increasingly the object of that distrust.

If one reflects on why the law-mental health system has come under particular attack of late, the answer which suggests itself is that it is a mirror in which the observer can see the ills of the entire society. There is the pseudotechnical solution of human problems as though that could substitute for personal care and involvement. There is the increasing concern about autonomy and the fear of governmental intrusion symbolized by involuntary civil commitment. There are the growing and unresponsive bureaucracies which seem to defeat their own goals. There is the churning of values which undermines all sense of united enterprise. There is neglect of the young, which diminishes hope, and abandonment of the aged, which erodes integrity. There is the degeneration of law into legalism as rules replace responsibility. And, of course, there is the racism and the uneasiness of the relation between the caretakers and the subjects.

This monograph, then, deals largely with failures, but it does so with the expectation that those failures must be recognized or they will be repeated.

References

1. See *Practicing Law Institute* and *The Mental Health Law Project: Legal Rights of The Mentally Handicapped* (B. Ennis, et al., eds). (New York: Practising Law Institute, 1973); Stone, Psychiatry and the law, 1 *Psychiatric Annals* 19 (1971).

2. See, e.g., T. *Szasz, Law, Liberty, and Psychiatry* (New York: MacMillan Co., 1963).

3. T. Szasz, *The Myth of Mental Illness* (New York: Dell Pub. Co., 1961); *The Manufacture of Madness* (New York: Harper and Row, 1970).

4. See, e.g., *Argersinger* v. *Hamlin*, 407 U.S. 25 (1972) (right to counsel whenever imprisonment is imposed); *Gideon* v. *Wainwright*, 372 U.S. 335 (1963) (right to counsel in felony cases); *Miranda* v. *Arizona*, 384 U.S. 436 (1966) (rights of suspects); *Mapp* v. *Ohio*, 367 U.S. 643 (1961) (rights against unreasonable searches and seizures).

5. See, e.g., *Gideon* v. *Wainwright, supra* note 4.

6. See, e.g., *Lessard* v. *Schmidt*, 349 F.Supp. 1078 (E.D. Wis. 1972).

7. J. Hogarth, *Sentencing As A Human Process* (Toronto: University of Toronto Press, 1971). *See also* Stone, Book Review, 86 Harv. L. Rev. 1352 (1973) (reviewing Hogarth); M. Frankel, *Criminal Sentences: Law Without Order* (New York: Hill and Wang, 1973).

8. Becker, Deviance and the response of others. In: D. R. Cressey and D. A. Ward (eds.), *Delinquency, Crime and Social Process* (New York: Harper and Row, 1969) pp. 585-589.

9. Penrose, Mental disease and crime: Outline of a comparative study of european statistics, 28 *Brit. J. of Med. Psychology* 1 (1939).

10. Biles and Mulligan, Bad or mad—the enduring dilemma, 13 *Brit. J. Crim.* -275 (1973).

11. See, e.g., H. Packer, *The Limits Of The Criminal Sanction* (Stanford, Cal.: Stanford University Press, 1968); Lemert, *Instead of Court* (DHEW pub. No. (HSM) 72-9093 (Rockville, Md.; NIMH, 1972); Symposium; dismantling the criminal law system: Decriminalization and divestment, 19 *Wayne L. Rev.* 253 (1973); Kadish, The crisis of overcriminalization, 374 *Annals* 157 (1967).

12. Center for the Study of Responsive Law, *The Mental Health Complex*, Pt.1: Community Mental Health Centers (1973).

13. Romano-V., O.I., Institutions in modern society: caretakers and subjects, 183 *Science* 722-725 (Feb. 22, 1974).

14. Reich and Siegel, The chronically mentally ill shuffle to oblivion, 3 *Psychiatric Annals* 35 (1973).

15. XXV *Social Security Bulletin* 10 (Oct. 1962).

16. Government Printing Office, *Studies in public welfare*, paper No.5, pt.2, 114 (1970).

17. See, e.g., Michelman, Foreword: On protecting the poor through the fourteenth amendment, 83 *Harv. L. Rev.* 7 (1969); In pursuit of constitutional welfare rights: One view of Rawls' theory of justice, 121 U. of *Pa. L. Rev.* 962 (1973), Morris, New horizons for a state bill of rights, 45 *Wash. L. Rev.* 474 (1970).

18. *Housing Act of 1949*, 42 U.S.C. sec.1441 (1971).
19. J. Rawls, *A Theory Of Justice* (Cambridge: Harvard University Press, 1971).
20. *Id.* at 535.
21. See, e.g., R. Sennett and J. Cobb, *The Hidden Injuries Of Class* (New York: Random House, 1973); S. de Grazia, *The Political Community: A Study Of Anomie* (Chicago: University of Chicago Press, 1969) pp. 162-183.
22. As to equal protection, see, e.g., cases discussed in developments in the Law-Equal Protection, 82 *Harv. L. Rev.* 1065 (1969). As to agencies rules, see, e.g., *Arizona Grocery Co.* v. *Atchison, Topeka and Santa Fe Ry. Co.*, 284 U.S. 370 (1932); Administrative Procedure Act, 60 *Stat.* 237 (1946), 5 U.S.C. sec.551-559, 701-706. As to due process, see e.g., cases discussed in P. Freund, et al., *Constitutional Law* (Boston: Little, Brown and Co., 1967) Vol. 2, pp.1321-1352.
23. See, e.g., L. *Fuller, The Morality Of Law* (New Haven: Yale University Press, 1963) pp.33-94.
24. A. de *Tocqueville, Democracy In America* (J. P. Mayer, ed.; G. Lawrence, trans.) (Garden City, N.Y.: Doubleday and Co. 1969) vol.1, p.241.
25. See A. Hamilton, et al., *The Federalist* (E. M. Earle, ed.) (New York: Modern Library, 1937) Nos. 79 and 81.
26. *In Re Gault*, 387 U.S. 1, 77-78 (1967) (Harlan, J. concurring).
27. 42 U.S.C. sec.401 et seq.
28. 42 U.S.C. sec.1320o-4(a)(1)

Chapter 2

Dangerousness

One "progressive" approach to civil commitment was described in chapter 1 as the preventive confinement analysis. That analysis is premised on the moral and constitutional argument that the only legitimate justification for civil commitment of any kind should be a proven likelihood of dangerous acts. Thus, this progressive approach rejects the medical model, rejects the treatment rationale, and puts forward the narrow John Stuart Mill libertarian point of view, which suggests that in principle civil commitment can be continued if the State can justify the loss of liberty in light of its traditional police function. The emphasis on dangerousness as the salient variable is compatible with the modern jurisprudence of criminal law and is central to the sentencing premises of the American Law Institute Model Penal Code (1) and the Model Sentencing Act (2). It is also a critical theme in the President's Commission on Law Enforcement and Administration of Justice (3).

It is easy to understand why the generic concept of dangerous-. ness has emerged as the paramount consideration in the law-mental health system. At first glance it seems to transcend all of the ideological disputes· which currently confound the law-mental health system. The assumption is that all sides will agree on dangerousness, violence, or harmful conduct as valid criteria for State intervention. Dangerousness seems to be a concept separable from one's belief system; however, reflection makes it clear that it is not such a transcending and acceptable concept. Skolnick (4), for example, points out that violence

> is an ambiguous term whose meaning is established
> through political process.

Geis and Monahan (5) elaborate this point in a comparison of street violence and suite violence. They discuss the difference in legal sanctions applied to someone who assaults another person on the street, and the executive who knowingly fails to replace defective gas tanks in airplanes. The criminal law treats the *latter* violence quite differently than the former. It is unlikely that such an executive will be thought of by anyone in the law-mental health system as a dangerous person and a fit subject for involuntary civil confinement. Ralph Nader emphasizes these arbitrary definitions of dangerous crimes:

> "Smogging" a city or town has taken on the proportions of a massive crime wave, yet federal and State statistical compilations of crime pay attention to "muggers" and ignore "smoggers" (6).

These are instances of dangerous acts of great social impact which have not been a traditional focus of the criminal law. But even within the traditional criminal law the ambiguous treatment of harmful conduct is ubiquitous. The sanctions against drunken drivers, who kill and maim more victims than any other group of offenders, is the most obvious example. At the other extreme is the reaction of the criminal law to certain kinds of sexual conduct; e.g., exhibitionism.

These examples are sufficient to make it clear that dangerousness, like beauty, is to some extent in the eye of the beholder. Thus there are problems of definition which have not been surmounted in the progressive quest for a transcendent standard. These troubling substantive considerations should be kept in perspective in the analysis which follows.

It was pointed out in chapter 1 that it is possible to describe a wide variety of legal decisions which when narrowly construed are based on the prediction of dangerous acts. The argument is made by Dershowitz (7) that all of these decision-prediction points should be clearly identified, be treated as a homogeneous group, and attempts be made to develop through empirical study, predictive tables which would delineate the percentage of success and failure and particularly the costs in terms of unnecessary loss of liberty. These objective tables would replace subjective judgment, and eventually become predictive devices used in civil commitment and other prediction-decision situations. All of these situations would call for the same procedural safeguards, and in that regard there would be no distinction between civil and criminal trials.

No one can quarrel with a call for more research based on sound experimental data. But what it means is that statistically meaningful samples of persons thought to be very dangerous must be returned to the community. If society is willing to take that step, it will require that the criminal justice system permit the randomized approach that good experimental research requires. This will be difficult without doing damage to every legal tradition. In addition, if we examine the few good existing empirical studies and the constraints of objective statistical prediction, it becomes clear what more study is likely to reveal. Indeed, by isolating as the salient variable at all these judicial decision points the likelihood of dangerous acts, the preventive confinement analysis when coupled with empirical data, as I will show, is an intellectual tour de force which reveals that all forms of civil commitment, whether or not treatment is provided, are unconscionable. Indeed, all judicial predictive decisions turn out to be unacceptable.

Base Rates for Dangerousness and Prediction

It is doubtless true that lay opinion associates dangerousness with mental illness (8). However, the American Psychiatric Association has indicated that no more than 10 percent of the hospitalized mentally ill are dangerous (9). This "guesstimate," arrived at by a committee, is itself grossly inflated. The most thoughtful review of the relevant literature is by Gulevich and Bourne. (10). They concluded that the base rate of violent behavior (except for suicide) by those labeled mentally ill is no different than the general population. Data gathered before 1950 revealed that ex-mental patients, if anything, had lower crime rates than the population in general (11).

Recent data suggests that there may be slightly higher base rates for violent crimes among mental patients, particularly aggravated assault among women (12) and robbery for men (13). Giovannoni and Gurel (14) have similar data. Gulevich and Bourne (15) do not place great weight on these findings and, as they point out, even if one were to accept them, the overall picture is that violent crimes among mental patients do not have a high base rate in any absolute sense.

Since violent behavior among the mentally ill in fact has a very low base rate as all empirical study suggests, then it follows that any prediction tables will grossly overpredict. This statistical point was made years ago by Rosen (16), and by Meehl (17), and has been reiterated by many sophisticated methodologists thereafter (18). The statistical problem is one of false positives when predictions of rare events (low base rates) are attempted. In those circumstances even a predictive approach that seems to have a very high cutting point; e.g., 95 percent accurate in detecting the salient trait, is unworkable. Thus, as Livermore and co-workers point out in their discussion of this problem:

> Assume that one person out of a thousand will kill. Assume also an exceptionally accurate test is created which differentiates with 95 percent effectiveness those who will kill from those who will not. If 100,000 people were tested, out of the 100 who would kill, 95 would be

isolated. Unfortunately, out of the 99,900 who would not kill, 4,995 people would also be isolated as potential killers. (19)

These 4,995 people are the so-called false positives, the innocent victims of the test. A test which would predict with 95 percent accuracy is by behavioral science standards an extraordinarily high cutting point. Surely in the mental health area one would have to hope at best for a 60 percent or 70 percent rate. That would produce a cutting line in this example which would produce tens of thousands of false positives. As we shall see, what we now have is much more crude than even that. The validity of the statistical cutting point argument seems compelling, and has been adopted by other legal scholars (20).

Rubin (21) has made a rough estimate that there are now 50,000 persons each year who, via the civil commitment system, are involuntarily confined on the basis of predictions of dangerousness. Whether these were subjective or objective predictions, based simply on the statistical cutting point argument, one can assume that the majority are false positives improperly confined.

Wenk and co-workers (22) summarized some of the most relevant studies which demonstrate the objective statistical cutting point within the criminal justice area where one might assume higher base rates for violent crimes. The California Department of Corrections developed a violence prediction scale to predict parole violation by violent acts. It identified 86 percent false positives. A second study of parolees by the same group using histories and psychiatric reports produced 99 percent false positives. A California Youth Authority study using 100 variables, including a psychological test battery, led to 95 percent false positives.

What one can conclude from this is that if dangerousness is the sole criterion for civil commitment or other preventive detention, and if an empirical study demonstrates violence is a rare event (low base rate), then even if we had a very good predictive technique or device, we would end up confining many more false than true positives.

The Predictive Techniques

I have already indicated that techniques with a high cutting line, e.g., 95 percent accurate, are inefficient when applied to low base rate events. Now I shall consider the accuracy of clinical prediction, the "cutting line" of psychiatrists, psychologists, and other mental health technicians (23). Halleck, speaking for psychiatrists who are designated as the decisionmakers by most courts in all forms of civil commitment, and in as many as 10 percent of the 600,000 annual criminal cases (24), writes as follows:

> Our criteria for predicting who will commit a dangerous act are totally inadequate (25).

George K. Stürup, a psychiatrist of great clinical experience with dangerous persons, states the situation as follows:

> Little is known, however, about assessing dangerousness beyond intuitive feelings . . . (26).

Even psychiatrists who claim predictive capacity concede that standard diagnostic nomenclature is of no value:

> The terms used in standard psychiatric diagnosis are almost totally irrelevant to the determination of dangerousness. (27).

Instead, the typical global and clinical approach is offered:

> There are no rigid criteria of dangerousness, there are only clues gleaned from a meticulous inquiry into multiple aspects of the personality. (28).

This last description is characteristic of what one finds in the literature. The inquiry utilizes a variety of mental health professionals who pool their expertise and observations of the supposedly dangerous persons. Since part of the claim of success is based on experience, there is no way that others can simply follow their methods. In addition, the emphasis on knowing as much as possible (i.e., meticulous inquiry) in order to make a prediction has been challenged by Dershowitz. He points to studies in other contexts where more information leads to less successful prediction (29). The desire for more and more information is understandable since the decision is so critical. However, if the information load relates only to aspects of personality, there is no valid evidence that more will increase the precision of prediction. One thoughtful critique of such views emphasizes that violent behavior is at least as much a function of social context as it is a function of personality (30). This would explain why the traditional psychiatric approach emphasizing personality would have limited predictive value even at its best.

This is not meant to suggest that no traditional psychiatric clues are valid; only that such validity has not been established.

Two typical dynamic patterns that are associated with violence in the clinician's mind are morbid jealousy, particularly in men (*31-33*), and a sense of helplessness and being trapped, with rage as a defense against or a response to that feeling (*34*).

Many clinicians are impressed with the triad of enuresis, pyromania, and cruelty to animals as events in childhood which are predictive of later violence (*35*). Parents' brutality is also often cited as a predisposing factor (*36*). Alcohol seems to be the single variable most often indicted as predisposing to violence, but even here there are serious questions of cause and effect and base rate (*37*). Drug abuse, including amphetamines, barbiturates, heroin, etc., has been linked to violence—but except for amphetamines the link is rather ambiguous (*38*). There has also been recent interest by clinicians in what has been called the body buffer zone by Kinzel (*39*).

Much of this scattered clinical wisdom about violence has, as mentioned, never been proved valid in controlled studies. The clinician in the end often relies heavily on his own empathic talent, his emotional response, or countertransference (*40*); those are the clinician's stock in trade. However, one wonders what happens to these delicate antennae when there is great social and cultural distance between the clinician and his patient.

The traditional forensic psychiatrist, when pressed to the wall, will acknowledge the difficulty in his predictions. His rejoinder, however, is that "someone has to do it," and he is better at it than anyone else would be. Dershowitz claims that is not the case, but his data is less than convincing. Indeed, there is so little good methodological research it is as difficult to disprove as to prove the claims of the forensic psychiatrist.

Illustrative of the difficult problems of proof is a recent natural experiment often erroneously cited as clear evidence by critics of psychiatric predictions of violence. As a result of a court order it became necessary to transfer a large group of persons who were being confined at the Matteawan facility in New York for the criminally dangerous. Several followup reports have appeared of these dangerous patients. These have been summarized by Monahan who concludes that after 4 years, 20 percent had been reported as assaultive in the civil hospitals to which they were assigned, and thus presumptively 80 percent were not dangerous and needlessly confined to maximum security (*41*). The value of this conclusion is questionable, however, particularly in light of his own views about the social context of violent behavior (*42*).

Thus, it may well be true that confinement in a nonmaximum security facility is sufficient to keep dangerous persons out of the social context in which violent acts will be triggered. Furthermore, there is no question about the fact that institutions like Matteawan have enormous inertia. They knowingly retain patients long past the point in their lives where dangerous acts are likely. In fact, the behavior of released patients may say more about institutional inertia than about poor predictions. Thus, the enthusiasm of Rubin, Monahan, and others about the conclusive results of this natural experiment is not entirely justified. This criticism would seem to be confirmed by the Steadman and Keveles (43) finding that in their followup of ex-Matteawan patients the mean age of those still institutionalized or returned to institutions was 41.9, and those in the community 47.1.

This criticism of the Matteawan and similar studies is not to be read as implying a defense of the initial predictions of dangerousness. Rather it points up the broader methodological problem of natural experiments in which it is often difficult to limit or even precisely define the independent variable.

Since there are very few studies available of the predictive success or failure of psychiatrists or other mental health professionals, it is worth discussing in some detail one recent study (44) which lays claim to diagnostic reliability. It dealt with men who were thought to be sexually dangerous, and the mean age at discharge was about 35, thus they were not burned out.

Sexually dangerous men

	Number	Recidivists Number	Recidivists Percent
Recommended for release:			
At time of initial diagnosis	304	26	8.6
After commitment and therapy (average stay 43 months)	82	5	6.1
Total, recommended for release	386	31	8.0
Not recommended for release:			
At time of initial diagnosis	31	12	38.7
After commitment and therapy (average stay 30 months)	18	5	27.8
Total, not recommended for release	49	17	34.7
Total, all patients released	435	48	11.0

The authors conclude, based on these results, that dangerousness can be reliably diagnosed and effectively treated.

If we translate this claim into the cutting point concept demonstrated earlier, and look at the persons who were released against the staff's recommendations at the time of the initial diagnostic evaluation, we find that they were correct in 38.7 percent of cases.

This, of course, means that they had 61.3 percent false positives despite the fact that the patients invariably had already committed dangerous sex crimes before being admitted, and despite the fact that they had 60 days to examine the patients; and these predictions under these circumstances were made by five mental health clinicians who had long experience with dangerous persons. Contrast that with the usual situation of one examining psychiatrist after a 1-hour or less interview of an alleged mental patient who has not yet committed a dangerous act, attempting to make this same sort of prediction as required by statute.

Even enthusiastic predictors like Kozol and co-workers write:

> The difficulty involved in predicting dangerousness is immeasurably increased when the subject has never actually performed an assaultive act. This is particularly relevant to involuntary mental hospitalization and to proposals for preventive detention.

The authors conclude:

> No one can predict dangerous behavior in an individual with no history of dangerous acting out (45).

This, however, is exactly the task assigned to the committing psychiatrist in most of the reform oriented new civil commitment statutes. One court whose efforts we shall discuss at length in the section on civil commitment has recognized the impossibility of administering such a substantive standard as "likely to be harmful to others." Instead, the court asks proof beyond a reasonable doubt that a harmful act has occurred. It is only by that mutation of the legal standard that any civil commitment for the mentally ill as dangerous can occur.

In California, which employs fairly strict civil commitment standards, the criterion of dangerous to others is invoked in only 2 percent of the cases. If that were to become the sole criterion as the civil libertarian view suggests, we would confine only 2 percent of those now being confined, and many of those would be false positives.

These limitations on prediction are not simply applicable to clinical judgment; it is also true of all psychological tests as well. Megargee, in 1970, did a detailed review of such tests. He concluded:

> Thus far no structured or projective test scale has been derived which, when used alone, will predict violence in the individual case in a satisfactory manner. Indeed, none

has been developed which will adequately postdict, let alone predict, violent behavior (46).

It can be stated flatly on the basis of my own review of the published material on the prediction of dangerous acts that neither objective actuarial tables nor psychiatric intuition, diagnosis, and psychological testing can claim predictive success when dealing with the traditional population of mental hospitals. The predictive success appropriate to a legal decision can be described in three levels of increasing certainty: preponderance of the evidence, 51 percent successful; clear and convincing proof, 75 percent successful; beyond a reasonable doubt, at least 90 percent successful. Even if actuarial devices reduce the amount of predictive error none can claim to meet even the lowest of these legal standards. The best prediction studies of criminal offenders are reviewed and evaluated by F.H. Simon, Home Office Research Studies, London, 1971. This excellent methodological analysis confirms the minimal value of actuarial devices in low base rate contexts.

The mental health professionals whether or not they use such devices simply have no demonstrated capacity to generate even a cutting line that will confine more true than false positives; i.e., the preponderance of the evidence standard. It is doubtless true, as Halleck suggests, that there are rare clinical constellations in which a psychiatrist or other mental health practitioner can make better predictions than that, but when the attempt is made over a broad spectrum of patients, intuition and clinical experience are not enough. There are, on the other hand, a group of patients in which anyone could predict dangerous acts; e.g., drug addicts who regularly support their habit by mugging, but that prediction does not require a mental health professional.

It may well be that in many other situations a lay person can predict dangerousness at least as well as a professional. Hakeem (47) has shown that in certain circumstances laymen do as well or better than parole officers in predicting parole outcome. Rappeport (48) in a somewhat similar vein, suggests that courts may do better than psychiatrists in predicting when it is safe to discharge mental patients.

I have dealt here only with dangerous acts done to others because that is the thrust of the preventive confinement analysis. It is my own conviction that the prediction of dangerous acts to the self is somewhat better accomplished (49). But still that predictive success does not have a high enough cutting line to meet the standard of confining more true than false positives. I have also ignored those arguments which point out the importance of defining the gravity of the dangerous act and the degree of likelihood that it will in fact occur in a given period of time. All of these points only make it more obvious how imprecise and unreliable clinical and actuarial predictions are.

Monahan (50) has enumerated the variety of reasons why the mental health professional, since he has no reliable criteria, will tend to grossly overpredict dangerousness. Among the most obvious:

Lack of corrective feedback. If the person is confined, the predictor has no chance to learn if he was right or wrong.

Differential consequences to the predictor. If someone suspected of violence is confined, the predictor can never be proved wrong. If he is released and commits a violent crime, the predictor can expect to read about it on the front page.

Differential consequences to the subject. The predictor can rationalize overprediction as a vehicle for getting people who need it into treatment.

Monahan argues persuasively that psychiatrists have stereotyped notions of the personality attributes of dangerous persons which in fact have no valid relationship to the occurrence of dangerous acts. They are committed to these stereotypes because of theoretical constructs which cause them to selectively attend to certain data. Without feedback one can only assume that this bias will remain unchanged.

In contrast to these pragmatic considerations there is a hypothesis favored by a variety of social and behavioral scientists that the poor and the minorities, such as the blacks, are more apt to be labeled as dangerously mentally ill. As Rubin reiterates this thesis in the context of his study of a chronic inmate population of 17 criminally dangerous persons, labeling is:

> unrelated to any violent behavior, but rather to society's need to find objects who represent projections of its own violence, or who can be scapegoated for a number of reasons (51).

I find this hypothesis simplistic at best; at worst it is misleading and wrong. Szasz (52), of course, makes the same argument. The psychiatrist decisionmaker is seen as a conduit for an organic social entity which needs to project its violence on scapegoats. First, our society is not an organic entity rather it is a complex and heterodox amalgamation of groups with conflicting views. It has no collective unconscious except in some metaphysical sense.

Second, as already emphasized in Monahan's discussion of psychiatric bias toward overprediction, there are more important pressures on the psychiatrist; i.e., public humiliation if he predicts a false negative.

Third, psychiatrists have their own agenda, they derive status and power from being decisionmakers, they lose that power and status by false negatives.

Fourth, despite the adage that hindsight is always superior to foresight, the retrospective view of Rubin and others who look at a population that has been confined for an average of 25 years is misleading. Twenty-five years after a murder the killer may well seem like the kindest and most innocent of men, and the brief charges contained in his file may, when reviewed through his current mental status, seem preposterously weak and exaggerated, as Rubin claims to have been the case in his survey. Violence may be difficult to predict, but it is a tangible reality of daily life.

Fifth, to the extent psychiatrists do share the biases of middle class professionals, that bias works in complicated ways. As Shah (53) points out, the dangerous mentally ill label is used by psychiatrists to get people into treatment. When so used the label may be withheld from blacks whom the white psychiatrist defines as untreatable. It is interesting in this respect to note that blacks are dramatically underrepresented in some State institutions for the sexually dangerous (54), and the published reports of Patuxent in Maryland, an institution for the broader group of the dangerously mentally ill, demonstrate that blacks were not overrepresented (55). A national survey of admissions to State and county mental hospitals for the criminally insane reveals that nonwhites are not in fact overrepresented as they are in all other State criminal facilities (56). (Admissions to State prisons in 1970, 21,276 white and 16,161 nonwhite). Admissions to State hospitals for the criminally insane in 1972, 9,207 white and 2,541 nonwhite.) This point will be amplified in the discussion of the juvenile court system.

Sixth, where a large number of ongoing psychiatric predictions of dangerousness have actually been studied, it seems clear that the most important variable is the actual past criminal conduct or charge (57). Kozol also emphasized the importance of careful study of criminal behavior as crucial (58). Indeed, if psychiatrists have no valid predictive indices, one can easily understand that they would look to past acts since there seems nowhere else to look. Furthermore, there is the clinical maxim that the best predictor of future acts is past acts.

Finally, if one turns from the clinicians to existing actuarial tables, one finds that they instruct the objective decisionmaker to look to race. For example, a most detailed actuarial study contrasting assaultive and nonassaultive juveniles disclosed that:

> From the data presented in this report, the most promising areas for further investigation of differences between assaultive and nonassaultive juvenile offenders seems to be race (59).

Violence is for a variety of reasons, endemic among poor Americans, a group in which minorities are overrepresented. We know that the victims of violence are also predominantly the poor and minorities. This tragic social situation cannot be explained or understood by theories about psychiatric scapegoating.

Can Dangerous Behavior Be Treated

One consequence of a preventive confinement system that in fact worked would be that it would confine dangerous persons only. Based on the evidence already considered, one can conclude that such a group would be quite different than the current population of the hospitalized mentally ill. Presumably there would be few psychotics (e.g., Kozol (60) found only 7 percent of the sexually dangerous to be psychotic) and many with personality disorders; e.g., sociopaths (61). It is a truism in psychiatry that treatment success with personality disorders, particularly sociopaths, is quite limited. Some psychiatrists prefer to see such individuals in maximum security facilities where they can be more readily controlled (62, 63). Few psychiatrists are motivated or interested in treating the dangerous personality disorder (64). These patients are neither amenable to psychotropic drugs, nor to brief individual psychotherapy. Even the few therapeutic optimists who utilize everything in the mental health armamentarium, including behavior modification, admit that years of treatment are necessary and they insist on maximum controls (65, 66).

There is considerable irony in the various discussions of limiting civil commitment and prison sentences to dangerous persons. Among those who urge it, the National Council on Crime and Delinquency in its latest policy statement—"The Nondangerous Offender Should Not Be Imprisoned"—states as to dangerous persons: "Neither mental hospitals nor prisons are now capable of treating such offenders(67)."

At the same time, the president of that Council wrote that the identification of dangerous persons was "the greatest unresolved problem the criminal justice system faces"(68).

It is a bizarre system of criminal justice which confines only those who cannot be identified, and it is an equally bizarre mental health system which commits only those who cannot be treated.

The question that arises is: Why confine dangerous persons to mental hospitals at all? If society were to decide that this was the only proper group for confinement on legal grounds, then a decision would still have to be made as to what facility could best deal with them. If they are truly dangerous, and if treatment is unlikely to succeed, or will take years, then surely a prison is better than a community mental health center. If a prison, then why not keep such persons in the criminal system from the outset?

That, of course, is what the preventive confinement model is in part meant to do—to restore civil commitment to the criminal system. But the logical force of that model leads to the conclusion that predictive judgments be abandoned and all confinement be based on past dangerous acts which have been proved beyond a reasonable doubt. The basic premise, of course, is not based on helping people, it is based on a professed fair balancing of individual freedom against protecting the public. In fact, since there is no valid method for predicting dangerousness, reform that moves toward making the predicting of dangerousness the sole criterion for civil commitment is not reform; rather, it is abolition disguised as reform. As I shall indicate, it may be appropriate to abolish many forms of civil commitment, and in some cases for reasons suggested by the preventive confinement analysis. But if there are in fact reasons for society to provide treatment to people whose mental illness prevents them from accepting such treatment, then there may yet be a role for civil commitment in a free society.

References

1. American Law Institute, *Model Penal Code,* 1972.
2. Model Sentencing Act, 1963.
3. *The Challenge Of Crime In A Free Society* (Washington, D.C.: U.S. Government Printing Office, 1967).
4. J. Skolnick, *The Politics Of Protest* (New York: Simon and Schuster, 1969). p. 4
5. Geis and Monahan, The social ecology of violence, a chapter to appear in T. Lickona (ed.), *Man And Morality* (New York: Holt, Rinehart and Winston, in press).
6. Nader, Foreword, in J. Esposito, *Vanishing Air* (New York: Grossman, 1971) p. 8.
7. Dershowitz, On preventive detention, *New York Review Of Books,* March 13, 1969, p. 22.
8. J. C. Nunnaly, *Popular Conceptions Of Mental Health* (New York: Holt, Rinehart and Winston, 1961).
9. Position statement on the question of adequacy of treatment, 123 *Am. J. Psychiat.* 1458 (1967).
10. Gulevich and Bourne, Mental illness and violence. in D. Daniels, M. Gilula, and F. Ochberg, *Violence And The Struggle For Existence* (Boston: Little, Brown, 1970), p. 390.
11. Summarized in Rappeport and Lassen, Dangerousness arrest rate comparisons of discharged patients and the general population. 122 *Am. J. Psychiat.* 776 (1965).
12. Rappeport and Lassen, The dangerousness of female patients. 123 *Am. J. Psychiat.* 413 (1966).
13. Rappeport and Lassen, *supra* note 11.
14. Giovannoni and Gurel, Socially disruptive behavior of ex-mental patients. 17 *Arch. Of Gen. Psychiat.* 146 (1967).
15. Gulevich and Bourne, *supra* note 10.
16. Rosen, Detection of suicidal patients: An example of some limitations in the prediction of infrequent events. 18 *J. Consult. Psychol.* 397 (1954).
17. Meehl and Rosen, Antecedent probability and the efficiency of psychometric signs, patterns, of cutting scores. 52 *Psychol. Bull.* 194 (1955).
18. Wenk, Robison, and Smith. Can violence be predicted? 18 *Crime And Delinquency* 393 (1972); C. Kelley, *Crime In The U.S.* 1972. Washington, D.C.: Government Printing Office, 1973; J. Monahan, *The Prediction And Prevention Of Violence.* (Pacific Northwest Conference on Violence and Criminal Justice. Issaquah, Wash., December 6-8, 1973, in press.)
19. Livermore, Malmquist, and Meehl, On the justifications for civil commitment, 117 *U. Pa. L. Rev.* 75, 84 (1968).
20. Morris, Psychiatry and the dangerous criminal. 41 *So. Cal. L. Rev.* 536 (1968).
21. Rubin, Prediction of dangerousness in mentally ill criminals, 27 *Arch. of Gen. Psych.* 397 (1972).
22. Wenk, *et al.,* supra note 18.
23. J. Rappeport (ed.), *The Clinical Evaluation Of The Dangerousness Of The Mentally Ill.* (Springfield: Thomas, 1967).
24. Rubin, *supra* note 21, p. 397.
25. S. Halleck, *Psychiatry And The Dilemmas Of Crime.* (Berkeley: University of California Press, 1971), p. 348.

26. Stürup, Will this man be dangerous? In: De Reueck And Porter (eds.), *The Mentally Abnormal Offender*. (Boston: Little, Brown, 1968), p. 17.
27. Kozol *et al.*, The diagnosis and treatment of dangerousness, 18 *Crime And Delinquency* 371, 383 (1972).
28. *Id.*, p. 383.
29. Dershowitz, Preventive confinement: A suggested framework for constitutional analysis, 51 *Tex. L. Rev.* 1306 (1973).
30. Geis and Monahan, *supra* note 5.
31. Lanzkron, Murder and insanity: A survey. 119 *Am. J. Psychiat.* 754 (1963).
32. R.R. Mowat, *Morbid Jealousy And Murder*. (London: Tavistock, 1966).
33. Shepherd, Morbid jealousy: Some clinical and social aspects of a psychiatric symptom, 107 *J. Ment. Sci.* 687 (1961).
34. J.R. Lion, *Evaluation And Management Of The Violent Patient*. (Springfield: Thomas, 1972).
35. Hellman and Blackman, Enuresis, firesetting, and cruelty to animals: A triad predictive of adult crime, 122 *Am. J. Psychiat.* 1431 (1966).
36. Silver, Dublin, and Lourie, Does violence breed violence? 126 *Am. J. Psychiat.* 404 (1969).
37. Gulevich and Bourne, *supra* note 10.
38. Tinklenberg and Stillman, Drug use and violence. In: Daniels, Gilula and Ochberg, *supra* note 10.
39. Kinzel, Body buffer zone in violent prisoners. 127 *Am. J. Psychiat.* 59 (1970).
40. Lion, *supra* note 34.
41. Monahan, *supra* note 18.
42. *Id.*
43. Steadman and Keveles, Community adjustment and criminal activity of the Baxstrom patients: 1966-1970. 129 *Am. J. Psychiat.* 304 (1972).
44. Kozol *et al.*, *supra* note 27; see also J. Rappeport, *supra* note 23 at 52.
45. *Id.*
46. Megargee, The prediction of violence with psychological tests. In: C. Spielberger (ed.), *Current Topics In Clinical And Community Psychology*. (New York: Academic Press, 1970), p. 98.
47. Hakeem, Prediction of parole outcome. 52 *J. Crim. L. Criminology and Police Science* 145 (1961).
48. Rappeport, Lassen, and Grunewald, Evaluation and followup of state hospital patients who had sanity hearings. 118 *Am. J. Psychiat.* 1078 (1962).
49. Stone, A syndrome of serious suicidal intent, 3 *Arch. Gen. Psychiat.* 331 (1960); Stone and Shein, Psychotherapy of the hospitalized suicidal patient, 22 *Am. J. Psychother.* 15 (1968); Monitoring and treatment of suicidal potential within the context of psychotherapy, 10 *Comp. Psychiat.* 59 (1969); Stone, Treatment of the hospitalized suicidal patient, In: J. Masserman (ed.), *Current Psychiatric Therapies* (Vol. IX) 209, New York: Grune & Stratton, 1969.
50. Monahan, *supra* note 18 at p. 9.
51. Rubin, *supra* note 21.
52. T. Szasz, *The Manufacture Of Madness* (New York: Harper and Row, 1970).
53. Shah, Crime and mental illness: Some problems in defining and labeling deviant behavior. 53 *Ment. Hyg.* 21 (1969).

54. *See also*, Brief of Amicus Curiae The American Psychiatric Association, *Legion* v. *Weinberger*, U.S. S. Ct. No. 73-5467, *appeal from* 354 F. supp. 456 (S.D.N.Y. 1972) (Three-judge court).

55. E.g., A report of the Oregon experience with the Sexually Dangerous Persons Act notes as one of its most remarkable findings "all the sex offenders civilly committed as sexually dangerous were white." Bradley and Margolin, The Oregon Sexually Dangerous Persons Act 8 Williamette L.J. 341, 384. State of Maryland, Department of Public Safety and Correctional Services, Maryland's Defective Delinquent Statute: A progress report (1973).

56. National prisoner statistics, state prisoners: Admissions and releases, 1970 Federal Bureau of Prisons, Wash., D.C. Taube, Unpublished survey of hospitals for mentally disordered offenders.

57. Steadman, Some evidence on the inadequacy of the concept and determination of dangerousness in law and psychiatry. 1973 *J. Psychiat. And Law* 409.

58. Kozol *et al.*, *supra* note 27.

59. Molof, Differences between assaultive and nonassaultive juvenile offenders. Research report No. 51, State of California Department of Youth Authority, 1967, p. 62.

60. Kozol *et al.*, *supra* note 27 at 383. Only 7 percent of sexually dangerous are psychotic.

61. Kloek, Schizophrenia and delinquency, In: De Reueck And Porter (eds.), *The Mentally Abnormal Offender, supra*, note 26.

62. Kozol et al., *supra*, note 27.

63. Patuxent study, *supra* note 55.

64. P. L. Scheidemandel and C. K. Kanno, The mentally ill offender: A survey of treatment programs, publications of the *Joint Information Service of the APA and the NIMH*, (Washington, 1966).

65. Kozol et al., *supra*, note 27.

66. Patuxent study, *supra*, note 55.

67. *Crime And Delinquency*, vol. 19, Oct. 1973, No. 4, pp. 449-456.

68. Rector, Who are the dangerous? 1 *Bull. Am. Acad. Of Psychiat And Law* 186 (1973).

Chapter 3

Statistics on Inpatient Care

Recent court decisions all too often cite statistics which are long outdated and which create the impression that psychiatric patients inevitably spend years in confinement. I shall therefore briefly summarize some of the most recently available data (1971-73) to create a numerical sketch of inpatient care. As of June 30, 1973, there were approximately 248,562 patients in State and county mental hospitals. This represents a 26.4 percent decrease since 1970 and is less than half the 600,000 number cited in contemporary cases and legal literature.

Episodes

During 1971 at least 1,755,816 psychiatric inpatient episodes were recorded in the United States. Three-fourths of these were in facilities under public auspices and one-fourth were private. Although similar data are not available for 1973, there is every reason to assume that such episodes continue at that level or higher. The most frequent specific diagnosis applied at hospitalization in 1971 was schizophrenia (23 percent of cases).

Length of Stay

During 1971 in State and county mental hospitals which presumably have less good care and serve the sickest population, 86.9 percent were discharged within 6 months of admission. The median length of stay for all such admissions was 41 days. The per resident patient expenditure has increased from less than $15 to more than $25 per day (1970-73 average for all States). In contrast, the median stays in general hospitals and community mental health centers was approximately 16 days and the costs were enormously higher.

First Admissions

The total number of first admissions to State and county mental hospitals increased from 130,000 in 1962 to 164,000 in 1969. The

25 percent increase occurred despite the development of community mental health centers which began in 1967. Since 1969 the trend has, however, reversed and in 1972 had dropped to 141,000.

Number of Beds

As of January 1972 there were approximately 471,800 psychiatric beds (30 percent of the total hospital beds) in the United States. Seventy-seven percent of these were still in State and county mental hospitals. At that 1972 date only 2 percent of the available beds were in federally funded community mental health centers. The latter, of course, have a more rapid turnover.

Where Are Patients Hospitalized?

During 1971, of the 1,755,916 inpatient episodes: 745,259 were in State and county mental hospitals; 542,642 in psychiatric wards of general hospitals; 176,800 in Veterans Administration hospitals; 130,088 in community mental health centers; 97,963 in private mental hospitals; 28,637 in residential treatment centers for emotionally disturbed children; and 34,427 in other multiservice facilities. Although similar data is not available for all facilities in 1973, there is evidence indicating a diminishing reliance on State and county mental hospitals.

All of the aforementioned data are derived from the statistical notes of the Department of Health, Education, and Welfare, Public Health Service, Alcohol, Drug Abuse, and Mental Health Administration, National Institute of Mental Health, Office of Program Planning and Evaluation, Biometry Branch, Survey and Reports Section. Particularly cited are reports numbers 74, 92, 97, 98, and 106. I am indebted to Carl A. Taube for supplying not only this published material, but also unpublished data cited in subsequent chapters.

Chapter 4
Civil Commitment

Current reports suggest that involuntary civil commitment is rapidly declining (1). The most recently available statistics on the subject are for 1972 (see table). As of that date, it was clear that the pendulum had swung such that voluntary admission had come to outnumber involuntary, and that swing seems to be continuing.

There are many reasons for this, not the least of which is the legal agitation of the past 10 years. Psychiatrists who once committed people because it was the easiest thing to do are increasingly diffident. Courts are apt to be more scrupulous in reaching their decisions; lawyers are more frequently involved in preventing confinement; and hospitals are more fastidious about their own role.

Nonetheless, the data suggest that two of every five persons admitted to State and county mental hospitals during 1972 were there against their wishes. And it is difficult to know how many of them chose to enter voluntarily only because of a threat of commitment. It is my own impression that where mental health services have been upgraded and psychiatrists have become sensitive to the legal issues, involuntary confinement can and has become a rare event. That impression forms the backdrop for the analysis which follows—i.e., *the best remedy for reducing wholesale involuntary confinement is good treatment in a decent local facility where the staff acknowledges and respects the legal rights of the patients.* However, even under those circumstances some involuntary confinement will be necessary.

Unfortunately, in many parts of the country such conditions do not exist and the result is a battle over legal standards and procedures for admission. Often, such battles achieve nothing for the mentally ill except the freedom to suffer outside an institution.

I shall, in what follows, examine the traditional goals of civil commitment, the procedural safeguards suggested by those who seek to legalize the process, the California experience as an attempt at reform, and my own views. The unique problems attending the confinement of children are discussed in the chapter on mental retardation.

43

Admissions to State and county mental hospitals by legal status of admission, sex, race, and age, United States, 1972

Sex, race, and type of admission	Total	Percent of total	Percent V+N+I	Less than 18 years		18-24 years		25-34 years		35-44 years		45-64 years		65 and over	
				Number	Percent V+N+I	Number	Percent V+N+I	Number	Percent V+N+I	Number	Percent V+N+I	Number	Percent V+N+I	Number	Percent V+N+I
Both sexes															
Total admissions	403,924			23,121		61,712		90,161		83,477		115,992		27,702	
Voluntary	196,346	49	51	11,427	49	29,215	52	47,156	56	38,892	48	58,340	51	11,316	—
Nonprotesting	23,095	6	6	3,447	15	2,993	5	4,980	6	5,562	7	4,534	4	1,579	—
Involuntary	169,032	42	44	8,247	36	24,108	43	32,544	38	37,311	46	52,015	45	14,807	—
Prison transfers	5,793			*		1,331		2,841		815		806		*	
Incompetent for trial	7,899			*		4,065		2,640		897		297		*	
Male															
Total admissions	249,005			14,728		42,248		57,918		53,591		65,319		13,298	
Voluntary	120,551	48	52	8,037		19,625		29,214		27,088		31,715		4,872	—
Nonprotesting	8,797	3	3	2,218		1,184		1,319		1,683		1,845		548	—
Involuntary	104,642	42	45	4,473		16,304		22,108		23,210		30,669		7,878	—
Prison transfers	5,632			*		1,196		2,828		815		793		*	
Incompetent for trial	7,480			*		3,939		2,449		795		297		*	
Female															
Total admissions	154,919			8,393		19,203		32,039		29,784		50,660		14,404	
Voluntary	75,795	49	49	3,390		9,590		17,942		11,804		26,625		6,444	—
Nonprotesting	14,298	9	9	1,229		1,809		3,661		3,879		2,689		1,031	—
Involuntary	64,390	42	42	3,774		7,804		10,436		14,101		21,346		6,929	—
Prison transfers	*			*		*		*		*		*		*	
Incompetent for trial	436			*		*		*		*		*		*	
White															
Total admissions	326,112			18,236		46,859		73,347		64,497		99,437		23,285	
Voluntary	168,807	52	53	8,973		23,620		40,285		32,799		51,979		11,151	—
Nonprotesting	16,386	5	5	2,176		2,047		3,393		4,148		3,888		734	—
Involuntary	132,182	41	42	7,087		19,165		25,391		26,577		42,562		11,400	—
Prison transfers	4,575			*		1,167		1,977		638		793		*	
Incompetent for trial	3,711			*		860		2,301		335		215		*	
Nonwhite															
Total admissions	77,812			4,885		14,853		16,814		18,241		16,460		4,252	
Voluntary	27,374	35	39	2,454		5,595		6,871		6,093		6,361			—
Nonprotesting	6,709	9	9	1,271		946		1,587		1,414		646		845	—
Involuntary	36,850	47	52	1,160		4,943		7,153		10,734		9,453		3,407	—
Prison transfers	1,028			*		164		864		*		*		*	
Incompetent for trial	3,544			*		3,205		339		*		*		*	

NOTE: V = voluntary, N = nonprotesting, I = involuntary. —— = not applicable.

*Fewer than 5 sample cases.

SOURCE: Taube, unpublished material.

Traditional Goals

Traditionally, civil commitment of the mentally ill has advanced four distinguishable social goals: (a) providing care and treatment to those who require it, (b) protecting allegedly irresponsible people from themselves, (c) protecting society from their anticipated dangerous acts, (d) relieving society—or the family—of the trouble of accommodating persons who, though not dangerous, are bothersome. Of these four goals only the third, dangerousness, meets the standard set by John Stuart Mill (2) in his famous essay, "On Liberty":

> The only purpose for which power can be rightfully exercised over any member of a civilized community, against his will, is to prevent harm to others. His own good, either physical or moral, is not a sufficient warrant. He cannot rightfully be compelled to do or forbear because it will be better for him to do so, because it will make him happier, because in the opinion of others to do so would be wise, or even right. These are reasons for remonstrating with him, or reasoning with him, or persuading him, or entreating him, but not for compelling him, or visiting him with any evil in case he do otherwise.

And Mill set a high standard of imminent danger:

> The preventive function of government . . . is far more liable to be abused, to the prejudice of liberty, than the punitory function, for there is hardly any part of the legitimate freedom of action of a human being which would not admit of being represented, and fairly too, as increasing the facilities for some form or other of delinquency. Nevertheless, if a public authority, or even a private person, sees any one *evidently preparing to commit* a crime, they are not bound to look on inactive . . . [If they] see a person attempting to cross a bridge which had been ascertained to be unsafe . . . they might seize him and turn him back, without any real infringement to his liberty . . . . Nevertheless, *when there is not a certainty, but only a danger* of mischief, no one but the person himself can judge of the sufficiency of the motive which may prompt him to incur the risk . . . (*emphasis added*) (3).

Mill's arguments challenge every instance in which the law coerces a man for his own good, and this, I must emphasize, is exactly the domain of the law-mental health system except in those rare instances where dangerousness is a central issue.

Even if one endorses benevolent coercion as a legitimate goal of government there is a large group of persons now confined for whom no such rationale can be advanced. They are not being coerced for their own good.

This is the group who are simply bothersome or troublesome to their families or to society. The major justification for confining such persons can only be for the supposed benefit of the family or of the community. Indeed, this is a generally acknowledged legal standard for confining the mentally retarded, and in a few jurisdictions it is an explicit justification for confining the mentally ill. (See chapters 8, Mental Retardation, and 10, The Aging.)

I shall denote the function of this social goal as the "convenience function" to make it clear that this must not be construed as paternalism, nor defended on the same moral, legal, or mental health grounds.

This convenience function has seldom been explicitly acknowledged, rather it has been hidden behind a promise of technical treatment, although at some points during the past century it has been the only goal actually achieved. Its implementation all too obviously calls for a macrosocietal policy judgment of a type which a free society is unwilling to confront in an open forum. It is, therefore, a typical instance of the clandestine decisionmaking role of mental health practitioners which allows society to do what it does not want to admit to doing, i.e., confining unwanted persons cheaply. Whatever the diverse goals of civil commitment may be, the historian can document that confinement of bothersome, obnoxious, or worrisome persons for no reason but convenience has a steady and perhaps proliferating, if ignoble history (4).

Despite such abuses, I shall assert in what follows that some paternalism is in fact justifiable; indeed, even Mill acknowledges that his argument is not meant to apply absolutely to the insane or to children (5). But I shall, later in this chapter, suggest a three step test for a justifiable paternalism. Its outlines are:

First: Does the law-mental health system know what is good for the given individual?

Second: Does the law-mental health system have the resources to do what it believes is good?

Third: Even if one and two are answered in the affirmative, is there evidence that in this case the person substantially lacks the competence to reject the paternalistic intervention?

Legal Criteria

The various social goals have been articulated, indeed, codified in State statutes. Eighteen jurisdictions provide for judicial hospitalization based either upon need for care and treatment or danger to self or others; nine jurisdictions do so only on the basis of dangerousness; six States rely solely on the need for treatment, while six more States order commitment based on whether the person should be confined "for his own or others" welfare (6) (what I have called the convenience function).

The problem, which has now reached crisis proportions, is not simply that these criteria for commitment partake of the definitional ambiguity and classificatory imprecision of all legislative formulations. Worse yet, there is increasing doubt, spawned by research and practice in a wide array of fields, as to whether these criteria really mean anything at all. As one critic has concluded, "The commitment decision is a process of social definition, of rejection, by society . . . ; there is nothing honestly scientific, let alone medical, about it" (7).

The first criterion, "in need of care or treatment," is often treated as though synonymous with "mentally ill," or even "insane" (8). This raises a spate of difficulties. Even apart from the Szaszian mental-illness-is-a-myth group, there has been growing confusion in the mental health professions about which disorders are to be regarded as mental illness. Unless some clarity can be brought to that concept, everything which follows from it will fatally infected with ambiguity.

Obviously there is no reason for the facile equation of need for care with mental illness or insanity. It is easy to think of persons not mentally ill (and surely not insane), but merely emotionally unbalanced or volatile, upset, tired, aggrieved, confused, or physically impaired, who would be helped by treatment.

Now it is often rebutted that care and treatment is only involuntarily bestowed on those incompetent to make a reasoned decision on whether to seek voluntarily such help as they need. I believe this should in fact be the practice—the Draft Act, developed as a model for reform, so provides (9)—but it is not now the case in many real-world jurisdictions. Actual capacity to make such decisions is not the standard applied; nor is it even likely to be one of several factors inquired into. Rather, the typical process for involuntary confinement is by an initial emergency provision of the statute. The need for such temporary or emergency care and treatment is presumptively established by the statement of any person (14 States), a relative, friend, spouse, or guardian (seven

States), or a public official (32 jurisdictions). The feeling of crisis which attends the process of emergency confinement rarely permits the full exploration of the patients' competence. Judicial approval which might promote such inquiry is a requirement in only 14 States. In most of those 33 jurisdictions where a medical certificate is provided for, the physician need not be a psychiatrist (*10*).

Even when judicial consideration is invoked, usually to ratify longer-term confinement, factors relevant to the stated goals of confinement—such as the amenability of the patient to treatment, the length of time which may be therapeutic, and the ability of the available institution to treat him—are not investigated. Finally, little attention is given to whether care and treatment in a total institution is really required. Though in one major case, the U.S. Court of Appeals for the District of Columbia declared that a committing court has an affirmative duty to search for alternative dispositions to full inpatient commitment (*11*), the prevailing view so far has been that expressed by then Judge, now Chief Justice Burger, in dissent in the same case; that the courts should limit themselves to confining or not confining since they are not "equipped (in this case) to carry out the broad geriatric inquiry proposed or to resolve the social and economic issues involved" (*12*).

The second social goal adduced to the commitment process is that of protecting the committed individual from himself. Lamentably, few statutes prescribe the nature of the harm which must be anticipated, its likelihood, or the ability of the individual to comprehend and reject or assume such danger. It is unclear whether the harm must be suicide, the danger of getting lost or physically injured, or merely of occasionally making imprudent economic or sexual decisions. Many young people were involuntarily confined over the past decade because drug experimentation was considered harmful by the older generation.

Also, the statutes do not require consideration of whether the harm anticipated is due to an absolute impoverishment of capacity to care for oneself which the individual is unlikely ever to overcome, or to what is suspected to be a relative and temporary incapacity. Nor do the statutes require, nor in practice do many courts indulge, an inquiry into the considerable harms that may befall the individual because of involuntary confinement. These may include stigmatization, collapse of self-esteem, separation from family and community, loss of job and impairment of future employment prospects, as well as, in our current state of institutional care, a not insubstantial chance of brutalization or mere physical deterioration in the total institutions to which many such persons are sent. Despite massive empirical evidence that long term confinement is debilitating (13) the view persists among many practitioners that "there is no harm in playing it safe" by recommending commitment when there is the slightest suggestion it may be helpful (14). The point I want to emphasize is that if the justification of commitment is to protect the individual from himself, the court has a responsibility to weigh the risks on both sides carefully.

Since it does not, we are witnessing another way in which the law-mental health process fails to advance its stated goals. Lip service has often been paid to the stringent requirements which our legal system demands before the State will intervene to protect an individual against his own bad judgment. But if the State is to intervene in the role of parens patriae, there is shockingly little proof required in the determination of existing criteria as to whether the individual is really a childlike person in need of help, or whether the institution to which he is sent really satisfies any of his needs. But here the pendulum is swinging in the other direction. The standard of dangerousness to self has been increasingly narrowed in its effect by those who are involved in legal reform. The State of Washington, for example, now allows no longer than 17 days confinement for a person who is dangerous to himself (15). This suggests that the right to commit suicide has been given some legal recognition. I shall return to this problem below.

Finally, commitment is buttressed by the rationale of protecting society from anticipated dangerous acts; indeed, this is the wave of reform. Since the difficulties of predicting harmful conduct were dealt with in the previous section, they will receive but brief treatment here. It is surprising how long the notion of a unitary, calculable quantity known as dangerousness has persisted, both in statutes and judicial decisions. Only rarely have courts asked the component questions of the magnitude, likelihood, preventability, and likely victims of the alleged dangerous conduct (16). Furthermore, surrounding the process of civil commitment of dangerous persons is the profound question of why only the allegedly mentally ill should be subject to this form of preventive confinement—especially since the evidence suggests that of all the candidate variables, mental illness is an especially poor indicator of future criminal conduct (17).

One court has said that without

> an analytical framework to guide . . . courts in applying the
> conclusory term 'dangerous to others'. . . (it) . . . could

readily become a term of art describing anyone who we would, all things considered, prefer not to encounter on the streets (18).

And the current system seems to confirm this concern. But a careful definition of dangerousness as the sole standard to be proven by a preponderance of the evidence will solve none of the important problems, except in the sense that it would put an end to involuntary civil commitment.

The trend of the courts toward objective standards, be they dangerousness to self or to others, does not permit an escape from the ambiguity of the standard of mentally ill. All of the statutes and judicial interpretations require that the patient be mentally ill and . . . (something). Thus, in the end, substantive content must be given to that concept unless we are to opt for the preventive confinement model. Obviously all of the reformers seek to give the concept of mental illness less importance, but the fallacy of that approach is that it ignores the question of who is an appropriate subject for treatment in a mental hospital. That question is central to my own suggestions below.

The Supreme Court recently expressed, somewhat disingenuously, its surprise that considering the vital interests at stake in civil commitment, so few cases challenging the State's power in this area had come before it (22). The fact is that for decades mental patients did not exist for the Supreme Court. Their commitment and care was viewed as a matter of local beneficence, and certiorari was denied repeatedly in cases challenging either the manner of commitment or institutional conditions (23). Until 1972 the Supreme Court had dealt with only four cases bearing on commitment procedures—one case requiring minimal statutory precision, two based on equal protection and the right to a hearing, and one other case (24).

For a long time the debate over the appropriateness of applying various due process safeguards to the commitment process was a seemingly ritualized arabesque. Lawyers, on the few occasions they were involved, intoned that individual rights were paramount and their infringement never excusable, while psychiatrists argued that any incursion on unmitigated medical discretion was, by definition, antitherapeutic (25). Unfortunately, along the way there seems to have been a considerable distortion of roles. Lawyers, by focusing solely on deprivations of procedural rights, have sometimes forgotten the other roles they may play in advancing the patient's interests (e.g., seeing that patient-clients get better care voluntarily), while psychiatrists, so impressed with their legally conferred role in the commitment decisions, seem to have been involved in making social dispositions rather than psychiatric or therapeutic decisions. Whether they perceived such pressure or not, physicians acted as though under pressures to satisfy the social control function (26).

Putting aside these needlessly polarized views, it is appropriate to ask: Which procedures, at what stage, might have an importance in the protection of individual rights? How and to what degree would the invocation of such rights create an adverse emotional or therapeutic impact? In addition to the specific points set forth below, one recurring but often overlooked factor worth mentioning is the medically debilitating effect of not providing due process safeguards at some point. A system in which persons are committed for long periods of time on the basis of a hearing which they often do not attend, and are represented, if at all, in summary fashion, before an impatient and skeptical judicial officer, would be profoundly frightening to any person, and is conducive to promoting the kinds of paranoid, persecutory emotions which many mentally ill persons experience.

While the contradictions, excrescenses, and perhaps even hypocrisies of the civil-criminal distinction are manifest (19), there are still important purposes served in a variety of contexts by a system which deals differently with those who are ill. The trenchant points are that we have not as yet adequately defined a standard for commitment nor assured that the consequences of confinement under any of the models fit the rationales.

Procedural Developments in Civil Commitment

Perhaps because of the moral and epistemological problems of making headway in clarifying or justifying the substantive criteria of involuntary hospitalization, recent attention has focused powerfully on the procedures. Of the substantive criteria, only dangerousness to self and others has been the subject of major legislative efforts at tightening and redefinition, and these only in jurisdictions traditionally in the forefront of mental health developments (20). In contrast, reformation of procedural safeguards attending the commitment process has been undertaken by courts and legislatures in many States (21). This involves giving the patient procedural rights similar to those now given the criminal defendant.

One major recent decision, reversed and remanded by the Supreme Court, but now back again for their consideration, deals with virtually all the due process safeguards which might be asserted. In *Lessard* v. *Schmidt* (27), a special three-judge district court declared Wisconsin's civil commitment statute unconstitutional, and ordered that those committed have the rights to (a) timely notice of the charges justifying confinement, (b) notice of right to a jury trial, (c) an initial hearing on probable cause for detention beyond 48 hours, (d) a full hearing on the necessity of detention beyond 2 weeks, (e) aid of counsel, (f) the fifth amendment protection against self-incrimination, (g) proof of mental illness and dangerousness "beyond a reasonable doubt," and (h) an inquiry into less drastic alternatives before commitment for inpatient care is ordered.

Lessard would invalidate the provisions of commitment laws in virtually all States, and would if followed exactly, put a virtual end to involuntary confinement. *Lessard* serves as a useful catalogue of points by which to evaluate the legal and mental health implications of procedural safeguards. It is not, however, unique. The laws of the State of Washington now duplicate many of its holdings (*28*).

Notice and opportunity to be heard. Notice and the opportunity to be heard are so fundamental an element of adversary justice that the Supreme Court's decisions show an accelerating trend toward applying it to ever more contexts, indeed to all in which there is a "significant . . . interest" at stake (*29*). But even the Court has acknowledged that the "formality and procedural requisites for the hearing can vary,"(*30*) and the problem is that civil commitment has long been regarded as not really an adversary process.

Most States permit emergency detention after notice merely to relatives of the individual and without a hearing (*31*). Such confinement (during which there is usually observation and treatment) may range from 1 to 30 days, with 5 to 10 days the median (*32*). Clearly, this is a major curtailment of liberty; the defense is that emergency measures may be required to protect against imminent danger, and that telling a paranoiac that he is to be committed, and forcing him to immediately engage in an argument as to his mental state is dangerous, cruel, and antitherapeutic. However, these psychiatric justifications can be overstated. Emergency detainment may be proper, but only for the length of time necessary to arrange for an initial hearing before a judge at which probable cause for continued confinement should be demonstrated. The *Lessard* court said that this period should not exceed 48 hours (*33*). And while surely no grossly psychotic person should be forced to take part in a hearing against his will that is no reason not to give the individual the opportunity to choose whether or not to participate in the hearing. This cursory probable cause hearing would not justify long term commitment. It would simply mean that a legal authority had ratified the decision temporarily to deprive a person of his freedom.

If every case of emergency confinement in every jurisdiction required a hearing in which the judge must meet with all patients within 48 hours and find probable cause for continuing that confinement, the life of the judiciary would certainly be transformed. I can see no reason why any mental health practitioner should object to this judicial participation, which might at the least provide a useful interdisciplinary experience. Futhermore, it is always unpleasant to commit a patient, and this places that burden more squarely on the judge.

I shall discuss the legal nature of this hearing below under right to counsel.

Medication. The *Lessard* court, in its attempts to transform the loose commitment procedures into stringent criminal procedures, held that at this initial hearing within 48 hours, the patient should also be allowed to appear without being incapacitated "by medication." Some Wisconsin judges have attempted to comply with all of the Lessard procedures; others have not. I shall, as we consider each of these procedures, describe the attempt of one intelligent judge to comply (hereafter Judge I). Judge I was immediately confronted by complaints from the mental health personnel that although he and an assistant were in fact available within 48 hours, emergency situations arose within that period.

A violently disturbed patient can disrupt not only an entire ward, but an entire hospital, if staff have to be brought to subdue him and struggles ensue. Without medication, mental hospitals would be back to straitjackets, padded cells, and the 19th century. What such struggles do to the staff in terms of physical injury, morale, and therapeutic attitude are critical costs which affect other patients as well. The uneasy compromise allowed by Judge I was to permit drugs to be used at dosages or of a kind which would "restrain" but not "treat." It is possible to translate this legal distinction into pharmacology. One might administer sodium amytal intramuscularly rather than phenothiazines. But query, which drug would permit a more effective hearing? Clearly, this is one of those human situations where human judgment rather than rigid rules are the sensible alternative. If even Judge I's solution were to be found legally unacceptable, then mentally ill patients who are violent should be taken to jails rather than hospitals until their probable cause hearing. Bad as that would be, it surely would be more sensible than transforming hospitals into jails.

Evidentiary rights. The *Lessard* court took the view that 10 to 14 days was the maximum acceptable period for confinement for examination without a second and full hearing, saying:

> If the facilities of the State hospitals do not permit full examination within this period because of inadequate

personnel, it is difficult to see how continued detention can be said to be beneficial to the patient (*34*).

That conclusion seems eminently justified, but the procedures to be followed in the second hearing present staggering problems.

The fifth amendment bar against self-incrimination is based on a policy of the legal system that all the facts are more likely to emerge if the State is put to the test of discovering extrinsic evidence to support incarceration of the individual than if it is permitted the easier route of gathering or coercing evidence from the person's own mouth. Although the fifth amendment by its terms forbids only the compelling of incriminating testimony in criminal cases, the Supreme Court has held that it may apply in other contexts where loss of liberty on inculpatory remarks is possible (*35*).

The *Lessard* court chose to apply it to civil commitment, requiring the examining psychiatrist to warn the patient that anything he told the psychiatrist might be used to confine him. The court blandly ignored the difficulty this might pose:

> The patient should be told by counsel and the psychiatrist that he is going to be examined with regard to his mental condition, that the statements he may make may be the basis for commitment, and that he does not have to speak to the psychiatrist. Having been informed of this *danger*, the patient may be examined if he willingly assents. *It may be expected that most patients, like Miss Lessard in the present case, will desire to talk* to a person they believe they can trust (*36*). (emphasis added.)

The court cites the expert testimony of Bruce Ennis and Dr. Szasz to the validity of this expectation of trust, although both are on record as opposed to all involuntary confinement.

Judge I's solution to the fifth amendment problem was to have for the second (full) hearing a psychiatrist not on the hospital staff interview the patient. That psychiatrist gives the patient a warning similar to the Miranda warning the police give to those they arrest. But that psychiatrist, after conducting his "independent" examination, is permitted to consult the patient's medical record. Whether this is the best use of limited psychiatric time, or whether, as practiced by Judge I, it protects the fifth amendment rights of the alleged patient, is dubious.

Some civil libertarians would argue in any event that the "alleged" patient should have his fifth amendment rights before his initial hearing. If so, the patient would have to be greeted at the door of the hospital with a Miranda-type warning. What this does, in effect, is to ask the mental health professions to forego their traditional identity and declare themselves as potential adversaries in the same role as the police. The alternative which would respect the legal right and avoid this role distortion is to have separate psychiatrists who do not have access to the hospital records, and who do warn the patients, be the only expert witnesses testifying at both hearings. There is little doubt in my mind that such an arrangement would mean that in many instances it would be impossible for the examining psychiatrist to make an informed decision and thus it would be a restraint sufficient to preclude most involuntary civil commitment.

Courts have wrestled with similar questions in the context of quasi-criminal confinement, (I use quasi-criminal to include sexual psychopath, defective delinquent, etc., procedures which are nominally civil but are triggered by "crimes.") and in situations where a defendant is subjected to a mental examination before a criminal trial(37). A variety of legal solutions have been suggested, but none of them completely resolves the difficult problems that the fifth amendment poses in the mental health setting. The essential nature of that dilemma is this: When there is a clear conflict, should the relationship between mental health practitioner and involuntary patient be defined so as to advance treatment and diagnostic goals or to protect rights? The courts may balance the scales as they deem necessary under law, but there seems to be no simple formula which reconciles these interests. What this analysis does, however, is force us to reconsider the reasons the courts have given for introducing procedural safeguards like the fifth amendment. The important cases in the Supreme Court—*Gault, Kent, Jackson*, (38) and the *Lessard* opinion as well—all refer to the failures of the promised treatment which makes civil commitment no different than criminal incarceration. The invocation of procedural rights is based on a concern about the quality and effects of confinement. My own suggestion, of course, is that the Court develop methods which deal with that concern and not retreat to an invocation of procedural rights. We shall examine the fifth amendment problem in greater detail in the chapter on quasi-criminal confinement. Here I would suggest that if the court could assure itself that helpful and acceptable treatment (to be defined below) is a real possibility, then the purposes of the fifth amendment are mooted.

A second evidentiary issue is the role, if any, which may be accorded to hearsay evidence in the commitment process. The hearsay rule, which excludes testimony as to out-of-court statements, is more than a procedural nicety; it rests on the basic doctrine that the truth of a statement can really be evaluated only if the asserter can be cross-examined. Now, of course, there are exceptions to this rule, and it can always be said that a decision-maker, especially when so broad and subtle an issue as mental health is at issue, is entitled to have all the information possible, even if the veracity of some of it cannot be tested ideally. He can, it is thought, discount for this factor.

There are, of course, other reasons why in a civil commitment hearing hearsay has been allowed. First, expert testimony as by the psychiatrist has traditionally been exempt from the hearsay rule. Second, it has been considered unwise to place close friends and relatives on the stand and ask them to repeat statements which attest to the mental illness of the "alleged" patient.

Mental health practitioners no longer are in total agreement about this latter issue. Some who favor open confrontation would regard this reluctance as ill-advised. Here again, there is room for judgment. An alternative might be to allow hearsay where a psychiatrist convinces the judge that the alternative testimony, though available, ought not to be required because it might be destructive of family relations. There are, however, other problems that would attend a strict interpretation of the hearsay rule. It might mean that all of the staff who had direct contact with the "alleged" patient and reported to a decisionmaking psychiatrist would themselves have to testify in court. The cost in treatment time would be inexcusable.

A third vital evidentiary question is the standard of proof which must be met in order for commitment to be mandated. The problem can be set out quite simply. The law had devised three basic standards of proof, or degrees of certainty with which a party must convince the factfinder in order to prevail: (a) "Preponderance of the evidence," or, theoretically 51 percent certainty. This is the standard applied to civil suits in which the stakes are often economic, and in which "we view it as to be no more serious in general for there to be an erroneous verdict in the defendant's favor than . . . in the plaintiff's favor (39). (b) "Clear and convincing proof," perhaps something like 75 percent certainty. This is applied in cases in which society's interests are balanced against infractions of individual liberties (40). (c) "Beyond a reasonable doubt," or something above 90 percent certainty. This is applied, as is commonly known in criminal trials, but also, as is less well known, in other proceedings in which rights of "transcending value" are at stake (41).

There are two basic ways in which the proper standard to apply in civil commitment can be determined. The first is to compare the individual and State interests at stake, and decide whether the pattern of interests is more congruent with the aforementioned first, second, or third models. There can really be little question that the third standard should apply when there is no guarantee of treatment. Both commonsense and judicial opinion recognize that commitment affects "fundamental rights"(42) and is a "massive curtailment of liberty" (43). And the State's interest in incarceration, based on its failure to provide treatment, is far less than in criminal prosecutions.

In the *Winship* case(44), the Supreme Court made much of the fact that the beyond a reasonable doubt standard was essential to commanding the respect of the community for the criminal justice system, and to insuring, in a free society, that individuals feel secure that the government cannot grab them and incarcerate them without convincing the factfinder of the basis therefor "with utmost certainty." Given the record of past performance with the tragic parody of legal commitment used to warehouse American citizens, it is equally important that the individual feel sure that the mental health system cannot be so used and abused. Indeed, it may be more important, for while the average citizen may have some confidence that if called by the Grand Inquisitor in the middle of the night and charged with a given robbery, he may have an alibi or be able to prove his innocence, he may be far less certain of his capacity, under the press of fear, to instantly prove his sanity. In view of these and other considerations, the D.C. Court of Appeals has recently held that the beyond a reasonable doubt standard is required in commitment(45).

The problem is, what is it that should be proved beyond a reasonable doubt? Is it that a person is both mentally ill and dangerous? If it is, then we are faced with a standard for prediction of dangerousness which, as indicated, is impossible of fulfillment. Judge I interpreted *Lessard* as requiring proof beyond a reasonable doubt not of the predicted danger but of some dangerous threat or act which had already occurred prior to confinement. But when we add proof beyond a reasonable doubt as a standard for the vague criteria used in other jurisdictions we have simply multiplied 95 x 0.

Trial by jury. The *Lessard* court noted that Wisconsin provides for jury trial and that at the second hearing the alleged patient was entitled to a jury. I see no objection to that, at this point. Its repugnance to the mental health professions rests on two concerns, first, the privacy of the patient, and second, the time costs for the mental health personnel. The answer to the first is that if the patient wants to waive his privacy he should have that right. The answer to the second is more problematic. Each new legal procedure is, in effect, a decision on the allocation of limited mental health resources.

Given the limited staff at many State and county mental hospitals, the cost in patient care would be inexcusable and thus, the result will often be that the mere request for a jury trial would lead to release. Therefore, I would suggest that if jury trials are deemed necessary, the legislature should appropriate funds for new positions for a cadre of expert witnesses whose major role would be to participate in these trials. The State and county mental hospital should not bear the burden in loss of staff. Such legally trained psychiatrists are, for example, available in Sweden(46).

Right to counsel. Without the right to appointed counsel, regardless of ability to pay, any other rights granted in commitment are likely to prove bootless. And beyond the genuine systemic importance of this right, one suspects it has been hotly debated because it is especially central to the ego of the attorney and especially threatening to the psychiatrist. The paramount importance of the right to appointed counsel must be acknowledged; its role as the enforcement mechanism for all other rights has led the Supreme Court to extend it, in rapid succession, to felony defendants, juveniles, misdemeanor defendants, and others(47). And a U.S. Court of Appeals recently held that a person subject to involuntary civil commitment is entitled to the "guiding hand of counsel at every step of the proceedings"(48). The evidence is that the presence of counsel has a profound effect on the likelihood of commitment, the treatment received, and length of stay in the institution(49). And prior case law suggests that where such fundamental liberties are in peril, permitting indigency to deny this right might be held to violate due process. But at present, while 42 jurisdictions provide that the patient has the right to be represented by counsel, only 24 provide for appointment of counsel for those who have none(50).

The toughest issue is whether there is a right to counsel at all stages of the proceedings for all purposes. The notion of such a right is bitterly opposed by many mental health personnel who feel that it wholly abdicates medical considerations in favor of a monolithic dedication to legalisms. But, it is a mockery of legalism to insist that a hearing be adversarial and then to have a lawyer for only one side. Thus, what is needed is the development of a mental health bar capable of providing the court with both sides. If courts were to adopt the two-hearing system of *Lessard*, the position endorsed here is that the role of defense counsel at the initial hearing should be similar to his role in a grand jury hearing. He would be available to advise his client, but not be allowed to be present at the hearing.

If the necessity of an attorney at all other stages of the commitment process is to be justified, his role must be seen as wider than just the avid cross-examiner so often portrayed. Fortunately, much attention has been given recently to the variety of functions—not merely legal, but social—which the attorney can serve(51). They include: (a) explaining the proceedings to the individual; (b) investigating the background of the case, assuring that it is not brought frivolously or for malice; (c) speaking for an inarticulate or frightened patient, assuring that temporary aberrations in his bearing or behavior are perceived as such; (d) asserting defenses, demanding a jury trial; (e) arranging for independent psychiatric examinations to develop rebuttal evidence, insure that privileges are respected and that procedures are regular; (f) producing evidence and cross-examining; (g) if civil commitment is ordered, preparing the patient for it, acting as liaison to family, employer, etc., assuring the patient that his rights and interests will be protected after commitment as well; (h) investigating or insuring inquiry into alternatives to confinement, and assuring that a treatment plan is followed.

Surely some of the aforementioned functions are social service roles which far transcend what has traditionally been viewed as the attorney's function. But if the attorney does not fill some of these needs, it is unlikely that anyone else will; and without aid of counsel, commitment can easily become a summary or self-fulfilling process. There are, increasingly, lawyers who understand and are willing to fill these needs. And if counsel come to be perceived as co-workers in the mental health system, dedicated to the aforementioned array of purposes, and not merely as righteously contentious obstructors, their presence during the commitment process will be welcomed rather than dreaded.

If one looks back at the various procedural recommendations in the light of the statistics on involuntary confinement presented at the outset, a staggering vision emerges. Hundreds of thousands of hours would be spent by lawyers, judges, and mental health personnel. Vast sums of money would be poured into the decision-making process, duplicating all the waste and failure of the criminal courts. On the other hand, is it not more likely that the mental health profession will simply back off and give up? Neither of these seem like the road to progress. I turn, therefore, to other alternatives.

The California Law

An alternative to that of simply injecting the procedural safe-guards of the criminal law into long-term civil commitment has been the effort of a few States, led by California, to overhaul the entire process and, most dramatically, to limit the length of commitment.

In 1969, California passed the Lanterman-Petris-Short law (here-after LPS) which made more stringent the criteria for involuntary commitment, and increased the legal rights of the committed as well as localized the State's mental health funding apparatus. The intent was to create financial incentives under which a local county would want to keep its citizens out of large State institutions while providing alternative outpatient care. LPS limited involuntary commitment to those believed to be, by virtue of mental illness, addiction, or chronic alcholism, dangerous to themselves, dangerous to others, or "gravely disabled" (52). A series of graduated categories was created, requiring increasingly severe impairment or dangerousness to justify longer period of confinement.

Its major provisions are as follows: A person may be detained 72 hours(53), on the request of any private person or police officer, and the written application, following a preliminary screening, by a mental health professional designated by the county. The staff of the psychiatric facility may then certify the person for an addi-tional 14 days of treatment and observation.

After 17 days any further confinement requires judicial review. If the court believes the person is suicidal, he can be held for 14 more days and then must be released. If the court finds a person imminently dangerous to others, another 90 days of confinement is allowed, and if gravely disabled, a conservatorship is granted, the person detained, and his status periodically reviewed(54).

LPS was the result of legislative distrust of the decisionmaking process in commitment. It brought together political groups on the right and the left who felt that the loss of civil rights attending commitment was excessive and unnecessary (55). Since other States (e.g., Washington) are following this version of reform, it is important to ask what implications California's experience has for the development of mental health programs. Unfortunately the preliminary data now available are conflicting(56), and the picture has been muddied by other ongoing efforts. I shall present what I take to be the major trends reflected in reports which are otherwise discrepant.

Looked at from the provision of mental health care perspective, LPS seems designed to implement the concepts of community mental health for those who are and might be committable: Screen and refer those who can be treated without inpatient care, provide intensive short term inpatient care for those who need it, and retain only those who are gravely disabled (whatever that means). However, there is still a huge gap between the concepts of community mental health and their successful implementation, particularly when applied to those who meet the substantive standards erected by California.

What the California mental health system was expected to do, then, was to bridge that gap and make community mental health a reality. This herculean effort was to be made at the same time that deinstitutionalization of chronic patients was absorbing community mental health resources. Demand for services was in fact escalating as a result of three different trends. First, the discharged chronic patients; second, LPS itself required immediate services and considerable paperwork; and third, the very existence of community mental health centers created a new demand by groups never before serviced, because of neglect or because their problems had never before been defined as mental health problems.

It is against this background, and I have vastly simplified the facts, that one must attempt to evaluate the new procedures of LPS. But it should be clear that LPS is not the only variable in the changes that have taken place and this may help to explain some of the conflicting opinions about its effects.

The screening system. It was anticipated that the flow of mental patients into inpatient facilities would be diminished since LPS made screening mandatory, and screeners would refer all those suitable to alternative (outpatient) facilities. This anticipation has only been partially fulfilled.

A. The most important change has been in the duration and locus of hospitalization rather than the numbers hospitalized. The value of this change depends on the quality of the care at the new locus. The ENKI report indicates grave reservations about that quality (56a). The only solid conclusion is that the length of hospitalization has been markedly reduced.

B. While some who would formerly have been committed are undergoing outpatient care, a significant number have refused referral and have found their way into the criminal system. Indeed, the California legislature is now struggling with this problem(56b).

C. Finally, there is evidence that the creation of local community care has expanded the demand for mental health services by reaching segments of the community never before covered (57).

Thus, the raw figures on the inpatient admissions are not an accurate measure of the effectiveness of the Lanterman-Petris-Short law. Obviously, these results, standing alone, are susceptible of many interpretations, and are only illuminated by the added findings sketched below.

Use of the established standards for admission. This aspect of the new law has not done what was intended. Physicians' own judgments about the desirability of commitment were, by their own report, a more frequent basis for commitment than any of the statutory criteria so painstakingly defined by the legislature(58). Perhaps this continued confinement of persons the statute was designed to exclude was due to insufficient short-notice referral service and alternative facilities, or to institutional inertia, or to the intransigence of individual judgment—or even to the physicians' apprehension that there was widespread public anxiety about the presence on the street of persons who, though apparently non-dangerous, nevertheless exhibited bizarre and bothersome behavior. Whatever the explanation may be, it demonstrates the inability of the health system to cope with the nonmedical model. But the opposite can be reported as well. Anecdotal data in the ENKI study makes it clear that psychotically disturbed individuals were turned away because mental health professionals felt they did not meet the legal criteria.

Fourteen-day certification. The major success of LPS—as noted previously—has been the marked decline which the mandatory hearing after 17 days has wrought in the average length of stay. That average has declined from 107 days to 15 days(59). One danger cited by the ENKI study is that since voluntary patients can and customarily do stay longer, there may be some considerable pressure exercised by the staff in getting patients to sign voluntary papers(60). I do not consider that a danger.

Indeed, if patients can, as here, be persuaded to cooperate in treatment when there is no long-term commitment hanging over their heads, I consider it a therapeutic achievement. But a persisting, lamentable flaw of the process is that treatment has not been provided as had been hoped in a quick, intensive 72-hour spurt; rather, it was provided only as the 14-day release hearing approached. Thus, within the resources available and the constraints of LPS, what was meant to happen in 3 days took 17.

Dangerousness to self. Originally LPS had allowed only the 72-hour confinement of suicidal patients. That provision was twice amended during passage of the law to permit 14-day certification, and then an added 14 days. After 31 days citizens of California are free to kill themselves. But the ENKI study of 335 patients who had been released for at least 6 months found that none had committed suicide, and recertification for 14 extra days had been necessary in less than 1 percent of the cases in 11 counties.

The ENKI report on the California experience concluded that early mandatory release had not shown any effect on the suicide rates over the prior prolonged confinement system (61). Many psychiatrists dispute this, but no hard data are yet available. Since a small percentage of those who commit suicide are confined, hard data may never be available. Thus, the real question is whether the mental health system shall be allowed discretion to treat when it has identified someone it believes to be mentally ill and suicidal, or whether an arbitrary time limit should be set. The legal formula adopted in California makes no distinction between rationally and irrationally motivated suicide, (e.g., terminal cancer vs. a delusion of terminal cancer) and it does not inquire into the question of whether one more month of involuntary treatment would save a life. Of course, since it is difficult to predict suicide, the argument can be made that the law reflects the problem of false positives rather than an insensitivity to irrational suicide. Whatever the rationale of the law may be, I am convinced that its arbitrary limits ignore and compound the problems of treatment.

Imminent danger to others. If one examines only the mental health system, one finds that the additional postcertification as dangerous to others was invoked in only 2 percent of the cases. Given the base rates I have discussed, this is what one might expect. (But presumably many of these are false positives.) However, more than one study (62) has found that there was a concomitant increase in resort to the criminal processes to deal with the mentally ill: Referrals of mentally disordered persons to the Los Angeles Police Department, for example, increased about 80 percent in the first 2 years following the enactment of LPS (63). Most of the charges were for disturbing the peace, vagrancy, and other quasi-offenses. Overall, the number of bookings of mentally disordered persons declined, as the police often refused to become involved. However, there was a dramatic increase in arrests followed by incompetency to stand trial commitment which allows for longer periods of confinement than LPS. This resort to criminal processes fulfills the hypothesis that the penal-mental health system operates as an overlapping reciprocal system for the control of deviance.

Conservatorship. The conservatorship aimed at the "gravely disabled" seems to have produced the most discrepant practices. ENKI reports difficulty and confusion in implementing it, and an unpublished study suggests that in at least one jurisdiction a high percentage of patients end up in this long term confinement (64). Often the gravely disabled standard was attached to the senile patient who may not belong in the mental health system to begin with. Quite obviously, given the structure of the law, applying for conservatorship is the only way that the mental health system can avoid the rigid time constraints. Since the time constraints are obviously arbitrary when viewed against the realities of mental illness and the limited service resources, it was inevitable that all the stresses for prolonging confinement would be directed at that one escape hatch.

Aftercare. Contrary to the intent of LPS, there has not been established any greater continuity of care. Community facilities seem not to be serving in any greater degree those who have formerly been hospitalized, and readmission rates have not declined (65). This is cause for great dissatisfaction among mental health practitioners who feel that LPS had made continuity of care more difficult with patients wandering in and out of hospitals. However, it can be argued equally that it has only made that problem more obvious, and that it can be solved only by coordinating alternative local services and not by uniformly lengthening inpatient stay.

Conclusion. In my judgment, the California experiment should not be considered a model for other States. The available studies are neither conclusive nor entirely encouraging. What is known suggests that the persons in need of treatment who would previously have been committed are not being diverted by screening to outpatient care, and continuity of care and effective treatment is still largely a vain hope. That conclusion is in large measure shared by a committee of the California legislature (65a) which has proposed amendments of LPS including mandatory outpatient treatment.

But California has not been the disaster some psychiatrists predicted, and in fact its experience suggests one absolutely crucial fact. Short term involuntary confinement may be all that is necessary in many cases; once the patient is over the initial crisis he may be quite willing to accept treatment voluntarily (66). Obviously that acceptance is enhanced if the facility offers decent and humane treatment.

I would like to extrapolate one conclusion from the California data that admittedly is suggestive at best. Two percent of the patients were found dangerous to others and 1 percent were found dangerous to self at the hearing held at the end of 17 days. My own judgment is that if the hearing had been held at the end of 3 days; i.e., close to the time required by the Lessard court, those numbers would have been no more than doubled. Thus, involuntary confinement based on the objective measures of dangerousness would affect only 6 percent of those actually confined. Perhaps that estimate is too low, but surely not by much based on the data presented in the chapter on dangerousness.

Anyone reading the various studies, whatever their bias might be, would have to conclude that such a limitation would mean that many overtly psychotic persons would go without treatment. There can only be two justifications for accepting such a result. First, that mental illness is a myth and its treatment is therefore impossible. Second, that civil rights are so important that the State can only interfere when danger is imminent. I reject both those views, as do most mental health professionals.

In fact, in what follows I shall propose a return to certain premises of the much maligned medical model as the only valid approach to involuntary confinement.

The Medical Model

Diagnostic Criteria

Despite controversy and suggested innovation, the last few years, if anything, has produced a renewed confidence in the traditional diagnostic nomenclature of psychiatry, particularly as they relate to psychoses. This in part derives from a variety of biological and genetic studies, as well as the accepted effectiveness of psychotropic drugs which seem to confirm aspects of the medical model.

As Phillips and Draguns point out (67) this resurgence of traditional diagnostic categories has taken place in the face of three kinds of global objections. Existentialists see diagnosis as dehumanizing; behaviorists interested in symptomatic acts find diagnosis irrelevant; and, lastly, students of the sociology of deviance look to social competence measures rather than disease concepts. Diagnosis is considered a transformation of social identity by social degrada- is considered a transformation of social identity by social degradation.

The counterargument is that it is not the diagnostic label which dehumanizes and stigmatizes; it is the mental conditions and resulting interpersonal disability. What seems to be a majority view among those doing research in the somatic aspects of mental illness is that genetic and biological studies will give new meaning to the current diagnostic system rather than dismantling it.

Unfortunately, perhaps because of the global criticism, there has been comparatively little recent study of the reliability of psychiatric diagnoses, given its continued significance in the lives of those labeled. Ash (68) and Mehlman (69) in early studies emphasized the unreliability of specific diagnosis. Others, like Schmidt and Fonda (70), found 80 percent reliability for major categories such as organic, psychotic, and characterological but they also found that when greater precision of diagnosis is demanded, reliability dropped to about 50 percent. In 1962, Beck (71) reviewed all previous studies and concluded that the narrow diagnostic reliability was no greater than 42 percent. But he emphasized that even Ash had found 64 percent reliability for the three major categories (psychosis, neurosis, and personality disorder).

Zubin (72) whose authoritative review of psychiatric diagnosis is often cited, reports:

> The overall level of agreement for broadly viewed diagnostic categories ranges from 64 percent to 84 percent.

This confirms what Hunt and co-worker (73) had found earlier:

> The more difficult a judgment is to make, the less valid it will be. In our study of the reliability of diagnosis we found that reliability diminishes as we proceed from broad inclusive class categories to narrower more specific ones.

My argument is that in principle, at least, reliability could be improved if for purposes of civil commitment psychiatrists would confine themselves to the broad diagnostic categories and in addition diagnose only severe conditions. This latter point is made by Babigian and co-workers (74), who report:

> It appears that a sizable proportion of the persons contacting psychiatric services presents a type and severity of illness that is easily recognizable and classifiable.

Kreitman and co-workers (75) also point out that the more severe the illness, the greater the diagnostic agreement.

In principle, then, it would be possible to develop even higher reliability than that reported in the literature for the broad categories by including degrees of severity, and accepting the diagnosis only when a given level of severity was present. Involuntary confinement could then be limited to only those who can be reliably diagnosed as having a severe mental illness.

A Five-Step Procedure

Reliable diagnosis of a severe mental illness, which has already been discussed, would be the first step in the scheme I shall develop.

The second would be whether the person's immediate prognosis involves major distress.

The third would be whether treatment is available.

The fourth would be whether the diagnosable illness impaired the person's ability to accept treatment; e.g., the person was either too disturbed to communicate, or because of incapacity arising from the illness such as delusions and hallucinations, the person was unable to comprehend the possibility of treatment.

The fifth and final step would be to decide whether a reasonable man might reject such treatment (see Chapter 6, The Right to Refuse Treatment).

I. Reliability, of course, means no more than that several diagnosticians would agree on a label. It does not mean that the label is a valid indicator of anything. But if diagnostic categories have any validity in psychiatry, it is because they indicate something about etiology, prognosis, and treatment.

II. The law-mental health system should be particularly interested in the second and third steps—prognosis and treatment—as relevant to involuntary confinement. If, as I suggest, involuntary confinement is limited to severe pathology where there is high reliability, there is also likely to be convincing evidence that short-term prognosis absent treatment, will include profound anxiety, depression or other painful affects, deterioration of the personality, and the proliferation or intensification of symptoms. Furthermore, where mental illness is the result of toxic conditions such as delirium tremens, failure to treat may result in brain damage and death.

The law, influenced by the reforms I have described, asks the psychiatrist to prognosticate dangerous behavior. That is absurd because it is a rare event, and the capacity for such prognostication is absent. What the mental health profession can prognosticate is the mental state and the likely course of the illness of the patient. Something is known about the deterioration of the decompensating schizophrenic, and the intense suffering of the agitated depressed patient. A compassionate law and a compassionate psychiatrist should direct attention to the issue of human agony rather than the behavior which may or may not flow from it. The nature of a prognosis justifying involuntary confinement should include human suffering; i.e., profound anxiety, panic, depression, and frenzy which are already manifest or incipient.

III. The next step is to ask the hospital if treatment is available, and if so, what kind and how effective. I have emphasized that mental health practitioners cannot predict dangerousness, but they can keep records of previous treatment for patients in similar diagnostic categories—its duration and effectiveness. Indeed, PSRO, which I shall discuss, will require a similar establishment of records and procedures.

What the psychiatrist would do in this system, then, is first make his diagnosis. If it cannot readily be demonstrated that this is a reliable diagnosis of a severe condition, the process would go no further. Reliability and severity could be challenged and/or demonstrated by independent psychiatric examination.

Diagnosis is the product of a present evaluation and not a future prediction. It does not ask the psychiatrist to do something he is unable to accomplish. Treatability of any psychiatric patient, of course, is, like dangerousness, a predictive judgment. But at least the actuarial tables already exist, or the data to make such tables exist. And although it is a prediction, it is a different kind of prediction. The prediction is: If the psychiatrist is allowed to treat this patient in a hospital where he can control the social context, what will happen to the patient's mental state based on his experience in similar cases where he has considerable experience? This, as opposed to the supposed reforms which ask the psychiatrist what dangerous acts will occur when he cannot know or control the social context and when there exists no backlog of useful experience.

IV. Severe illness reliably diagnosed, and prognosis and treatability are, however, not enough to justify involuntary confinement. It must also be shown that the alleged patient's decision to refuse treatment is an incompetent refusal.

I suggest the following as tests of incompetent refusal:

1. There should be a burden on the reliably diagnosed severely ill person to articulate a reason for refusing treatment.

2. Those patients who are unwilling or unable to consent, or object (the so-called nonprotesting patient), should be considered as having made an incompetent refusal.

3. If the alleged patient is able or willing to state a reason for objecting to confinement, the psychiatrist should be asked to demonstrate that the refusal is irrational and is based on or related to the diagnosed illness; e.g., the voices tell me the doctors are going to transplant my brain into an android; the doctors are really F.B.I. men who are part of the conspiracy against me; I am radioactive and no one should come near me; I have to kill myself because everyone thinks I am a homosexual; I don't deserve to be treated, I am worthless.

4. If the patient has a reason which is not a product of his illness; e.g., I have been a Christian Scientist all my life: I do not believe in medicines or physicians. Even though a physician might consider

this irrational, it is not based on his current misperception of reality, and it should therefore be considered a competent refusal.

Obviously, under this procedure only seriously psychotic—irrational—patients would be confined. No patient with a personality disorder, neurosis, or behavior problem would be incompetent. The same would be true of alcoholics and addicts, absent toxic syndromes.

The questions of the judge (or jury) would be deciding are:

1. Do the psychiatrists make a convincing diagnosis of serious illness?
2. Is the patient suffering?
3. Is treatment available and how long will it take?
4. Does the patient's objection to treatment seem irrational and based on his illness?

As I shall further explicate in the discussion of the right to treatment and the right to refuse treatment, (cf. chapters 5 and 8) the following questions comprising the fifth step would be answered as well:

V. Would a reasonable man accept the treatment being offered in that hospital? Might a reasonable man object to a proposed treatment method even though the alternative is more costly to the State and/or less apt to be successful?

All of these questions could be addressed at a hearing and with counsel within a few days of confinement. It would not preclude an earlier probable cause type hearing on the same issues.

The balancing test I propose, then, is: Would a reasonable man, given the patient's serious illness and suffering, be willing to give up a certain amount of freedom in that particular institution in exchange for a treatment that in similar cases produces a specific range of results? Such a test takes into account the quality of life and the treatment provided in the given treatment facility, and it means that a person might be committable to one institution and not to another. It means that no one could be committed to some State and county hospitals given the conditions and treatment which now exist.

It is my contention that the criteria of serious, reliably diagnosed mental illness, incompetent refusal, reasonable expectation of treatment in a decent institution are the essential ingredients which give moral content and legal justification to the doctrine of parens patriae.

It is also my contention that those criteria, if followed, would moot the many metaphysical arguments about the ambiguous line between mental illness and eccentricity, political and ideological dissent, religious conversion, etc. It moots those arguments by saying that in cases where those arguments can be raised convincingly, the criteria cannot be met.

This is the Thank You Theory of Civil Commitment: it asks the psychiatrist to focus his inquiry on illness and treatment, and it asks the law to guarantee that treatment before it intervenes in the name of parens patriae. It is radical in the sense that it insists that society fulfill its promise of benefit when it trenches on human freedom. It is also radical in that it divests civil commitment of a police function; dangerous behavior is returned to the province of criminal law. Only someone who is irrational, treatable, and incidentially dangerous would be confined in the mental health system.

A difficult problem which had until recently confounded the Thank You Theory was how could some of the baseline perspectives on disease and treatment be approached by a court. What general standards could they turn to so as to evaluate specific medical opinions? That obstacle has now been resolved, in my view, by the beginning development of PSRO standards.

When psychiatrists were asked to develop standards of treatment under PSRO they turned to exactly the issues I suggested are crucial to civil commitment: diagnosis, treatment, length of stay, etc. These PSRO standards provide the court with guidelines that permit the commitment decisions I have outlined to be applied intelligently to individual cases. A sample of model forms (as developed by an American Psychiatric Association task force) to suggest what the eventual process might be for schizophrenia and manic depressive illnesses, two severe illnesses, are shown in the model criteria tables starting on page _____ . Each diagnosis requiring involuntary treatment would be considered in light of the following:

1. Conditions, including mental suffering, which justify the necessity for hospitalization
2. A description of hospitals services critical to and consistent with the diagnosis, including:
   a. Present illness
   b. Past history
   c. Examinations
   d. Laboratory studies
   e. Special diagnostic studies
   f. Consultations
   g. Medications
   h. Special treatment
   i. Specific nursing services
   j. Discharge plan
3. Minimum and maximum length of stay

4. Suggested time of initial review to determine need for continued hospitalization

These criteria are expected eventually to be adaptable to computerization and to initial review by a nonphysician.

Two sample forms indicate the kind of data which PSRO makes available to the courts. Some of the data is responsive to current standards for commitment, but I have emphasized those relevant to the Thank You Theory. I do not mean to suggest that the new bureaucracy created by PSRO will promote health care. I assert only that it will generate treatment standards—not useful procedures.

Model criteria, Schizophrenia:

Justification for admission[1]
    Required [1] :
        Impaired reality testing
    In addition to the required, one or more of the following must be present:
        Paranoid thinking
        Bizarre behavior
        Potential danger to self, others, or property
        Impaired social, familial, or occupational functioning
Need for electroconvulsive therapy or high-dose medication
        Need for therapeutic milieu
        Need for continuous skilled observation
        Failure of outpatient management
        Inadequate social support
        Inaccessibility of outpatient psychiatric care
        Legally mandated admission
History of present illness
    Comment required[1] :
        Reality testing
        Delusions and hallucinations
        Disordered thinking and affect
        Drug and medication history
        Potential danger to self, others, or property
        Current social, familial, and occupational functioning
        Treatment and course of illness to date
        Current medical status

---

[1] Please see "Interpretation of Model Criteria Sets."

Past history
    Comment required:
        Psychiatric
        Medical
        Family
        Social and occupational
Examinations
    Required:
        Physical
        Mental status

Laboratory studies
    Required:
        CBC
        Urinalysis
        Serology
    Consistent with diagnosis[1] :
        Chest X-ray
        Blood chemistry profile
        Endocrine or hormone studies (e.g., thyroid)
        Toxicology (blood or urine)
Special diagnostic studies
    Required:
        None
    Consistent with diagnosis:
        Electrocardiogram
        Papanicolaou stain test
        Spinal tap
        Spine X-ray
        Electroencephalogram
        Psychological testing
Treatment plan
    Required:
        Specific treatment plan
Consultations
    Required:
        None
    Consistent with diagnosis:
        Medicine
        Neurology
        Social service
        Anesthesia
        Obstetric-gynecological examination

---

[1] Please see "Interpretation of Model Criteria Sets."

Medications
    Required:
        None
    Consistent with diagnosis:
        Major tranquilizers
        Hypnotics
        Antidepressants
        Anti-Parkinson drugs
        Non-narcotic analgesics
        Laxatives or stool softeners
        Contraceptive medication
Special Treatments
    Required:
        None
    Consistent with diagnosis:
        Electroconvulsive therapy
        Psychotherapy (individual, group, family, couples)
        Psychodrama
        Behavior modification
        Activities therapy
        Educational therapy
        Vocational rehabilitation
        Therapeutic milieu
        Therapeutic assignment (e.g., home, school, work, etc.)
Specific nursing services
    Required:
        Physician-approved nursing care plan
Discharge plan
    Required:
        Written discharge plan
Suggested screening points
    1. *Within 24 hours of admission*

    2. *At 50th percentile (median) for length of stay* (locally determined)

    3. *At intervals of one-half the median length of stay thereafter.*
       E.g., for diagnosis with local median length of stay of 30 days,
       screening will take place at 30 days, and if patient continues to
       be hospitalized, every 15 days thereafter until discharge.
Model criteria, Manic Depressive Illness, Manic:
Justification for admission
    Required[1] :
        Mania and impaired reality testing

---

[1] Please see "Interpretation of Model Criteria Sets."

In addition to the required, one or more of the following must be present:
    Physiological impairment
    Potential danger to self, others, or property
    Impaired social, familial, or occupational functioning
Need for Electroconvulsive therapy or special drug therapy (lithium or high-dose antipsychotic)
    Need for continuous skilled observation
    Failure of outpatient management
    Inadequate social support
    Inaccessibility of outpatient psychiatric care
    Legally mandated admission

History of present illness

    Comment required[1] :
        Symptoms and signs of mania
        Reality testing
        Depression
        Sleep and appetite disturbance
        Drug and medication history
        Current social, familial, and occupational functioning
        Treatment and course of illness to date
        Current medical status
Past history
    Comment required:
        Psychiatric
        Medical
        Family
        Social and occupational

Examinations
    Required:
        Physical
        Mental status
Laboratory studies
    Required:
        Complete blood count
        Urinalysis
        Serology
    Consistent with diagnosis[1] :
        Chest X-ray
        Blood chemistry profile
        Endocrine or hormone studies (e.g., thyroid)

---

[1] Please see "Interpretation of Model Criteria Sets."

Laboratory Studies
 Consistent with diagnosis[1] (Continued):
  Toxicology (blood or urine)
  Serum lithium
Special diagnostic studies
 Required:
  None
 Consistent with diagnosis:
  Electrocardiogram
  Papanicolaou stain test
  Spinal tap
  Spine X-ray
  Electroencephalogram
  Psychological testing
Treatment Plan
 Required:
  Specific treatment plan
Consultations
 Required:
  None
 Consistent with diagnosis
  Medicine
  Neurology
  Social service
  Anesthesia
  Obstetric-gynecological examination

Medications
 Required:
  Major tranquilizer or lithium or both
 Consistent with diagnosis:
  Minor tranquilizers
  Hypnotics
  Antidepressants
  Anti-Parkinson drugs
  Nonnarcotic analgesics
  Laxatives or stool softeners
  Contraceptive medication
Special treatments
 Required:
  None

---

[1] Please see "Interpretation of Model Criteria Sets."

Consistent with diagnosis:
   Electroconvulsive therapy
   Psychotherapy (individual, group, family, couples)
   Activities therapy
   Educational therapy
   Vocational rehabilitation
   Therapeutic milieu
   Therapeutic assignment (e.g., home, school, work, etc.)
Specific nursing services
   Required:
   Physician-approved nursing care plan
Discharge Plan
   Required:
   Written discharge plan

Suggested screening points
   1. *Within 24 hours of admission*
   2. *At 50th percentile (median) for length of stay* (locally determined)
   3. *At intervals of one-half the median length of stay thereafter*[1]

---

[1] E.g., for diagnosis with local median length of stay of 30 days, screening will take place at 30 days, and if patient continues to be hospitalized, every 15 days thereafter until discharge.

SOURCE: *Diagnostic and Statistical Manual II* (Schizophrenia, 295 except 258.8: Manic Depressive Illness, Manic, 296.1, 296.33), American Psychiatric Association, January 1974.

Interpretation of model criteria sets
(the numbers refer to steps in chart which require interpretation)

The enclosed criteria sets were designed to be utilized in the following frame of reference. Charts will be screened initially (1) by a trained person using a handbook of terminology and general model criteria as a guide (usually within 24 hours after admission). This initial screening will be conducted by comparing the information appearing in the chart with the list of criteria. In order to pass this initial screening a chart must include at least one of the combinations listed under "Justification for Admission" (2)—the required item plus at least one of the additional items.

At the point of median length of stay (by diagnosis) for a given PSRO, the chart will be screened again as before. At this point it should:

1. Include mention of all criteria listed under "comment required" (3). This does not imply that the findings must be positive; however, if findings are negative, a note to that effect should be present in the chart.

2. Include all procedures listed as "required" (4).

3. Not include any procedures that are not listed as either "required" or "consistent with diagnosis" (5).

A chart not meeting any of the above points will cause the chart to be selected for physician review. (7). The criteria have been constructed so that review should be needed on less than 10 percent of all psychiatric charts undergoing initial screening. It should be stressed that selection for review does not imply any deficiency in the quality or appropriateness of care. The only meaning of such selection is that there is something unusual about this case and that a quick review by a physician is in order. In most instances the reason for any deviation from the usual range of clinical management will be readily apparent to the reviewer. Occasionally the reviewing physician (member of the peer review committee) will want to check with the attending physician and only rarely should there be a significant disagreement which needs further review by a review committee.

In this frame of reference, criteria provide no more than a basis for selecting cases for physician review. Failure to pass the initial screen does not imply improper care or utilization or that payment should be disallowed for cases outside the usual range. The attending physician may and should take whatever action he feels is best for each of his patients. If that differs from the model criteria, the only additional responsibility is to tell a colleague why.

The following definitions are offered:

1. Initial screen—comparisons of information appearing in the chart must be made against the list of criteria. This comparison is performed by a nonphysician.

2. Justification for admission—reasons listed are sufficient for hospitalizing a patient without the need for review beyond screening. Some are specific to a particular diagnosis, though most are not. These factors when noted in the chart make admission appropriate without further review. They do not imply that such patients must be hospitalized, only that if they are, there is no question that they should have been. Patients not meeting these criteria may be admitted to the hospital, however, their charts will be reviewed by a physician.

3. Comment required—points listed must be mentioned in the chart. The form and content of the physician's notes on each are up to him. Only if he fails to comment at all will the chart be selected for physician review. Similarly, some sort of physical examination, mental status examination, nursing care plan, and discharge plan must be recorded.

4. Required—required laboratory studies must be done on each patient to pass initial screening. The results of these studies and their interpretation are up to the attending physician. He may omit any item he feels inappropriate to a particular patient (i.e., a serology on a patient who had a similar test the preceding week). In that event a brief explanatory note for the reviewer should suffice.

5. Consistent with—criteria listed as "consistent with" may be performed or omitted at the attending physician's discretion without leading to physician review. Tests, medications, or treatments not listed on the "consistent with" list may be ordered for a particular patient, however, some reason for doing so should be recorded or made available to the reviewing physician.

6. Suggested screening points—the time of screening of patients will be based on length of stay and will occur automatically at the 50th percentile (median) for similar patients as locally determined. If the patient is still hospitalized, the case will be reviewed again at half the median length of stay beyond the median, and at subsequent periods which equal half the median length of stay. Thus, hospitalized patients are reviewed to determine whether continued hospitalization is indicated at the median and subsequently every half median number of days.

Progress notes in the chart will be required to show the reasons for continued hospitalization.

For example, if a patient has a condition for which the local median length of stay is 30 days, review will take place at 30 days, and if the patient continues to be hospitalized, every 15 days thereafter until discharge.

7. Review—charts not passing the initial screening will be reviewed by a physician to determine the reason for the deviation of the information listed in this chart.

These are tentative models and may be changed, but their fundamental assumptions are such that they are admirably suited to the goals of the "Thank You Theory." Since the forms are to be available after 24 hours, the court could hold its hearing at any point within the first few days. As I shall point out in Chapter 6, The Right to Refuse Treatment, these forms would also allow the court to identify treatments which a patient could refuse.

The problem with PSRO is that each geographic area is to establish its own standards for length of stay and appropriate treatments. However, since national standards will be available for comparison, the court need not be locked into one arbitrary and regressive system. PSRO standards are meant to be applicable only when Federal funds are to be used, but that should not prevent a court from relying on them for guidance in any situation where the State imposes involuntary confinement on one who is alleged to be mentally ill. (Cf. Chapter 5, The Right to Treatment.)

I have proposed a theory and a set of standards which advance what I believe to be a legitimate role of the State, benefiting citizens while respecting their rights. It attempts to combine the threshold questions and the outcome questions. It directs the mental health system to a narrower purview in imposing treatment than now exists. Were it to become a reality, the procedural rights of the criminal system would lose much of their significance, and they would be replaced by truly civil procedures; procedures which allow the officers of the court to insure a just and reasonable use of imposed treatment. Almost as important, it would allow the mental health professions to reassert their traditional identity—alleviating human suffering.

References

1. Joost and McGarry, Massachusetts Mental Health Code: Promise and performance 60 American Bar Association Journal 95.
2. J. S. Mill, On Liberty. In: *The Philosophy of John Stuart Mill* (M. Cohen, ed.) (New York: The Modern Library, 1961) p. 197.
3. *Id.*, at 296.
4. See, e.g., Amsterdam, federal constitutional restrictions on the punishment of crimes of status, crimes of obnoxiousness, crimes of displeasing police officers, and the like, 3 *Crim. L. Bull.* 205 (1967); Foote, Vagrancy-type law and its administration, 104 *U. Pa. L. Rev.* 603 (1956).
5. J. S. Mill, *supra,* note 2, at 197, 296.
6. S. Brakel and R. Rock, *The Mentally Disabled And The Law* (Chicago: University of Chicago Press, 1971) p. 36, table 3.2.
7. Shaffer, Introduction, symposium: mental illness, the law and civil liberties, 13 *Santa Clara Lawyer* 369 (1973).
8. S. Brakel and R. Rock, *supra* note 6, at 36.
9. *Id.*
10. *Id.*, at 39-43.
11. *Lake* v. *Cameron,* 364 F.2d 657, 660 (D.C. Cir. 1967).
12. *Id.* at 663.
13. *See,* Hearings of the constitutional rights of the mentally ill before the subcommittee on constitutional rights of the senate committee on the judiciary, 91st Cong. 1st and 2nd sess., 214-215, 319, 409 (1969-70); Chambers, Alternatives to civil commitment of the mentally ill: Practical guides and constitutional imperatives, 70 *Mich. L. Rev.* 1108, 1126-1129 and n. 83 (1970).
14. *See,* Roth, *et al.,* Into the abyss: Psychiatric reliability and emergency commitment statutes, 13 *Santa Clara Lawyer* 400, 430 (1973).
15. *See,* Wash. Rev. Code Sec. 71.05.200 (1), 71.05.230 (1973); Note, progress in involuntary commitment, 49 *Wash. L. Rev.* 617 (1974.).
16. *But see, Cross* v. *Harris,* 418 F.2d 1095 (D.C. Cir. 1969).
17. *See generally,* J. Rappeport (ed.). *The Clinical Evaluation Of The Dangerousness Of The Mentally Ill* (Springfield: Thomas, 1967).
18. *Cross* v. *Harris, supra* note 16, at 1099.
19. Compare, for example, the cases of Bong Yol Yang, p. 493 and Dallas Williams, p. 526, Katz, *et al., Psychoanalysis, Psychiatry and Law* (New York: Free Press, 1967).
20. See, e.g., *Cal. Welf. and Inst. Code* Sec. 5300 et seq. (1971).
21. *See,* S. Brakel and R. Rock, *supra,* note 6, table 3.3 and notes thereto.
22. *Jackson* v. *Indiana,* 406 U.S. 715, 738 (1972).
23. See, e.g., Cases cited in hearings, *supra* note 13 at 58 n. 15.
24. *Minnesota* v. *Probate Court,* 309 U.S. 270 (1939); *Lynch* v. *Overholser,* 369 U.S. 705 (1962); *Specht* v. *Patterson,* 386 U.S. 605 (1967); *Baxtrom* v. *Herold,* 383 U.S. 107 (1966).
25. *Cf.* Katz, *et al., supra* note 19, at 767.
26. R. Rock, *et al., Hospitalization and Discharge of the Mentally Ill* (Chicago: University of Chicago Press, 1968).

27. *Lessard* v. *Schmidt*, 349 F. supp. 1078 (E.D. Wisc. 1972); vacated and remanded, 94 S. Ct. 713 (1964).
28. *See* Comment, Progress in involuntary commitment, 49 *Wash. L. Rev.* 617 (1974).
29. *Boddie* v. *Connecticut*, 401 U.S. 371, 379 (1971). *See also, Mullane* v. *Central Hanover Bank and Trust Co.*, 339 U.S. 306 (1950); *Goldberg* v. *Kelly*, 397 U.S. 254 (1970); *Fuentes* v. *Shevin*, 407 U.S. 67 (1972).
30. *Boddie* v. *Connecticut, supra* note 29 at 378.
31. S. Brakel and R. Rock, *supra* note 6 at table 3.2.
32. *Id.* at 44.
33. *Lessard* v. *Schmidt, supra* note 27 at 1091.
34. *Id.*, at 1092.
35. *In re Gault*, 387 U.S. 1, 49-50 (1967).
36. *Lessard* v. *Schmidt, supra* note 27 at 1101.
37. Note, Requiring a criminal defendant to submit to a Government psychiatric exam, 83 *Harv L. Rev.* 648 (1970).
38. *In re Gault*, 387 U.S. 1 (1967); *Kent* v. *United States*, 383 U.S. 541 (1966); *Jackson* v. *Indiana*, 406 U.S. 715 (1972).
39. *In re Winship*, 397 U.S. 358, 371 (1970).
40. *See Woodby* v. *Immigration and Naturalization Service*, 385 U.S. 276, 284 (1966).
41. See, e.g., *In re Winship, supra* note 39 at 358; *Denton* v. *Commonwealth*, 383 S.W.2d 681 (Ky. 1964).
42. *Baxtrom* v. *Herold*, 383 U.S. 107, 113 (1966).
43. *Humphrey* v. *Cady*, 405 U.S. 504, 509 (1972).
44. *In re Winship, supra* note 39.
45. *In re Ballay*, 482 F.2d 648 (D.C. Cir. 1973).
46. Moyer, The mentally abnormal offender in Sweden, 22 *Am. J. Comp. L.* 71 (1974).
47. *See Gideon* v. *Wainwright*, 372 U.S. 335 (1963); *In re Gault, supra* note 38; *Argersinger* v. *Hamlin*, 407 U.S. 25 (1973); cf. *United States* v. *Wade*, 388 U.S. 218 (1967).
48. *Heryford* v. *Parker*, 396 F.2d 393, 396 (10th Cir. 1968).
49. See, e.g., Gupta, New York's mental health information service: An experiment in due process, 25 *Rutgers L. Rev.* 405 (1971); Cohen, The function of the attorney and the commitment of the mentally ill, 44 *Tex. L. Rev.* 424 (1966).
50. S. Brakel and R. Rock, *supra* note 6, at 54.
51. See, e.g., Cohen, *supra* note 49; *see also* chapter 12 (Lawyers in the Mental Health System).
52. *See,* Cal. Welf. and Inst'ns Code sec. 5000 *et seq.*, sec. 5150.
53. Since week-ends and holidays are exempted from this period, it may in fact last for 5 or 6 days.
54. Cal. Welf. Code sec. 5250. Those "imminently dangerous" who are assaultive during hospitalization may be retained for added 90-day periods. "Gravely disabled" is defined as "unable to provide for one's basic personal needs for food, clothing, and shelter."
55. *See California Legislature, Assoc. Interim Committee on ways and means, subcomm. on mental health services*, The dilemma of mental commitment in California (1966).
56. See, e.g., ENKI Research Institute, A study of California's new mental health law (1972) (hereinafter ENKI Study); Abramson, The criminalization of mentally disordered behavior, 23 *J. Hosp. and Comm. Psychiat.*

101 (1972); Topinka, Conservatorship in Santa Clara County (unpublished, 1972); Final report, the Senate Select Committee on proposed phaseout of state hospital services, California legislature, March 15, 1974.

56a. See, e.g., ENKI Study of Sacramento County, pp. 54-62.

56b. *See* final report, cited *supra*, note 56.

57. ENKI Study at 196 and table 50 at 197.

58. *Id.* at 116, table 27.

59. *Id.* at 194.

60. *Id.* at 122.

61. *Id.* at 153.

62. *See* sources cited supra, note 56.

63. ENKI Study at 185.

64. *Id.* at 156; Topinka, *supra*, note 56.

65. ENKI Study.

65a. Final report cited at 56.

66. Spensley, et al., Involuntary hospitalization: What for and how long? 131 *Am. J. Psychiat.* 219 (1974).

67. Phillips and Draguns, Classification of the behavior disorders. 18 *Ann. Rev. Psychol.* 447 (1971).

68. Ash, The reliability of psychiatric diagnoses, 44 *J. Abn. and Soc. Psych.* 272 (1949).

69. Mehlman, The reliability of psychiatric diagnoses, 47 *J. Abn. and Soc. Psych.* 577 (1952).

70. Schmidt and Fonda, The reliability of psychiatric diagnosis: A new look, 52 *J. Abn. and Soc. Psych.* 262 (1956).

71. Beck, Reliability of psychiatric diagnosis, 119 *Am. J. Psychiat.* 210 (1962).

72. Zubin, Classification of the behavior disorders, 18 *Ann. Rev. Of Psychol.* 373 (1967).

73. Hunt, Wittson, and Hunt, The relationship between definiteness of diagnosis and severity of disability, 8 *J. Clin. Psychol.* 314 (1952).

74. Babigian, et al., Diagnostic consistency and change in a followup study of 12,015 Patients, 121 *Am. J. Psychiat.* 895, 900 (1965).

75. Kreitman, et al., The reliability of psychiatric assessment and analysis, 107 *J. Ment. Sci.* 887 (1961).

76. The approach closest to the "Thank You Theory" is that of the British Royal Commission of 1957; its criteria and limitations are discussed in Muller, Involuntary mental hospitalization 9 *Comprehen. Psychiat.* 187 (1968).

Chapter 5

Right to Treatment

The thesis of the proposed civil commitment procedures is that the parens patriae doctrine can only be legitimately invoked when there is a firm guarantee of reasonably effective treatment at the time of involuntary confinement. The intent of this "Thank You Theory" approach is to anticipate the entire process of involvement between the State and the citizen. This is in sharp contrast with the traditional criminal law approach and with the preventive confinement model which focus only on the question of entry.

The criminal law, in seeking to do justice, insists that a man is innocent unless "it has been unequivocally shown that he voluntarily engaged in antisocial conduct proscribed by statute so as to warrant the imposition of criminal sanctions" (1). The criminal law, like the preventive confinement model, insists that a barrier must be hurdled and considerable energy is focused on that single issue. The additional goals of the criminal law are deterrence, rehabilitation, protection of the community, and retribution. At the level of empirical reality, few indeed are the sophisticated observers who believe that any of these other goals are reached. It is fair to characterize the criminal system then as one whose only effective function (even that is debatable) is its just inquiry into whether the first barrier of guilt has been hurdled.

Judges face up to this impossible reality only at the point of imposing sentence, and not surprisingly judicial sentencing behavior leaves much to be desired (2). Some commentators believe it has become totally irrational (3). If we realize that the vast majority of criminal defendants are in fact guilty, and have more than hurdled the barrier, then their sentence and their subsequent fate is the most important question to them and to us.

Of course, since the vast majority of criminal cases are resolved by plea bargaining, this refined procedural apparatus is invoked as a possibility rather than as the actual practice. Although as a nation America can take great moral satisfaction in its decisionmaking procedures as to the determination of guilt at trial, that pious decision currently bears little relationship to the goals of criminal justice.

The point is that as judges and legal scholars increasingly insist on imposing the criminal law model on civil commitment, they should be reminded that (a) as a system of justice it simply does not work, (b) in most cases the moral niceties of the system are not utilized, and (c) despite the low rate of utilization the courts are impacted.

Nonetheless, except for the right to treatment cases, the vast literature of legal decisions and scholarly analysis deals with the standard of civil commitment and the procedures by which that standard is to be reached in a court of law. But the problem posed by the mentally ill in society will not be solved or even ameliorated by imposing the procedures and standards of criminal law. We therefore turn to the right to treatment as a legal vehicle for inquiry into the results of the entire process rather than the standards for entry.

The right to treatment has now been formulated by the courts as an important legal question in all of the categories of noncriminal confinement (4).

The juvenile system is particularly instructive. Conceived at the turn of the century, it was an effort to divert young people from the criminal system into rehabilitative and reformative treatment programs. It was to be therapeutic rather than punitive. Thus, the rights of the juvenile and procedural safeguards of criminal law were given less emphasis. Somebody who was to be helped, it was thought, needed less protection of his civil rights than did someone who was to be punished. This identical trade-off exists in all the categories of noncriminal confinement. The famous *Gault* decision of the Supreme Court (5) recognized that the promise of treatment to juveniles was often illusory, and in that context justified some constitutional increase in the procedural safeguards. This and similar legal approaches invoking the criminal model obviously do not solve the problems of the juvenile court; they merely acknowledge defeat of the treatment model and make it somewhat harder for society to confine.

Outside the juvenile court system the first cases dealing with right to treatment arose in the category of civil commitment of sexual psychopaths. This entering legal wedge raised the issue whether someone confined as a sexual psychopath could challenge the place of his confinement (6). *Miller* v. *Overholser* held that it was illegal to lock a man up in a building for the violently insane in which no treatment was provided, since the statute promised treatment. The Court agreed.

The Massachusetts Supreme Court, again in the category of sexual offenders, affirmed and expanded the principle that where

84

the statute promises treatment, confinement must not be in a jail-like facility *(Commonwealth* v. *Page)*. It further held that nonpenal confinement is legal only when:

> ... the remedial aspects of the confinement have foundation in fact. It is not sufficient that the legislature announce a remedial purpose if the consequences to the individual are penal (7).

These initial rulings were not based on the invocation of a constitutional right to treatment, but rather an interpretation of the applicable statutes. Further, these decisions say nothing about the quality or quantity of treatment, only that it must in fact be provided. But they do begin to examine what happens to people after the court decides to confine them.

The next major legal decision was *Rouse* v. *Cameron* (8) which is often cited as the first holding by a court that the right to treatment has the force of a constitutional right. The case involved a man who claimed he was receiving no treatment after being confined subsequent to a finding of not guilty by reason of insanity. The legal analysis of the ruling is complicated. Judge Bazelon found the right to treatment in the statute, as in the previous cases, but indicated there might be a constitutional right as well, alluding to questions of due process, cruel and unusual punishment, and equal protection. Judge Fahy, in his concurring opinion, went further and relied on the constitutional arguments. The *Rouse* decision, in addition to suggesting these constitutional implications, extended the significance of the right to treatment by stating that continued failure to provide treatment cannot be justified by an insufficiency of resources. The court, however, did not articulate general judicial criteria for acceptable treatment. It did not demand cure, or even improvement, or that the treatment used be the best possible. It asked only for a bona fide effort to provide an individualized treatment program with periodic evaluation.

The next important legal case came in the category of confinement due to incompetency to stand trial *(Nason* v. *Superintendent of Bridgewater State Hospital)* (9). In *Nason* the court clearly saw a constitutional right to treatment on grounds of due process and equal protection, and threatened to free the patient-defendant, absent treatment.

These were the groundbreaking cases in the history of the legal right to treatment. Interestingly, none of them arose in the context of the more numerous and familiar cases of civil commitment of the mentally ill. Other relevant cases not discussed in this summary:

Benton v. *Reid* (*10*). (The Director of Public Health could not hold someone in a prison whose only failing was that he was dangerous to public health.) *In Re Maddox* (*11*) (right to trial by jury of persons confined without treatment); *Commonwealth* v. *Hogan* (*12*) (special treatment center required); *Millard* v. *Cameron* (*13*) (indefinite confinement of sexual psychopaths justifiable only if treatment is involved). *Lake* v. *Cameron* (*14*) is sometimes considered a right to treatment case contradicting the generalization in the text. However, there the court was seeking to avoid confinement by finding alternative facilities.

Perhaps it is no accident that these were all men who though shunted out of the criminal system had been originally charged with crimes and thus had had extensive access to legal counsel. These cases had little impact at first (*15*), although they articulate the right to treatment and provide a legal and constitutional rationale for it. No one was discharged because of lack of treatment and the courts gave little specific guidance to the psychiatrists or to the legislatures as to the general standard of treatment required. At best, Judge Bazelon in *Rouse* had demanded a bona fide effort and hinted at a possible case by case review, an ambiguous standard reiterated in *Nason*.

However, the recent case of *Wyatt* v. *Stickney* (*16*) pushed further in every respect, and at last directed attention to the plight of the large group of mentally ill patients involuntarily confined in less than adequate State hospitals.

Wyatt v. *Stickney* was a class action suit brought by guardians of patients involuntarily confined at Bryce Hospital, a State facility in Alabama. Civil commitment in that State takes place in the context of minimal procedural safeguards and the promise of treatment is properly considered a paramount consideration. A constitutional principle of due process was clearly stated by Judge Johnson:

> To deprive any citizen of his or her liberty upon the altruistic theory that the confinement is for humane and therapeutic reasons and then fail to provide adequate treatment violates the very fundamentals of due process (*17*).

Wyatt v. *Stickney* became *Wyatt* v. *Aderholdt* with the resignation of Dr. Stickney from the Alabama Department of Mental Health. Under that name it was first appealed to a three-judge panel of the fifth circuit court of appeals. (After 2 years its major holdings were upheld by that court. It had now become *Wyatt* v. *Hardin* since Aderholt had also departed.) Since *Wyatt* was a class action, Judge Johnson went much further than his predecessors, and attempted to spell out standards of adequate treatment for all patients in the facility, indicating a willingness at least in his court, to attempt to identify and supervise the vagaries and complexities of institutional psychiatric care and treatment. That complexity is superimposed upon a critical legal entanglement; namely, the separation of powers. How far can the judiciary go in setting standards of institutional practice which will require the legislature and the executive branch to raise new tax revenues, or reorder the fiscal priorities of social needs (18) as they have been established through executive and legislative decisionmaking?

These troubling legal questions are an appropriate transition to an important decision negating the right to treatment. *Burnham* v. *Department of Mental Health* (19) is a Georgia class action case now being appealed along with *Wyatt*. The court in *Burnham*, held that adequacy of treatment is solely a matter of State law and not a constitutional right. The right to treatment, that court states, is merely a claim to public services. The provision of government services is a matter of State law, and no constitutional issue is raised unless there is discrimination in the provision of such services based on "invidious criteria" such as race. Furthermore, even if there were a right to treatment, it would not be justiciable, which in this context means the court cannot ascertain specific manageable standards.

Although subtle distinctions can be made between the legal questions raised in *Burnham* and those in *Wyatt*, for all intents and purposes the two courts were at loggerheads, until the U.S. Court of Appeals of the Fifth Circuit resolved the conflict in favor of *Wyatt*. However, *Burnham* makes it clear that not all of the American judiciary is convinced that the right to treatment is a legal reality. That question will have to be decided by the Supreme Court.

If one focuses on the constitutional aspect of these various cases which have spawned similar litigation all over the country, one can decipher a series of cutting points for legally enforced change.

I. The first is cruel and unusual punishment; i.e., does confinement without treatment constitute unconstitutional punishment without even a criminal charge being filed? Here we rely on the eighth amendment.

This rationale is, perhaps, the simplest to demonstrate. Courts have held that even the most humane incarceration may constitute punishment (20). And confinement without treatment may be regarded as punishment for a mere status—mental illness—over which the patient has virtually no control, a punishment of the type declared unconstitutional by the Supreme Court in *Robinson* v. *California* (21). Or, nontherapeutic confinement of the nondangerous mentally ill may be regarded as cruel and unusual under the standards of "pointless and needless," "degrading to the dignity of human beings," or "unrelated to any valid legislative purpose" set forth recently by the Justices of the Supreme Court in capital punishment (22). Finally, and most simply, State mental institutions cannot be allowed to perpetuate conditions like those which have already been declared unconstitutionally cruel in prisons (23).

It is my view that if the simplest standard of cruel and unusual punishment were applied in existing total institutions, many would be found to fall well below it. Even if the right to treatment were only constitutionally justified when the conditions of confinement were cruel and unusual on a scale developed for prisons, considerable reform could be accomplished.

II. Judge Johnson recognized that eighth amendment argument, but sought a higher standard based in due process and equal protection. That standard would seek to do more than prevent destructive conditions; it would insure adequate treatment. This is the second cutting edge.

Thus, the *Wyatt* order detailed minimum "medical and constitutional" requirements to be met with dispatch. The decree set forth standards guaranteeing basic patient rights to privacy, presumption of competency, communication with outsiders, and so forth. Requirements were established governing staff-to-patient ratios, floor space, education, sanitation, and nutrition. The court also ordered that individual treatment plans be developed, that written medication and restraint orders be filed, and that these be periodically reviewed. Outside citizens' committees were appointed to monitor enforcement of patients' rights under the order (24).

The *Wyatt* decree was far from a generalized array of commands arbitrarily arrived at. It was formulated from study of the testimony of institutional personnel, outside experts, and representatives of national mental health organizations appearing as amici. Most of the specifics of the order were taken from a memorandum of agreement signed by the parties.

The most critical specifics, the model staffing ratios, approximate those last recommended by the American Psychiatric Association (25). That a floor for minimally adequate care can be rationally set is underscored by the congruence between the *Wyatt* standards and, for example, recent standards for psychiatric facilities formulated by HEW. These regulations require institutions seeking to be eligible for Medicaid and other Federal compensation to satisfy physical safety, and sanitary standards (26), staffing requirements (27), recordkeeping standards (28), and procedural and review regimens (29), similar to those mandated by *Wyatt*.

III. It is my view that unless a State meets this second standard necessary for even decent care, no new patient should be committed for therapeutic reasons. The compelling next question is whether on the same legal basis one can go further than Judge Johnson and demand effective therapeutic conditions as a third level of the right to treatment.

In at least 24 States the statutes altruistically promise to provide treatment to those who are in need of it (*30*). Therefore, it might be argued that due process demands that such a promise be honored. In addition, where only the need for treatment is invoked to justify commitment, due process is compromised when the State fails to require weighing of relevant factors such as the amenability of the patient to treatment, the capacity of the existing institutions to deal with his infirmity, and the term of confinement which, for his specific malady, may arguably be effectively therapeutic (*31*).

IV. Beyond destructive conditions, adequate treatment, and effective treatment within a total institution there is a fourth level argument; namely, that confinement should not be continued if alternative treatment outside the institution would be preferable (*32*). This is the thrust of a recent lawsuit brought against St. Elizabeth's Hospital in the District of Columbia (*33*).

Power of Enforcement

Even if, on the basis of the arguments and case law previously discussed, there is a right to treatment, it may be asserted that courts are not competent to enforce it. In legal parlance, the question is whether the right to treatment issue is justiciable—whether there are judicially ascertainable standards by which to measure the rights and duties of the parties, whether a judicial decision will transgress the proper sphere of another branch of government and whether the court has power to grant adequate relief (*34*). (This hurdle was overcome in *Wyatt* by stipulations agreed to by both sides.)

The criticisms of the developing right to treatment run generally as follows: Treatment is a term encompassing so many approaches and types of curative efforts that defining its adequacy can only be a post hoc judgment made without regard for the actual choices faced by the medical staff (*35*). Moreover, "the only feasible way in which the adequacy of treatment could ever be measured is against the needs of a particular patient" (*36*). Courts, therefore, could not hope to monitor the delivery of adequate care to each patient—even if general standards of some kind could be derived. And even the formulation of indicia of overall care would require weighing of medical data by inexpert judges.

In my judgment, however, these objections are overstated and can be successfully rebutted. First, while it is true that opinions vary concerning the preferred treatment modality for a given mental disorder, there is considerably more agreement as to when there is no treatment of any kind being afforded. Thus, for example, the court in *Wyatt* made it quite clear that it was not attempting to choose between arguably effective forms of therapy; it confined itself to eradicating conditions which made effective therapy impossible for any patient (*37*). Even those courts most friendly to the notion of the right to treatment acknowledge that the right does not adhere to the single, hypothetically best treatment, but merely to "adequate treatment" (*38*), "suitable treatment" (*39*), "a bona fide effort" to help the patient (*40*), or treatments such as give the patient a realistic opportunity to improve or be cured (*41*).

Thus, in determining whether a hospital has made a bona fide effort to cure its patients, the role of the court is really no different than in reviewing agency action in other areas. As Judge Bazelon has noted (*42*), the court merely looks to see whether the hospital has made a reasonably convincing effort, whether the patient has received an adequate degree of a mode of therapy which some reputable segment of the profession deems appropriate. While this overall review will still require judges to weigh technical testimony regarding the indicia of adequacy, this is not foreign to the judicial role in other fields. Few judges are truly expert with respect to the antitrust or ecology matters before them, yet they nevertheless are routinely called on to weight the conflicting testimony and resolve technical controversies in these areas. More relevantly, judges resolve matters of medical malpractice, the medical aspects of drug-related crimes, the adequacy of medical care afforded prisoners—as well as all the questions of sanity and psychiatric categorization, involved in commitment. It is implausible to contend that these same faculties suddenly atrophy when treatment—the purpose of the entire classification process—is brought into question.

The right to treatment cases discussed in this chapter all deal with the problems of those already confined. Often the court is trying to remedy conditions in institutions where years of neglect and resulting patient deterioration are involved. (See also right to treatment aspects in chapters on mental retardation and the juvenile system.) The briefs in *Wyatt* read like a description of the Augean stables. As tragic as the fate of the chronic mentally ill may be, it should not deflect our attention from considering the right to treatment of those who might become the next chronic generation.

A procedure which would avoid that result would require that the right to treatment be combined with the commitment decision as suggested in the previous chapter. I indicated there that PSRO standards, which apply to all federally funded health care, would allow the courts to supervise and monitor the right to treatment. Indeed, in my opinion, PSRO resolves the difficult problem of justiciability—at least for those who will enter the mental health system in the future.

The availability of PSRO standards, however, does not resolve the problem of how they are to be made part of the legal process. How will the standards be implemented, for example, in State hospitals that do not have Federal funds under medicaid? This raises the whole issue of "comity" and the separation of powers between branches of government. In this context the judiciary might be said to be imposing its priorities on the legislature. These considerations could keep PSRO standards from being applied to fully State supported mental health facilities.

There are, of course, replies to this view. When constitutional rights have been abridged, courts have been willing to enter decrees requiring affirmative action by State and local administrators of public schools (*43*), public assistance programs (*44*), political processes (*45*), public housing programs (*46*), and prisons (*47*).

Such relief is particularly appropriate where legislative and administrative bodies have been given an opportunity to choose among alternative remedial measures and have responded in a dilatory or patently insufficient manner. And though courts cannot directly order the appropriation of funds, they have entered injunctions, compliance with which requires expenditures (*48*). (This is the basic posture in *Wyatt*.)

Among the potential options open to an institution ordered to raise its standards to constitutionally minimal levels are reducing the patient population, which is the line of least resistance, or alternatively applying for new State and Federal funding, soliciting funds from families, and so on; all of which are far more difficult.

In this regard, the recent case of *Legion* v. *Weinberger* (*49*), though unsuccessful, is particularly interesting. *Legion*, as its pseudonymous title suggests, was a class action, brought by medically indigent patients who had been involuntarily committed to State mental institutions. The plaintiffs charged that medicaid violated their equal protection rights in that ample benefits were conferred on the already more fortunate voluntary patients in the psychiatric wards of general hospitals while it provided no benefits for the involuntary patients of State and county mental hospitals where the poor and minority groups are over-represented. The Supreme Court summarily affirmed the lower court's dismissal of the suit, though Justice Blackmun disagreed with this result. Had the suit succeeded, the Federal Government would have been obliged to pump millions more into State and local facilities.

Ironically the Federal Government through the Justice Department has recently embarked on a policy of bringing its own right to treatment suits. One such suit is on behalf of mentally retarded patients in the State of Maryland. The complaint charges that the Maryland Department of Mental Health has failed to provide treatment by failing to recruit enough qualified professionals to plan appropriate treatment programs, to offer essential psychiatric and social services to retarded delinquents and to provide a safe, clean, humane environment. *U.S.* v. *Solomon*, N74-181. (Citation not available at this writing.)

The charges are familiar. The origin of the suit is what is ironic, given the efforts of the Federal Government to impound funds essential to accomplishing exactly what such suits demand. It becomes all the more obvious that the real question is how can the proper resources be found to make the right to treatment a reality.

In addition to class action right-to-treatment suits, other strategies are available to assert specific patient's rights. Although most mental patients lack knowledge of their rights or access to counsel (50), obstacles which have severely limited the number of habeas corpus petitions filed (51), a habeas suit is still a relatively simple and sometimes expeditious means of securing better treatment for a given patient. Suits in the nature of mandamus have also been mentioned (52). But perhaps the most powerful legal wedge will be monetary damages against hospitals and mental health professionals for denial of constitutionally required treatment, for negligence, or for false imprisonment. Most prominently, in *Whitree* v. *State* a New York court granted the plaintiff $300,000 in damages against the hospital and staff after finding that:

> The lack of psychiatric care was the primary reason for the inordinate length of his incarceration, with the concomitant physical injury, moral degradation, and mental anguish (53).

And just recently, a Florida jury awarded $38,500 to a mental patient who brought a civil rights suit against his psychiatrists, alleging that he had been confined for 14 years with little or no treatment, a decision recently upheld by the Fifth Circuit Court

(54). (This case has recently been heard by the Supreme Court.) If these damage suits allow attorneys to receive contingency fees which are often one-third of the damages, there will be little need to recruit public interest lawyers. The possibility of such lawsuits, plus class actions like *Wyatt*, plus the revolving door policies favored by many State departments of mental health will all combine to bring quick action in the name of right to treatment. That action has followed the path of least resistance; i.e., reduction of the inpatient population.

The pattern of discharging the chronic mentally ill from total institutions without adequate alternatives and refusing to commit because of new standards is becoming a familiar pattern all over the United States. As indicated in chapter 1, the result is to place an intolerable burden on the welfare system. Equally unfortunate is that the few available alternatives in the mental health system are unable to cope with the seriously mentally ill. Thus, the adequacy of treatment deteriorates where it once existed, and there are large numbers getting no treatment—all this in the name of civil rights and the right to treatment.

There are, for example, an estimated 25,000 ex-mental patients living on welfare in New York City (55). The run-down hotels of the inner city where ex-patients enjoy their new freedom— unsupervised, unmedicated, and uncared for—have replaced the back wards of the State hospital.

A horrifying indictment of the New York situation includes the following charges (56):

1. Ambulatory mentally ill are housed in nursing homes geared to the physically handicapped.
2. The Bowery's alcoholic population has been joined by the mentally ill, many of whom have been discharged from State hospitals. Ninety-four of the first 100 such patients examined by a hospital team in 1972 were overtly psychotic.
3. Many of the mentally ill are in nursing homes where the cost per patient is $1,000 per month, and yet treatment is not geared to their needs.
4. Nursing homes for the care of the aged have taken in mentally ill young adults. Often the only tolerable solution for combining these disparate groups is massive medication of the mentally ill.

A similar pattern has been described in California in a report called "To the Lowest Bidder" (57). It documents in particular the way community facilities in the mental health system have deteriorated in the face of the large numbers and more disturbed persons whom they cannot assimilate.

The response of local communities to this new problem is reminiscent of times gone by when the mentally ill were set adrift in the legendary "Ship of Fools." Anywhere but here is all too often the response to the creation of halfway houses, foster homes, sheltered settings, etc. This is accomplished by zoning ordinances, harassment by local officials, and recently in Long Beach, N.Y., by a specific ordinance intended to prevent the mentally ill from moving into hotels in that community. (That ordinance has been recently overturned by the courts.)

The significance of the right to treatment litigation for the mentally ill remains ambiguous. Noble constitutional arguments and court decrees, after they have been translated into bureaucratic action, may have little resemblance to the original intentions.

The only certain result seems to be an acceleration of deinstitutionalization. Alabama, for example, has reduced its State hospital population dramatically after *Wyatt* (*58*). But that may in the end mean less rather than more treatment is offered to the mentally ill as we will have shifted from warehousing to abandonment.

There is a lingering ambiguity about the right to treatment cases which recurs in the section on mental retardation. Specifically, do the constitutional arguments apply only to those involuntarily confined by the State? That question is glossed over in much of the litigation. If subsequent legal decisions were to conclude, as suggested in chapter 1, that rights to anything become salient only when rights against the State have been obstructed as by involuntary confinement, then the States could avoid the burden of providing treatment by instituting the progressive civil commitment laws advocated by civil libertarians.

Given that possibility, and the pattern of deinstitutionalization already in evidence, it seems quite obvious that the ultimate solution of the right to treatment rests not in litigation but in national health insurance which does not exclude inpatient mental hospital care.

References

1. *In Re Ballay*, 482 F.2d 648, (D.C. Cir. 1973).
2. *See* M.E. Frankel, *Criminal Sentences: Law Without Order* (New York: Hill and Wang, 1973); Stone, Book Review: J. Hogarth, *Sentencing As A Human Process* (Toronto: U. of Toronto Press, 1971), 86 *Harv. L. Rev.* 1352 (1973).
3. See, e.g., Wilson, If every criminal knew he would be punished if caught, *New York Times Magazine*, January 28, 1973 at 9.
4. *See generally*, Hospitalization of the mentally ill: Due process and equal protection, 35 *Brooklyn L. Rev.* 187 (1969).
5. *In Re Gault*, 378 U.S. 1 (1967).
6. *Miller* v. *Overholser*, 206 F.2d 415 (D.C. Cir. 1953).
7. *Commonwealth* v. *Page*, 159 N.E.2d 82, 85 (Mass. 1959).
8. *Rouse* v. *Cameron*, 373 F.2d 451 (D.C. Cir. 1966).
9. *Nason* v. *Superintendent of Bridgewater State Hospital*, 233 N.E.2d 908 (Mass. 1968).
10. *Benton* v. *Reid*, 231 F.2d 780 (D.C. Cir. 1956).
11. *In Re Maddox*, 88 N.W.2d 470 (Mich. 1958).
12. *Commonwealth* v. *Hogan*, 170 N.E.2d 327 (1960).
13. *Millard* v. *Cameron*, 373 F.2d 468 (D.C. Cir. 1966).
14. *Lake* v. *Cameron*, 364 F.2d 657 (D.C. Cir. 1966).
15. *See* Katz, The right to treatment: An enchanting legal fiction, 36 *U. Chi. L. Rev.* 755 (1969).
16. *Wyatt* v. *Stickney*, 325 F.Supp. 781 (M.D. Ala. 1971); 334 F.Supp. 1341 (M.D. Ala. 1971); *enforced by* 344 F.Supp. 373, 344 F.Supp. 387, *appeal docketed sub nom. Wyatt* v. *Aderholt*, No.72-2634, 5th Cir., filed Aug. 1, 1973.
17. 325 F.Supp. at 785.
18. *See Wyatt* v. *Stickney* and the right of civilly committed mental patients to adequate treatment, 86 *Harv. L. Rev.* 1282 (1973).
19. *Burnham* v. *Department of Pub. Health*, 349 F.Supp. 1335 (N.D. Ga. 1972), *appeal docketed*, No. 72-3110, 5th Cir., Oct. 4, 1972.
20. See, e.g., *Cross* v. *Harris*, 418 F.2d 1095, 1101 (D.C. Cir. 1969); *Hamilton* v. *Love*, 328 F.Supp. 1182, 1193 (E. D. Ark. 1971).
21. *Robinson* v. *California*, 370 U.S. 660, 666 (1962); *see also United States* v. *Walker*, 335 F.Supp. 705, 708 (N.D. Cal. 1971).
22. *Furman* v. *Georgia*, 408 U.S. 238, 312 (White, J., concurring), 271 (Brennan, J., concurring), 331 (Marshall, J., concurring) (1972).
23. See, e.g., *Inmates of Boys Training School* v. *Affleck*, 346 F.Supp. 1354 (D.R.I. 1972); *Jones* v. *Wittenberg*, 323 F.Supp. 93 (N.D. Ohio, 1971).
24. *Wyatt* v. *Stickney*, 344 F.Supp. 373, 376, 379-385 (M.D. Ala. 1972).
25. *See* Hearings on the Constitutional rights of the mentally ill before the subcommittee on constitutional rights of the Senate Committee on the judiciary, 91st Congress 1st and 2nd Session 43 (1969-1970); 86 *Harv. L. Rev.* 1282, 1297-1299 (1973).
26. 45 C.F.R. sec. 405.1022 (1973).
27. 45 C.F.R. sec. 405.1023 (1973).
28. 45 C.F.R. sec. 405.1027 (1973).
29. 45 C.F.R. sec. 250.20-23 (1973).

30. *See* S. Brakel and R. Rock, *The Mentally Disabled And The Law* (Chicago: University of Chicago Press, 1971) tables 3.1-3.20

31. Cf. *Jackson* v. *Indiana*, 406 U.S. 715, 728, 732-733 (1972); *Lessard* v. *Schmidt*, 349 F.Supp. 1078, 1092 (E. D. Wis. 1972).

32. *See Aptheker* v. *Secretary of State*, 378 U.S. 500 (1964); *Shelton* v. *Tucker*, 364 U.S. 479 (1960); Wormuth and Mirkin, The doctrine of the reasonable alternative, 9 *Utah L. Rev.* 254 (1964).

33. Complaint for declaratory and injunctive relief filed in D.C. Feb. 14, 1974.

34. *Baker* v. *Carr*, 369 U.S. 198,217,236 (1961).

35. Szasz, The right to health, 57 *Geo. L. J.* 734 (1967).

36. *Burnham* v. *Department of Pub. Health*, 349 F.Supp. 1335, 1343 (N.D. Ga. 1972).

37. *Wyatt* v. *Stickney*, 344 F.Supp. 373, 375-376 (M.D. Ala. 1972).

38. *Nason* v. *Superintendent of Bridgewater State Hospital*, 233 N.E. 908 (Mass. 1968).

39. *Millard* v. *Cameron*, 373 F.2d 468, 472 (D.C. Cir. 1968).

40. *Covington* v. *Harris*, 419 F.2d 617, 625 (D.C. Cir. 1969).

41. *Wyatt* v. *Stickney*, *supra* note 37, at 374.

42. Bazelon, Foreword, A symposium: The right to treatment, 57 *Geo. L. J.* 673, 678 (1969).

43. See, e.g., *Swann* v. *Charlotte - Mecklenburg Bd. of Educ.*, 311 F.Supp. 265 (W.D.N.C. 1970), *aff'd* 402 U.S. 1 (1971).

44. See, e.g., *Goldberg* v. *Kelly*, 397 U.S. 254 (1970).

45. See, e.g., *Harper* v. *Virginia Bd. of Elections*, 383 U.S. 663 (1966).

46. See, e.g., *Fautreaux* v. *Chicago Housing Auth.*, 304 F. Supp. 736 (N.D. Ill. 1969), aff'd, 436 F. 2d 306 (7th. Cir. 1970), *cert. denied* 402 U.S. 943 (1971).

47. See, e.g., *Cruz* v. *Beto*, 405 U.S. 319 (1972); *Jones* v. *Wittenberg*, 330 F. Supp. 707 (N.D. Ohio 1971), aff'd sub. nom. *Jones* v. *Metzger*, 456 F. 2d 854 (6th Cir. 1972).

48. See, e.g., *Holt* v. *Sarver*, 442 F. 2d 304 (8th Cir. 1971); *Taylor* v. *Sterret*, 344 F. Supp. 411 (N.D. Tex. 1972); United States v. School Dist. 151, Cook Cy., Ill. 301 F. Supp. 201 (N.D. Ill. 1969).

49. *Legion* v. *Richardson*, 354 F. Supp. 456 (S.D.N.Y. 1972), summarily aff'd 94 S. Ct. 564 (1973). *See also*, Brief of Amicus Curiae, The American Psychiatric Association, *Legion* v. *Weinberger, U.S. Supreme Court*, No. 73-5467 (1973).

50. *See Bolton* v. *Harris*, 395 F. 2d 642, 649 (D.C. Cir. 1968); Golten, The role of defense counsel in the criminal commitment process 10 *Am. Crim. L. Rev.* 409 (1972).

51. *See Hearings, supra*, note 25 at 901.

52. *Rouse* v. *Cameron*, No. 287-365 (D.D.C., January 17, 1967, Judge Holtzoff's comments during rehearing); Drake, Enforcing the right to treatment: *Wyatt* v. *Stickney*, 10 *Am. Crim. L. Rev.* 387, 600 (1972).

53. *Whitree* v. *State*, 290 N.Y.S. 2d 486, 495 (Ct. CL. 1968).

54. *Donaldson* v. *O'Connor*, 493 F.2d 507 (5th Cir. 1974).

55. Reich and Siegel, The chronically mentally ill: Shuffle to oblivion, 3 *Psychiatric Annals* 35 (1973).

56. *Id.*

57. *To The Lowest Bidder*, Mimeographed Materials, Council for Community Action Planning, Inc. (1971).

58. Goodman, The Constitution v. the snakepit, *New York Times Magazine*, March 17, 1974. p. 21.

Chapter 6

The Right to Refuse Treatment

Together with the growing concern about the right to treatment has come a recognition of the need to respect and protect the right of psychiatric patients to refuse treatment (1). This is a subject of enormous complexity, involving legal, psychological, ethical and socioeconomic considerations, only some of which can be outlined and discussed below. But without further qualification, I should state my own conclusion that practical legal solutions must be linked to the development of PSROs and effective psychiatric utilization procedures described in the previous chapters.

Many of the issues pertinent to right to refuse treatment have been explored in the burgeoning literature on experimentation with human subjects (2). Unfortunately in the mental health area the lines drawn between experimental and accepted treatment are at times ambiguous and debatable: e.g., various psychosurgical procedures, carbon dioxide inhalation (3). Because it would take us too far afield we cannot here discuss the many administrative or regulatory schemes for medical experimentation which might be adapted to the right to refuse treatment (4). Rather the premises are that accepted treatments can be distinguished and will be in PSRO standards, and that accepted treatments require less cumbersome regulation than experimental procedures. One can presume, however, that in the future, legal battles will be fought for both economic and political reasons as to what constitutes a standard treatment under PSRO. The model to be proposed later in this section is one in which administrative guidelines are established utilizing mental health expertise as will be the case in PSRO, but individual decision making is left to the court on the request of a patient, his guardian, or attorney.

The right to refuse treatment poses legal problems such as the patient's competency to decide whether or not to undergo treatment (5), rights and constraints arising from the various legal statuses of confinement (6), religious objections, and other exercises of constitutional rights (7), the difficulty of defining and acquiring the "informed consent" of a disturbed if legally competent patient, and possible malpractice implications of administering or withholding involuntary treatment of various kinds (8).

Psychological complications include the potential for deluded or overly fearful decisions to refuse treatment on the one hand, and impulsive or masochistic decisions to accept on the other. Other issues are the proper allocation of scarce resources (e.g., shall treatment facilities be forced to provide psychotherapists for patients who refuse effective somatic therapy?), the definition of emergency situations where the patient's consent should not be necessary, and the lack of consensus within the profession on treatment methods—a disagreement which bewilders patients and third party decisionmakers asked to decide whether to accept assertedly necessary therapy.

Ethical issues include the nature of coercion and of informed consent in a psychiatric context (9), as well as the broader questions of whether a person has, if not a legal at least an ethical right to be mad and to control his own body (10). In this context, some techniques of behavior modification, e.g., the use of token economy programs throughout an entire institution, create particular problems (11). Economic difficulties arise from the added costs to the State of patients who refuse less expensive therapy, or therapy which might more quickly terminate confinement. These two are apt to become enmeshed in the PSRO debate. Assume that PSRO allows medicaid patients tranquilizers and group psychotherapy for a given condition but the patient refuses all drugs and insists on individual psychotherapy. Is the State to pay the added cost which might result? What is the State's remedy? Will the patient be discharged from the hospital?

Superimposed on substantive complexities such as these is the problem of public confusion and rightful apprehension about mind altering procedures. While the quieter, though undoubtedly greater problems of unnecessary commitment, nontherapeutic confinement, the paucity of institutional alternatives, and the disabling stigma of past confinement seldom cause a public stir in the public media, the single issue of involuntary mind alteration has leapt to the forefront of public concern. Anxiety has been exacerbated by the irresponsible, almost science fiction approach of certain writers, the exaggerated and oversimplified advertising claims of the drug houses, and the dramatization of these distortions in the mass media.

Measured policy on so intricate a problem can seldom be formulated in so excited a context; the only antidote for widespread confusion is a clear presentation of the facts. First, therefore, and with full appreciation of the inherent difficulty, it is essential that some national mental health organization prepare a single pamphlet describing in simple language all of the generally available psychiatric and psychological treatments. (Perhaps it might include majority and minority views.) This pamphlet should be given the widest circulation possible, and should be distributed to all patients and their families at the time of admission to public or private mental health facilities. It should also be widely available to courts and attorneys. Such a pamphlet, in addition to clearing the air, could serve as an aid, indeed one would think a prerequisite to an intelligent decision by a patient on whether to accept or refuse a recommended course of treatment.

Similar information presented on national educational television would be a valuable service to a public, one-tenth of whose members will at some time during their lives be in a mental health facility. Public apprehension has been coupled with widespread public indignation over alleged abuses of psychiatric treatment for disciplinary, punitive, or other nontherapeutic reasons. Ken Kesey's dramatic portrayal of degrading practices by mental health personnel has become a legend in this regard (12). If such abuse occurs (and I am not prepared to deny that it does) (13), it may be a criminal offense, as well as serving as the basis for civil suits for negligence, malpractice, or deprivation of constitutional rights. When proprietary hospitals are involved, administrative sanctions such as revocation of license may be resorted to (14).

Much of the furor concerning involuntary treatment has centered on the use of electroshock therapy. Since much of the malpractice literature on psychiatric treatment either focuses on or alludes to electroshock, and since it is in the view of some psychiatrists a valuable and widely practiced treatment, I consider it an appropriate vehicle for examining some of the broader issues (15).

At this time, very few States have legislation regarding the conditions under which physicians may employ electroshock treatment (or any other treatment) (16). A notable exception to this rule is California, which in 1971 guaranteed patients the right to refuse electroshock or lobotomy (17). Paradoxically, however, the very next section of the California code provided that such rights:

> may be denied for good cause . . . by the professional person in charge of the facility (18).

The high-handedness of this approach has reminded one commentator of the Biblical refrain, "And the Lord gave, and the Lord hath taken away" (19). [California has now passed strict legislation (AB 4481) regulating these treatments. That legislation is now being challenged on constitutional grounds, Doe v. Younger et al., 4th Civil #14407.] A number of States have, however, through their departments of health or similar administrative entities, formulated departmental regulations with respect to consent to electroshock. These provisions are varied and divergent. For example,

> Kentucky regulations state that obtaining consent is not necessary because the treatment is an accepted therapy beyond the stage of experimentation. Michigan and New York on the other hand require permission from a legally responsible person (20).

Recently, however, the Massachusetts Department of Mental Health has developed more specific and stringent regulations governing the use of electroshock treatment (21). These may serve as one model of substantive guidelines for medical care. The regulations provide that informed written consent must be obtained before proceeding with electroshock treatment of any voluntary patient, that a patient's consent may be withdrawn at any time, and that psychiatric facilities must report all administrations of electroshock to the department (22). The departmental regulations do not create criminal penalties for infractions, but do provide the possibility that nonpublic facilities not in compliance may lose licensure, as well as creating a basis for a persuasive civil suit.

In formulating these regulations, it also became necessary to develop a set of guidelines for an appropriate regimen of electroshock treatment—guidelines which, apparently, had never before been established in Massachusetts or any other jurisdiction. Such guidelines were enacted by a somewhat dubious psychiatric establishment so as to avoid the enactment of guidelines included in a bill pending before the State legislature. In addition to foreshadowing further legislative interventions in medical decisionmaking, it was felt that statutory guidelines would have been less flexible than administratively promulgated ones since a vote of the legislature would be necessary to alter or amend them.

Given the great need for flexibility in good clinical practice, I concur in the view that statutory regulation of nonexperimental psychiatric treatment is ill advised. On the other hand, in light of the great public concern with electroshock therapy, the regulatory steps taken by the Massachusetts Department of Mental Health were prudent. Such responsible efforts at regulation are ethically, legally, and psychiatrically long overdue. They enable the patient or other third party decisionmaker specifically to accept or reject a course of treatment whose parameters have been clearly defined by the medical officials of the State. PSRO guidelines extend this opportunity to all treatments if they are used as suggested here.

Despite the obvious virtues of such an effort to achieve informed freedom of choice, it does present significant obstacles to effective clinical practice, and immediately creates new problems. Almost as soon as these apparently sensible and flexible guidelines on electro-convulsive therapy were formulated, the following sort of dilemma arose: What does a hospital do when an acutely suicidal but voluntary patient refuses to give permission for electroshock treat-ment and his physician believes that it is the treatment of choice and is necessary? For the responsible physician such a situation may well be a psychiatric disaster. The regulations prevent him from providing what he deems likely to be life-saving treatment.

Without shock treatment he must provide the patient with around-the-clock suicidal precautions which may be enormously expensive and disruptive of the care of the other patients. Also, he may be forced to employ unnecessarily large dosages of presumably less effective medication—medication which is itself by no means free of side effects. Restraints, or high security measures con-siderably less humane than electroshock treatment may be required for an extended period of time at great cost and considerable psychic distress to the patient and his family. Nor will the Massachusetts Department of Mental Health regulations invariably insulate the responsible physician or the hospital from a malpractice suit if the patient under these circumstances does commit suicide. Even less is the physician protected from the understandable resentment of the patient's family or the community—no matter how many signed documents he can produce showing the patient's refusals of treatment. Nor can the hospital protect its other patients from the harmful emotional impact of a fellow patient's suicide (23). Some may argue that a person has the right to commit suicide (24); but must the hospital allow the patient to hang himself in its corridors?

The Massachusetts law on civil commitment provided that a patient who wished to be voluntary must be allowed that status, and that the hospital could not commit a voluntary patient (even though suicidally depressed) until he gave the hospital written notice of his intention to leave. Since all such voluntary patients had to give consent to electroshock, the responsible physician was stymied in the case of such voluntary nonconsenting patients. Therefore, the regulations were altered to permit the hospital to move for commitment when such patients refuse shock treatment. Such a procedure provides for judicial determination—which may be at least some form of safeguard of the patient's right to refuse treatment. This is not, however, the primary legal purpose of the judicial hearing; rather, it is to determine commitability (25).

Even in civil-liberties conscious Massachusetts, the regulations do not assure the involuntary patient the right to refuse electroshock. Consent may be given by the guardian or nearest relative over the patient's objection. But such a neat, pragmatic bifurcation of procedures for voluntary versus involuntary patients does not overcome the significant questions of personal rights.

If we shun the extreme positions—that the physician always knows best, or that every patient, no matter how disturbed or disoriented, has an absolute right to refuse therapy, then we are constrained to develop some concept such as "competent informed consent", to treatment. The first, and possibly dispositive question is whether the patient is competent to decide whether to undergo treatment. A person who is committable, because, for example, he is dangerous to himself or others by reason of mental illness may still be competent to decide on treatment. And just because a patient's status is formally voluntary, it does not follow that he is competent regarding treatment decisions; every psychiatrist has encountered masochistic patients eager to undertake any therapy, whether or not it is necessary. Though in some jurisdictions mere commitment still concomitantly establishes incompetency for various purposes (26), there has been a growing awareness that competency must be evaluated anew in each context with regard to the specific task to be performed (27). This is a difficult task, one which obliges us to define psychiatric dimensions of disturbance, delusion, and disorientation—and sometimes to make moral and political distinctions between dissent and disease. Yet, "competency to decide whether to undergo treatment" is a useful construct to work toward defining (cf. the attempt in chapter 2).

The second relevant element is the informed nature of the consent to treatment. It is now established that consent, to be effective, must arise from a decision based on adequate information concerning the therapy, the available alternatives, and collateral risks (28). From the physician's perspective, the question is, of course, which risks is he dutybound to know of, and to disclose. The physician is required merely to have the knowledge of a reasonably well trained and informed physician practicing in like circumstances (29). Surprisingly, few cases have involved the physician's failure to disclose risks of which he should have been but was not aware (30). However, where innovative or experimental (31) therapies are involved, the physician is more likely to be held responsible for knowing and disclosing all "material" risks (32). In addition to known risks, the physician ought to disclose the possibility of unknown risks, if it is salient (33). And within the array of known risks, he must disclose those which separately or in combination would be significant to a reasonable man (or which the physician has reason to know would be significant to the given patient) in deciding whether or not to undergo treatment (34). And, of course, disclosure must be in such a manner as to maximize the patient's understanding of it. (Recent decisions, however, seem to push further the doctor's responsibility to know and advise patients of minimal risks.)

The third element is the patient's consent. In order for the consent to be meaningful, the patient must have a reasonably specific notion of which particular dangers he is consenting to. Though as a psychological matter one might consent to be subject to a set of unknown risks, as a legal matter he may not (35). Clearly, the consent must be relatively freely given and not induced in a frenzied situation (36). Finally, since the question will often be whether the physician acted as a reasonable man in concluding from the patient's actions that the patient had, indeed, given his consent, it is clear that any prolonged objection by the patient during the course of therapy effectively revokes consent (37).

It would be possible to rank various psychiatric treatments according to criteria of severity, such as the gravity and duration of intended effects and likely side-effects, the extent to which a reneging patient can avoid these effects, and the sheer physical intrusiveness of the therapy. Presumably, as one moved from the more to the less severe treatments, the patient's consent would be less consequential. Such a ranking is consistent with recent malpractice criteria.

However, despite the value of such a ranking along a continuum of gravity, intrusiveness, finality, etc., there is an additional problem which confounds that formulation. Courts have suggested that physicians are not required to inform a patient of certain side-effects if that very information would be damaging to the health of the patient (38). Thus, the more disturbed the patient and the more severe the treatment and its side-effects, the greater the likelihood that a reason might exist for not fully informing the patient. But surely it is reasonable to conclude that some responsible person other than the treating psychiatrist should be fully informed. As it is, however, we lack clear guidelines as to how informed the consent should be, and this further complicates the problem of waiving or accepting consent.

Therefore, it is best to seek, albeit in an indirect way, a procedural solution, by answering the following questions: Who should have the role of deciding when there are no clear substantive guidelines? What information should the decisionmakers have available? What procedural safeguards, such as hearings, appeal, and so on, should the patient have in this context?

As I indicated at the outset, I believe these problems are best addressed through the development of PSRO and procedures for medical utilization review. This would require the hospital as soon as possible after admission to draw up a treatment plan setting forth the goals of treatment, making a prediction based on past therapeutic experience with similar disorders as to how soon progress toward each of the goals can be expected, and describing the treatment to be employed. Obviously the range of plans will differ with different therapeutic settings; but Richman and Pinsker (39) are right that "The definition of goals for a specific service setting is possible." Such a document prepared by the responsible professional would also be a useful part of the patient's record for consideration by all subsequent treatment personnel. The physician would review the information with the patient and if possible obtain his consent, whatever its ultimate legal efficacy. He would explain the expected therapy and its side-effects; where possible it would be desirable that the patient write a simple summary of his understanding of the treatment and its risks and benefits which could be appended to the record.

If the patient refuses to consent to a suggested treatment, or the physician believes that the patient's consent is not bona fide, or not fully informed, recourse should be available to a third party decisionmaker. The third party might be a legally appointed guardian, the nearest relative, a physician not on the hospital staff, an ethics or patients' rights committee, or a judge. A third party not professionally or personally affiliated with the attending physician would seem to be the minimally necessary ingredient of the process. If the decisionmaker is not a judge, I believe it will be difficult to insure the patient's civil liberties. Therefore, I shall outline a procedure similar to that suggested in the chapter on civil commitment.

I suggest a two step procedure; a preliminary judicial hearing at which a tentative decision is reached that observation, diagnosis, and preliminary treatment which may include pharmacotherapy are appropriate. The second hearing at which the patient would be represented by counsel would deal with three issues. First, does the patient require further involuntary confinement; second, is there a useful treatment plan; third, is there any part of that treatment plan which the patient objects to?

The judge would have to determine as to the third issue whether the patient has a valid reason to object. This would presumably require some inquiry into competence to decide the reasonableness of objections, and viable alternatives to the suggested course of treatment. The judge would also have to decide whether a reasonable man might object to the suggested treatment. Therefore, the treatment and its side-effects, etc., would have to be explained to the judge if they are not already in writing as earlier suggested.

The costs of this process in terms just of medical time spent in acquiring patients' consent or refusal, compiling the records, and appearing before the court, are likely to be huge. And there are always the possible dangers of delaying treatment. Therefore, for pragmatic reasons, the gravity of the treatment contemplated becomes relevant as a cutting line. Full procedural safeguards, including review by a judge as suggested here, might be made mandatory only for the more severe therapies.

Although the following list of treatments may not be acceptable to all, it represents a framework suggested by the recent medical and legal literature (*39a*). I would suggest that the following treatments not be permitted to be administered to a protesting patient until he has had an opportunity for a full judicial hearing:

1. Ablation or destruction of histologically normal brain cells by any medical or surgical procedure (There is a growing consensus that such psychosurgery is experimental and should be subject to stricter regulations governing experimentation on humans.)
2. Electroshock therapy or any other convulsive therapy
3. Coma or subcoma insulin therapy
4. Behavior modification utilizing aversive therapy
5. Inhalation therapy (CO_2, etc.)
6. Medically prescribed, highly addictive substances (e.g., methadone)

The emerging case law on informed consent and malpractice in psychiatry and medicine generally adds weight to the prudence of separating out these categories of treatment as indicated (*40*).

If a patient is being held as incompetent to stand trial, a full judicial hearing should be held before any of the aforementioned treatments are instituted—whether the patient, his lawyer, or guardian consents or not.

Similarly, if a person is confined in a quasicriminal setting (sex psychopath, defective delinquent, etc.) where consenting to treatment may be seen by that person as the means to obtain freedom from indefinite confinement, judicial review is also appropriate despite consent.

If this or any similar procedure for providing a right to refuse treatment is instituted, as I believe it should be, it is essential that the mental health profession begin to explore every legal remedy available to protect hospitals and their staffs from responsibility in civil suits when patients or third party decisionmakers reject a recommended course of treatment. Civil libertarians and mental health reformers as well would like the practitioner-patient relationship to be contractual rather than paternalistic (41). If that is to be the path of progress, then the practitioners' contractual rights must be reconsidered pari passu with the patients.

These recommendations offer no protection for those patients who voluntarily undergo various kinds of treatment on an outpatient basis. Presumably the standard of informed consent is applicable in those cases. Also, no protection is provided against the excessive use of pharmacotherapy within the mental health system. It is the view of this writer that unless the courts are to review every aspect of mental health intervention, some arbitrary lines must be drawn. I have drawn that line at what seems to me a reasonable point; others might draw it elsewhere. But if we protect patients' rights by all of the means already enumerated in other sections; e.g., commitment, right to treatment, periodic review, etc., then surely some leeway to the practitioner is justified.

Many practicing psychiatrists object to the kind of procedures suggested above in that they tend to make the judge a medical decisionmaker. They prefer drawing a sharp line which limits the judge to a determination of competence or incompetence. If the patient is incompetent, then a third party (relative, guardian, member of the hospital's committee on human rights, etc.) would be asked to choose for the patient. Obviously the choice between these two kinds of procedures involve important policy judgments, e.g., the court's proper role in regulating professional behavior and practice; the economy, time, and human costs of different procedural formats. The practicality of courts increasingly taking on administrative and legislative functions rather than the traditional function of dispute resolution is of concern. The most recent experience suggests that strict regulation leads the psychiatric profession to abandon the regulated treatments. The medical and social value of that is dubious.

References

1. *Cf.* N. Kittrie, The Therapeutic Bill of Rights, In: *The Right To Be Different* (Baltimore: Johns Hopkins University Press, 1971) pp. 402-404.
2. J. Katz, *Experimentation With Human Beings,* (New York: Russell Sage Foundation, 1972).
3. *Cf.* H. R. 6852, 93rd Congress, First session, April 11, 1973.
4. *See* Freund, Legal frameworks for human experimentation, Daedalus, *J. Am. Acad. Arts and Sci.,* Spring 1969.
5. *Natanson* v. *Kline,* 350 P2d 1093 (Kan. 1960).
6. *Kaimowitz for John Doe* v. *Michigan Department of Mental Health,* Civ. No. 73-1943-4, Slip. Op. 29-31 (Cir. Ct., Wayne County, Mich., May 10, 1973).
7. *Winters* v. *Miller,* 446 F2d 65 (2nd Cir.). *cert. denied* 404 U.S. 985 (1971).
8. D. J. Davidoff, *The Malpractice Of Psychiatrists* (Springfield: Thomas, 1973).
9. *Cf.* Katz, *supra* note 2, chapter 8, What are the functions of informed consent? pp. 523-608.
10. Kittrie, *supra* note 1.
11. Wexler, Token and taboo, 61 *Cal. L. Rev.* 81 (1973).
12. K. Kesey, *One Flew Over The Cuckoo's Nest* (New York: Signet, 1962).
13. *Cf. Wyatt* v. *Stickney,* 344 F Supp. 373 (M.D. Ala. 1972). *Appeal Docketed* sub nom. *Wyatt* v. *Aderholt* No. 72-2634 5th Cir., Filed Aug. 1, 1973.
14. This may be the sole sanction available under regulations promulgated by a Department of Mental Health.
15. Davidoff, *supra* note 8.
16. S. Brakel and R. Rock, *The Mentally Disabled And The Law* (Chicago: University of Chicago Press, 1971) pp. 161-164.
17. Cal. Welf. and Inst'ns Code sec.5325(F) (West Supp. 1971).
18. Cal. Welf. and Inst'ns Code sec.5326.
19. Note, Conditioning and other technologies used to "treat?" "rehabilitate?" "demolish?" prisoners and mental patients, 45 *So. Cal. L. Rev.* 616 (1972).
20. Brakel and Rock, *supra* note 16 at 163.
21. Massachusetts Mental Health Regulation 181, Effective May 1, 1973.
22. *Id.*
23. E. Stotland and A. Kobler, *Life And Death Of A Mental Hospital* (Seattle: University of Washington Press, 1965).
24. See Kahne, Suicide among patients in mental hospitals, 31 *Psychiatry* 32 (1968).
25. *Mass. Laws Ann.* ch. 123 (Supp. 1971).
26. *See,* S. Brakel and R. Rock, *supra* note 16, table 8.2.
27. *See, generally,* R. Allen, et al., *Mental Impairment And Legal Incompetency* (Englewood Cliffs: Prentice-Hall, 1968).
28. See, e.g., Waltz and Scheuneman, Informed consent to therapy, 64 *Nw. U. L. Rev.* 628 (1970), and sources cited therein at n.25; Comment, informed consent in medical malpractice, 55 *Cal. L. Rev.* 1396 (1967);

Davis, Duty of doctor to inform patient of risks of treatment: Battery or negligence, 34 *Cal. L. Rev.* 217 (1961).

29. *See, Kaplan* v. *Haines*, 232 A. 2d 840 (N.J. 1967): 2 F. Harper and F. James, *The Law Of Torts* sec.17:1-2 (Boston: Little, Brown, 1956 and Supp. 1968); McCold, The care required of medical practitioners, 12 *Vand. L. Rev.* 549 (1959).

30. *Waltz and Scheuneman, supra* note 28 at 632. *But see, Fiorentino* v. *Wenger*, 272 N.Y.S. 2d 557 (1966).

31. *See generally*, Katz, *supra* note 2.

32. See, e.g., *Board of Medical Regis.* v. *Kaadt*, 76 N.E. 2d 669 (Ind. 1948); American Law Institute, *Restatement (Second) Torts* Sec.295A and comment, and sec.300 (1965).

33. *Cf., Fiorentino* v. *Wenger, supra* note 30.

34. This approach requires the physician to attempt to understand the patient's expressed concerns. *See*, F. Harper and F. James, *supra* note 29 at sec. 17:1 n.15 (Supp. 1968). *See, DeFillippo* v. *Preston*, 173 A. 2d 539 (Del. 1961); *Natanson* v. *Klein, supra*, note 5.

35. *Cf. Roberts* v. *Wood* 206 F. Supp. 579 (S.D. Ala. 1962). *See*, Waltz and Scheuneman, *supra*, note 28; Comment, valid consent to medical treatment: Need the patient know? 4 *Duq. L. Rev.* 450 (1966).

36. *Cf. Gray* v. *Grunnagle*, 223 A. 2d 633 (Pa. 1966); *Bang* v. *Charles T. Miller Hospital*, 88 N.W. 2d 186 (Minn. 1958).

37. A possible exception would be the life-death situation. See, e.g., *Application of President and Directors of Georgetown Col.*, 331 F. 2d 1000 (D.C. Cir.), *cert. denied* 377 U.S. 978 (1964); Comment, Unauthorized rendition of lifesaving medical treatment, 53 *Cal. L. Rev.* 860 (1965).

38. Davidoff, *supra*, note 8 at 139.

39. Richman and Pinsker, Utilization review of psychiatric inpatient care, 130 *Am. J. Psychiat.* 900-903 (1973).

39a. *See* discussion of intrusive treatments in Developments in the law-civil commitment of the mentally ill, 87 *Harv. L. Rev.* 1190, 1316 (1974).

40. Davidoff, *supra*, note 8.

41. Glass, Restructuring informed consent: Legal therapy for the doctor-patient relationship, 79 *Yale L. J.* 1533 (1970).

Chapter 7
Institutional Peonage

The tradition of patient labor within the "total institution" is familiar to all mental health professionals. It can be justified on many scores: (a) that it ameliorates the passive state of patienthood, (b) that if the institution is in any sense a community, all should contribute, (c) that work brings the patient into contact with reality, (d) that work is an anodyne for depression, (e) that work can be an outlet for pent-up feelings, (f) that work makes the transition to the outside world less disrupting, etc., etc.

Whatever the rationales may be, I have no doubt that in the era of long hospital stays, work therapy was often acceptable to patients as a welcome alternative to institutional tedium. Work therapy, or, as some prefer to call it, forced labor, is in fact the major rehabilitative policy of the communist countries.

Recently, various lawsuits have charged that total institutions in America are using forced labor or, as it is called, peonage. The call is once again to legalize—this time the work relationship between the subjects and the caretakers. This chapter will examine some of this recent litigation and its implications. It is important to recognize at the outset, however, that the problems of peonage have been posed mainly in large total institutions which are, for many reasons discussed elsewhere, anachronistic. Whether advocates of legalizing the work relationship would be eager to apply this principle to the many small sheltered settings, the halfway houses, the many small therapeutic communities operating in a communal atmosphere, etc., is surely problematic. These small institutions have revitalized the ideology which was meant to infuse work in the megainstitution. If the strategy of peonage lawsuits is meant to dismantle the megainstitution, one wonders how in law it can be confined to that purpose.

Patient labor performed for little or no compensation, or peonage, as it has come to be known, is a practice at most of our large, public total institutions for the mentally impaired. Hence the recently asserted right of the mentally impaired to be compensated for notherapeutic institutional labor is a notion which both challenges and transcends this system. And the difficulty of eradicating peonage suggests the paradoxes and limits of the current treatment scheme.

In virtually all public institutions for the mentally impaired in the United States, patients are required to perform labor whose primary purpose is not therapy in the sense that it develops skills; rather, its goal is maintenance of the institution. A 1950 report of the Council of State Governments intoned:

> No hospital worthy of the name would regard a patient as a source of cheap or free labor, nor would it assign a patient to work except in his interest and in an occupation that was suitable for him in view of his condition and his requirements (1).

Yet a 1972 study of three-quarters of all America's institutions for retardates found that a fifth of the residents performed just such nontherapeutic labor, 30 percent receiving no pay at all, and an added 50 percent being paid less than $10 weekly (2). Numerous professional accounts report that the labor performed is not infrequently for long hours (40 or more hours weekly), and that those who do not labor usually do so either because they are unable to work, are not needed for institutional tasks, or have forcefully and repeatedly refused (3). The work is parimarily janitorial, sanitary, kitchen, or custodial (emptying bedpans, cleaning patients)—of the type disfavored by the institutional staff. As one hospital superintendent put it:

> No one pretends that most of the work patients do is to their advantage. It is dull, negative, and without therapeutic value (4).

Some would disagree, arguing that work is better than nothing; but if these institutions had active treatment or habilitation programs, limiting the work of patients to such activity would be inexcusable. Though most do not, a telling betrayal of the system is conjured by the image of a patient such as Ken Kesey's Chief Broom (5) who, though potentially quite competent, passes his life sweeping, sweeping, sweeping. Nor is this vision chimeric: a compensation suit was recently brought by a woman who was known to have an IQ of 134, who spent 16 years in a State hospital doing nothing more edifying than

> caring for elderly patients, serving beverages in the dining room, polishing floors, etc. (6).

Despite the ubiquity of peonage, most States have no laws (7) dealing with the labor or compensation of the patients! And the fact is that the entire economy of the mental hospitals is premised on the availability of barely compensated labor. One institutional farm happily reported a profit—without acknowledging that it was due solely to free labor (8). The dependence on peonage has gone beyond therapeutic considerations. It is a budgetary, and, hence, ultimately a political problem. Current mental health budgets simply do not provide either for sufficient staff (therapeutic or custodial) and certainly not for even minimally decent compensation for working patients. Legislatures have rejected the idea of adequate compensation based upon some sense that people become residents of State mental institutions because of the largesse of the State, that they should be thankful for the situation and make no demands on the State. And, of course, many may feel as well that the State should not have to pay for those tasks which are validly part of a therapy or vocational program (9). This may indeed be fair, and I limit my discussion of peonage to those tasks done primarily to benefit the institution and not the patient. The fact is that much patient labor seems to come within this category.

A number of reasons for insisting on a system of adequate compensation have been advanced. Compensation may promote therapeutic goals by giving a sense of dignity and purpose to the work, by substituting a mutual relation in which the patient may choose whether or not to perform such labor. It may abate the feelings of inadequacy, powerlessness, and persecution which are central to so many patients' illnesses. It may be used to teach the qualities of responsibility and wise money management which are deemed so important in determining the ability of patients to leave the institution and adjust to the world. Thus, it may hasten recovery and release and thereby save the taxpayers' money. It would eliminate numerous abuses which prevent the timely release of patients whom the staff is loath to lose because of their valuable labor.

A particularly chilling example is cited by one hospital psychiatrist: a patient-worker on an incontinent male ward who did much of the bed changing, cleaning of the old men, and so on. He was a homosexual caring for his harem. The staff refused to transfer him, however, until "someone else could be found to do his work" (10). Numerous examples have been recorded of patients retained years beyond what was necessary because their work was needed and "work is good therapy"(11).

In addition, adequate compensation would enable patients to pay something toward their care, contribute something to often shaky family relationships, and enable some to put aside money to ease their adjustment upon release. Finally, in a mental health system which always cries for more resources, compensation would make patients eligible for extra-systemic benefits now denied them, such as workmen's compensation, payroll social security, and State pension plans.

Despite these policy arguments, it is unlikely that significant numbers of States will institute adequate compensation schemes without the prodding of legal battles. So it is significant that there have emerged in recent years an array of arguments for the right to compensation for institutional labor to which at least some courts are prepared to respond.

Fair Labor Standards Act (FLSA). In 1966 Congress amended the FLSA of 1938. The Department of Labor has interpreted the changes as extending the coverage of the act to non-Federal hospitals and institutions for the aged, mentally ill, or retarded (*12*). Responding to this expression of Congressional purpose, suits have been brought on behalf of patient-workers denied minimum wage benefits in Delaware, Florida, Pennsylvania, Tennessee, and perhaps other States as well (*13*). If successful, these plaintiffs would be entitled to full back pay, plus damages. In the Tennessee suit, for example, the wage paid the patients was 6 1/4¢ per hour, and the recovery of wages sought is almost $9,000,000.

Some such suits may be more difficult in the future in light of the Supreme Court's recent ruling that the 11th amendment bars a Federal court from granting relief under the FLSA against a nonconsenting State (*14*). However, some compensation suits will still be possible: suits in State courts, suits against private institutions, or, though less likely, suits to compel action by the Secretary of Labor (*15*).

Assuming that patient-workers are to be compensated, the question is what tasks they shall be paid for. The most reasonable standard seems to be whether the tasks confer an economic benefit upon the institution. This is the standard embodied in the FLSA. While theoretically the most subtle standard might be whether the task is primarily assigned for therapy or institutional maintenance, this is an impractical guideline.

As one court which has dealt with the question and adopted the economic benefit test noted, any standard related to therapeutic benefits will necessarily be vitiated, since the staff may cast virtually any activity as potentially therapeutic under some treatment theory. As noted above, this has often occurred in practice. And the economic benefit definition of compensable labor is made less onerous by the fact that the FLSA does permit special wage rates for very handicapped workers whose efficiency is substantially

112

subpar. Institutions should have the burden of proving that challenged work is almost purely therapeutic and therefore noncompensable by pointing to such facts as these: the work does not displace what would otherwise have to be performed by hired staff; it is recorded; it is adjusted to the individual needs of the patient; it is changed frequently (the Department of Labor presumes that any work which continues for 3 months is an employment relation); it is part of a written or at least ascertainable treatment regimen.

There is, however, a trapdoor in legal efforts to obtain compensation for patient labor; namely, that the hospital would then expect patients to pay for their care in the institution. This practice, if accepted, could transform patient compensation into a complex accounting process with few benefits remaining to the patient. Many States, however, provide that payment should be proportional to the ability to pay. A major proportion of the chronic patient population is in fact indigent and thus if they are paid minimal wages they should be protected by those statutes.

Thirteenth amendment suits. A second approach to requiring compensation is via the 13th amendment and the statutes enacted under its aegis. Basically, these laws provide remedies for denials of civil rights. And since they are specifically authorized by acts of Congress, these suits may be brought in Federal court without the difficulties noted in regard to the FLSA.

At first blush, the relevance of the 13th amendment might not be clear. It merely outlaws slavery and involuntary servitude (except as punishment for a crime), though it was quickly construed to bar "every . . . form of compulsory labor . . . " (*16*). But the real key is found in the painstakingly ample wording of 42 U.S.C. sec. 1994:

> The holding of any person to *service or labor* under the system known as peonage is abolished forever . . . (and there is hereby declared void) any law *or usages* by virtue of which any attempt shall hereafter be made to establish, maintain, or enforce, *directly or indirectly*, the *voluntary or involuntary* service or labor of any persons as peons, in liquidation of any *debt* or *obligation* or otherwise . . . (emphasis added).

The historic link is established, as one psychiatrist put it:

> Today's institutional peons are the descendants of the 17th century able-bodied workhouse inmates who labored for their keep and, in turn, became 19th century inmates of the asylum for the insane paupers. Now such workers have been promoted. They are patients and the work is "therapy" (*17*).

The emphasized wording of sec. 1994 makes clear that inadequately compensated, unfree tasks may be peonage even though so light as to be "service," not "labor," even though enforced merely by practice, not law, though only indirectly enforced, and in some sense "voluntary," and though some institutional benefit is given (or obligation to pay discharged). This is crucial because some courts have too narrowly construed the requirement that labor be "compulsory."

The reality of the situation is that subtle psychological pressure may be brought to bear on patients who refuse to work, and that mental patients are particularly vulnerable to such pressures. More powerful still, institutional privileges or sanctions may be used to encourage useful labor; transfers to worse wards, denial of admission to special therapy or recreation programs, etc. The use of such coercive tools is not just a patient paranoia; there are a number of suits recording the withdrawal of privileges upon refusal to continue with work assignments (18).

Finally, release may be used as a carrot to induce compliance with a work regimen. Clearly questions of voluntariness are difficult, and unless the patient has established a continuing record of refusal, the court reviewing a situation will be hard put to deduce the exact level of coercive atmosphere that existed. But in commercial transactions where there is vast disparity of bargaining power, as well as in police station confessions, courts have been quick to set aside the results of inherently coercive situations. They should be similarly aware here.

A second point which a 13th amendment suit must prove is that there is no compelling State interest in the noncompensation system. Perhaps therapeutic work meets this test—if the patient was committed because of his need for treatment, is receiving it, and the work is related to the treatment. And personal housekeeping; i.e., making his bed, may likewise be uncompensated (19). But the current system of excessive work and little treatment may destroy this rationale—as even the courts which refuse to require compensation acknowledge (20). Unfortunately, the litigation record so far reveals too many examples where courts have agreed in theory that if the State has no important therapy interest in the work, it is probably compelled for institutional maintenance reasons and should be compensated—but then the courts have made a rather skewed judgment on the facts and denied recovery. (21).

Right to treatment suits. The right to treatment may be denied if untherapeutic labor takes up time, depresses the patient's spirit, and postpones release. Thus, in *Wyatt* v. *Stickney* the court declared that due process bars nontherapeutic work assignments because they constitute "dehumanizing factors contributing to the degeneration of the patient's self-esteem" (22). If such work discourages release, it may violate the patient's right to the least drastic means of being treated. And as one psychiatrist's confessions has stressed, it is quite easy for even well-meaning staff members to come to regard mere token compensation (gratefully accepted by the patients) as gratuities, to regard the work as necessary to a "well-functioning institution"— and in the process to overlook primary therapeutic goals (23).

Some have opposed the demand for compensation on the superbenevolent basis that

> it would not be satisfactory to attempt any anomalous relationship . . . which would in a legal sense detract from the patient status of the inmates (24).

It has been suggested that kindly aides will become hard taskmasters; that efficiency will be demanded, and thus patient shortcomings will be criticized rather than indulged; that in the long run hospitals will prefer to hire help and the patients will sit around with even less to do than before. All this is, indeed, possible—if one assumes the status quo will not change, nor be forced to change. This premise, and the recurrent budgetary inadequacies, were the reasons I initially stated that any solution to the peonage problem must transcend rather than work within the current State institution system.

This can be done. Perhaps a blanket ban on patient labor would be easiest to administer; but an effort to distinguish therapy from toil can be successful and detailed regulations can be formulated. Statutes recently enacted in a number of States guarantee compensation for patient labor, and it is expected that subsequent regulations will specify the details and set the actual wage rates (25).

Ultimately, of course, compensation will be debated as a measure which would greatly increase the present mental health budget. But in this context, too, it is necessary to transcend the mental health system and look at the whole range of social systems at work here. Cutting down on the mental health system merely displaces people and costs onto the welfare, juvenile, hospital, and prison systems. Conversely, compensating patients for nontherapeutic labor may permit them to send money to a family and help it keep together, thereby avoiding more social disintegration and institutional cost. The patient's sense of competence and integrity may be increased, speeding recovery, and he may put aside funds to ease his transition back to the community, or to pay for outpatient care. Within this perspective, budgeting is merely a circular process; the costs will be borne somewhere. Therefore, social policy should seek to maximize both rehabilitation and restoration of dignity whenever it spends. Compensation of patient labor seems to do this.

A Final Word About the Other Side

There is an ironic note to this brief chapter. As one reads the various peonage briefs and the burgeoning legal literature on the subject, one must conclude that the least redeeming work in our society is tending the physical needs of the aged and the incapacitated. This is the task that families recoil from and makes them press for institutionalization, that causes nursing homes to refuse patients, and that the hospital staff wants to impose as work therapy on the patients.

Anyone who has even walked the corridors of the State hospital system carries away vivid olfactory memories which attest to the desperate need for someone to do this labor. I doubt that many Americans are willing to do this work for the money—surely not the current generation of mental professionals who define themselves as technicians. But changing linen is only the last step in the continuum of labor essential to a hospital, much of which is viewed as degrading in our impersonal and technological society. The lawsuits I have discussed ask that these tasks be defined as paid work which patients will do if they choose. Presumably as they come closer to being in their right minds, they, like the sane members of society will refuse this degrading work. One wonders how the courts will solve the next round of problems!

References

1. Council of State Governments, The mental health programs of the forty-eight states 69 (1950).
2. Cited in Friedman, The mentally handicapped citizen and institutional labor, 87 *Harv. L. Rev.* 567, 568n.5 (1974)
3. See, e.g., Bartlett Institutional peonage: Our exploitation of mental patients, *Atlantic*, July, 1964 at 116; Bickford, Economic value of the psychiatric inpatient, *Lancet*, Mar. 30, 1963, at 714.
4. Bickford, *supra* note 3 at 714.
5. *See* K. Kesey, *One Flew Over the Cuckoo's Nest* (New York, Signet, 1962).
6. *Dale* v. *New York*, Cl. No. 51888 (N.Y. Ct. Cl., Mar. 30, 1973).
7. S. Brakel and R. Rock, *The Mentally Disabled And The Law* (Chicago: U. of Chicago Press, 1971) p. 166.
8. Hearings on the constitutional rights of the mentally ill before the subcommittee on constitutional rights of the senate committee on the judiciary, 91st Congress, 1st and 2d sess. 196 (1969-70) (hereinafter cited as Hearings).
9. See Friedman, *supra* note 2 at 570 n.16.
10. Hearings at 340.
11. Hearings At 194-198; J.M. Grimes, When Minds Go Wrong (New York: Devin Adair Co., 1954) pp. 79-80; Goldman and Ross, The patient who shouldn't be in, *Parade*, part I, Nov. 11, 1956.
12. Department of Labor, publication 1282, March 1971, *citing* 29 U.S.C. sec 203 (r) (l), (s) (4) (1970).
13. *See Carey* v. *White*, Civ. No. 4772 (D.Del., filed Sept. 5, 1973); *Roebuck* v. *Department of Health*, Civ.No. TCA 1041 (N.D. Fla., filed July 6, 1972); *Downs* v. *Department of Pub. Welfare*, Civ. NO. 73-1246 (E.D.Pa., filed June 5, 1973); *Townsend* v. *Cloverbottom*, Doc.No.A.-2576 (Ch. Nashville and Davidson counties, Tenn., filed May 22, 1973).
14. *Employees of the Dep't of Pub. Health and Welfare* v. *Missouri*, 411 U.S. 279 (1973).
15. *See Souder* v. *Brennan*, 42 U.S.L.W. 2271 (D.D.C., Nov. 14, 1973); 367 F. Supp. 808 (DDC 1973).
16. *Railroad Tax Cases*, 13F.2d 722, 740 (C.C.D.Cal. 1882), *error dismissed*, 116 U.S. 138 (1885).
17. Bartlett, in Hearings at 196.
18. See, e.g., *Dale* v. *New York*, supra note 6.
19. *See Jobson* v. *Henne*, 355 F.2d 129 (2d Cir. 1966).
20. *Id.*
21. See, e.g., *Krieger* v. *State of New York*, 283 N.Y.S. 2d 86 (Ct. Cl. 1966); *Jobson* v. *New York*, Cl. No. 49165 (Ct. Cl. 1966).
22. *Wyatt* v. *Stickney*, 344 F.Supp. 373, 375 (M.D.Ala. 1972), *appeal docketed subnom Wyatt* v. *Aderholt*, No. 72-2634, 5th Cir., Aug. 1, 1972.
23. Bartlett in Hearings at 339.
24. Hearings at 342.
25. See, e.g., N.Y. *Mental Hyg. Law* Sec. 15.09 (McKinney Supp. 1973); *Ind. Ann Stat.* 22-1315 to -1324 (Burns 1972).

Chapter 8
Mental Retardation

Introduction: Labels and the Unregulated System

Nowhere in the interaction between law and mental health is there more ambiguity, more confusion, and more failure to articulate and achieve goals than in the area of mental retardation. This is clearly demonstrated at the outset when one studies the legal standard of mental deficiency which is the threshold label invoked in statutes authorizing confinement. For example in at least five States the statutes with tautologic precision state: "Mental deficiency shall mean mental deficiency as defined by appropriate clinical authorities . . . " (1).

Here is the ultimate expression of the medical model, and therefore it offers one a chance to examine the results when the law abdicates responsibility to clinicians. First, let us consider the clinical literature which gives meaning to the labels. What one finds is a diverse group of disorders of multiple etiology with vastly different physical, psychological, and social problems whose sole unifying variable is intelligence quotient as measured by one of a variety of standardized tests (2). The Diagnostic and Statistical Manual II of the American Psychiatric Association neatly and statistically classifies by standard deviations as follows: Borderline Mental Retardation, IQ 68-85; Mild Mental Retardation, IQ 52-67; Moderate Mental Retardation, IQ 36-51; Severe Mental Retardation, IQ 20-35; Profound Mental Retardation, IQ under 20 (3).

Perhaps there is no other place in the mental health system where labels are more odious and more invidious. Yet, the label borderline mental retardation is statistically set in relation to the general population so that 16 percent of the children measured are so tagged. The result is that they will be tracked out of many of the most important social and educational opportunities available in our society (4). These labels are, of course, applied to a disproportionate number of disadvantaged and minority children. This clinical result is accomplished despite the fact that the tests measure achievement rather than ability and despite the fact that most of those in common use are culture bound instruments (5).

119

The tendency of the mental health clinicians to throw the broadest possible net, and label the largest possible number is demonstrated again here as in the case of base rate studies of the mentally ill. But here the arbitrariness of such decisions can be most readily discerned since there is a single variable, IQ.

Empirical studies of course demonstrate that there is in fact a correlation between a measured IQ of 68-85 and poor school achievement (6). But it is quite unclear what that correlation means. Furthermore the concept of mental retardation has obvious global implications and connotations, both for the lay public and even the professionals who use the term, which suggests a qualitative distinction and not just a quantitative standard deviation. The absurdity of this expansive category of Borderline Mental Retardation was recognized by the Expert Committee on Mental Health of the World Health Organization. They emphasized that the diagnosis not only damaged the individuals so labeled, but diverted the limited special services available to those actually in need (7).

Once again we see the sequence of expanded labeling by clinicians creating an arbitrarily high base rate which in turn leads to an expanded demand for special technical services.

The American Association on Mental Deficiency has recently faced up to this problem and eliminated the classification of Borderline Mental Retardation (8). That enlightened step, however, still leaves a statistical framework which relegates 2.5 percent of children to the various remaining categories of mental retardation. When one looks at the variety of disorders with totally different etiology (inborn errors of metabolism, congenital defects, cerebral palsy, deprivation syndromes, etc.) and totally different needs which go into these categories, even the clinical value of that narrow label becomes suspect.

The confusion inherent in the unitary classification is reflected in the struggle among the responsible clinicians as to who is in charge. The AMA Handbook for the Primary Physician (9) makes the primary physician the central figure. The APA makes the psychiatrist the central figure (10). That pediatricians, developmental psychologists, educators, and child psychiatrists have also laid claim to this field was obvious during the establishment of the National Institute of Child Health and Human Development (11).

Unfortunately, most of this territorial dispute developed only after it became obvious that significant Federal funding had become available. During the decades which preceded, the lament was that these various groups had abandoned their responsibility (12).

As Gunnar Dybwad (13) has suggested, if we do away with the label and ask what services this particular child requires, it becomes obvious that the unilateral claims of primacy are empty, and what is required "would vary depending on the type of case and would have to involve different combinations among the specialties."

If the label stigmatizes the child and confuses the clinicians, what value does it have for the law?

We began by looking at a typical statutory definition of mental deficiency; let us now consider what else the law requires before it allows confinement (14). The typical statute, if indeed it goes beyond a simple definition, adds only a phrase such as "incapable of managing himself and his affairs" (15). Or, in addition, it may add "and for whose own welfare or that of others, supervision, guidance, care, or control is necessary or advisable" (16).

These statutes recognize that the mentally retarded rarely are a danger to others, and thus their confinement, if it is to be justified, can only be based on the fact that it benefits them, their families, or the community. However, these statutes are irrelevant in practice since the confinement of the mentally retarded most often takes place when they are minors and thus they have no recourse to a court of law when they are confined. The juvenile who is mentally ill or mentally retarded is confined most often as the result of a judicially unregulated decision made by the clinician at the voluntary request of the parents.

> (A recent court decision in Tennessee holds that a parent cannot voluntarily commit a child . . . to institutions for the retarded or mentally ill without a court order. The court specifically uses arguments similar to those advanced in this chapter: "possible conflicts of interest between a mentally retarded child and even a parent." Cited in *Behavior Today*, Apr. 1, 1974, p. 87-88.)

The tragic consequence of such unregulated control is dramatically evidenced in the crowded conditions and the unmitigated failure of the total institutions expected to meet the needs of the mentally retarded (17). Recent lawsuits dealing with conditions at Willowbrook in New York, at Searcy in Alabama, at Belchertown in Massachusetts (18), all large institutions for the mentally retarded, reveal the demeaning, degrading, and even obscene conditions and practices which unregulated admissions have helped to create. Similar conditions can be found at even the "best" State funded large institutions for the mentally retarded.

The clinical philosophy of care which inspired the development of these large institutions was utopian in its inspiration (19). It was assumed that the mentally retarded should be removed from the complexities of urban life and transported to a rural setting in which the simple rhythm of nature would form a framework for their more benign adaptation to life. Some of our institutions for the mentally retarded still maintain farms and continue to attempt to reach this goal. But the intervening years have brought enormous change in their aspirations and population.

Many of the severely physically handicapped, mentally retarded who once lost their lives to intercurrent infections now live out their lives in these large rurally situated institutions which have become vast warehouses for them. These were not the group of retarded that the early protagonists of the utopian rural institution had in mind as appropriate for their therapeutic goals. Sequin (20), the great innovator in this field, wrote:

> The pupils . . . are chosen . . . in view of their possible improvement with the means at their command, those who are absolutely helpless . . . must, of course, be rejected; received, they would either be neglected or each would monopolize the entire time of an attendant.

But the failure of that vision which contained a recognition of its limitations and the willingness of clinicians to ease the burden of the family, foregoing the interests of the child, has bred this awful result. For these bedridden youngsters, large institutions at a distance from the urban centers where their families and the appropriate medical specialists reside not only fail to provide a therapeutic milieu but fail to meet even minimum health needs (21).

If one accepts the fact that the original function for which these institutions were established is largely unrealized, or has been met for only a very few, and if one adds to that recognition the horrid physical conditions which exist, it seems clear that the only reasonable legal, medical, and ethical policy to follow is one which is directed towards making entry into such large total institutions as difficult as possible, and attempting in every way possible to phase out these facilities.

When one suggests such goals, it rapidly becomes clear that here, as elsewhere, there are important conflicts of interest. I shall not deal with the political reality of the lobbying that can be mounted by the employees of these institutions, but shall focus on the families.

Although the concept of the rural utopia has proved largely unworkable, there remains an unwarranted public expectation that these large institutions have the expertise and capacity to provide the specialized resources and human care necessary to deal with the many different disorders designated as mental retardation.

The families of the mentally retarded have come to expect as a right, and even to lobby for, State institutions which provide total care. They may oppose efforts at deinstitutionalization and the development of small community residences. The reasons for this indicate some of the conflicting interests.

First, the very size and brute physicality of the megainstitution gives the parents a sense that it will endure after they are gone. This in contrast with the hastily organized residence run by an altruistic but perhaps transient staff.

Second, if the mentally retarded can be in such a small residence, then the question of why they are not in their own home is posed for the parent in a poignant and guilt inspiring way.

Thirdly, parents tend to treat the mentally retarded as infants or young children and err on the side of being overprotective, whereas the increased freedom of the community residence creates the possibility of sexual activity, accident, exploitation, etc. As one group of parents put it, in objecting to deinstitutionalization, the professionals "have been mesmerized by the theory of humanization for the retarded at the expense of the dehumanization of the parents" (22).

The current generation of clinicians also have conflicting roles. They are burdened by the legacy of these huge institutions and are often trapped by bureaucratic inertia. They are expected to upgrade care while they dismantle their own institution. This is a difficult task in the face of system maintenance constraints, particularly when the dismantling process produces resentment in the families as well as the bureaucratic staff. Thus, dismantling, if it is to come, usually must come from pressures outside the institution.

The basic social policy question is: Who will protect the interest of the mentally retarded child in not being confined to a total institution? Specifically, should we continue to allow the retarded to be institutionalized in infancy when there is convincing clinical experience to suggest that the ultimate fate of the mentally retarded individual is largely determined by the kind of early life experience to which he is exposed? Thus, for example, a child with Down's syndrome raised in a family or a family-like setting where he gets appropriate emotional stimulation and attention can expect to achieve an IQ perhaps as high as 60 or more, whereas a child raised in an institution without such stimulation can expect to attain a measurable IQ of less than 40.

In adolescence the former will enjoy radio and television, be competent to take care of his personal toilet, and perform simple chores. The latter may rock endlessly in an oblivion and seem uneducable (23). Looked at from that perspective, it is apparent that the interests of the mentally retarded child are not identical with the interests of its family, especially when the family has been led to believe, and wants and needs to believe a large State financed institution will provide and should provide appropriate care and habilitation. The clinicians of the past failed to recognize that. The clinicians of the present who know better have bent under their sympathy for the needs of the normal members of the family.

The concept of community based resources with the mentally disabled individual being retained in his home as much and as long as possible is the most appropriate social policy if we are to consider the child's best interest. Legislation, funding, and incentives which allow a variety of alternative facilities, such as day care, sheltered workshops, special education, etc., programs which support the family as the primary provider of care during the child's early years, are critical if the problems previously described are to be ameliorated (24). Intermediate care facilities for the physically handicapped mentally retarded which have access to quality medical care may be an improvement over the past but they present an uneasy compromise.

Beyond this general description of the nature of the institutional problem, it is important to emphasize that the mentally retarded individual presents an ongoing set of legal problems throughout his life. First, there is the problem of the label, how it is applied, and the criteria for its application. Second, there is the problem of protecting the labeled individual as to whether he is to be institutionalized or not, and at what age. Third, there is the protection of his rights while institutionalized. Fourth, for the mentally retarded outside total institutions there is the need to protect and supervise the exercise of their constitutional rights, and to insure that they are provided a decent living situation and are not exploited.

In this connection, but outside the scope of this monograph, are the private law rights of the mentally retarded which present a complex of ongoing challenges to the legal system (25). Beyond these desiderata there is the inescapable problem of the sexual adjustment of the mentally retarded adult, a problem which poses the deepest ethical dilemma. Many are unwilling to accept eugenic sterilization of the retarded female, and even the alternative of routine use of intrauterine devices or other contraceptive techniques. These procedures have become a subject of ethical controversy (26). The retarded male's sexual adjustment is equally problematic. All too often it brings him in conflict with the law because he is unable to express and gratify his sexual drives in a socially acceptable fashion. Indeed, it can fairly be said that the retarded male has no acceptable sexual behavior permitted to him by society.

Finally, there is the problem of guardianship for such individuals at such a point in time when their parents become disabled or incapacitated, or when there is an obvious conflict of interest between the child and its parents such as has been indicated.

The current watchword of clinicians is "normalization" (27). It implies an effort to reject the dehumanizing institutions of the past and to afford the mentally retarded person a life as close to the normal as possible. That goal returns the retarded to the community and intensifies their need for legal services.

The law as it relates to the mentally retarded then will be faced with a series of difficult questions ongoing from birth until death, and the solutions appropriate to the mentally ill cannot readily be applied to these difficult choices.

Let me illustrate the human dimensions of these problems by one highly charged ethical issue now being debated. Assume a fact situation in which parents have decided to keep a severely retarded female child at home. The child reaches adolescence and begins to menstruate. She cannot be trained by the parents to participate in this aspect of her personal hygiene; indeed, she is not reliably toilet trained. She leaves trails of menstrual blood around the home, refusing to wear appropriate hygienic devices. After a year of this, which her parents find intolerable, they take her to a gynecologist and request that he perform a hysterectomy.

Some approach such a problem from the perspective of individual rights, the girl's "humanity," and her right to be normal. They find such a surgical procedure inexcusable, and demand that a guardian of some sort be appointed to protect the child against her parents. Alternatively, they call for regulation of the surgeons who perform such procedures. Others would argue that if the parents are committed to caring for such a girl, they should be allowed to find a gynecologist willing to perform such a procedure, as long as it is first reviewed by some appropriate third party. Still others would allow either the parents or the institution in which the girl is confined to make such a decision without any prior review.

There are no easy solutions to such problems, but they are typical of the tragic choices confronting those who care for the mentally retarded. Here again it happens all too often that those who would protect the human rights of the mentally retarded either can or will do no more than that. Here, as in many other situations, such human rights may have little meaning. Thus, the rights of a young girl to retain her "normal" uterus will mean little if it results in her parents' abandoning her.

Although I do not take a position in this tragic dilemma, I present it because it is a poignant example of the inescapable problems confronting those who care for the mentally retarded. The one inescapable consideration for the decisionmaker is what will be the cost of his ethical decision to the person. How one balances absolute values against that consideration is a matter of both moral and legal significance. My own predilection is to allow considerable leeway to the judgments of that person who has assumed responsibility and is fulfilling that responsibility to the severely mentally retarded person by providing a high standard of care.

California: An Example of the Legal Process

With respect to the mentally retarded, as in many other areas of mental health, California has been a reformist State both in legislative planning and actual fiscal support. Thus, deficiencies which persist there, it may rightly be concluded, exist in exacerbated form in other States as well. A recent painstaking study of the process of institutionalization of the mentally retarded in California has revealed legal as well as medical flaws, irrationalities, and dubieties (28).

It is the practice in California for commitment orders to be sought and entered for institutionalized mentally retarded persons upon their reaching the age of 21, or before that time in cases where the parents are unknown, deceased, mentally ill, incompetent, or otherwise unfit to look after the child's interests.

The judicial commitment hearings occupy only a tiny percentage of the superior court judges' time; the study found the judges accorded it a correspondingly low degree of priority and attention. There was no consistent practice as to whether the patient, hospital officials, court clerks, social workers, or the District Attorney were present at the hearing; the only rule was that according to 38 of the 40 judges surveyed, an attorney for the patient was never present (29). Similarly, there was no established practice as to whether the patient was questioned, whether witnesses other than the parents testified, etc. The median duration of the "hearing" was between 5 and 10 minutes.

According to the judges interviewed, the factors foremost in their decision to commit the patient were a hospital or other institution's willingness to take the patient, and the individual's appearance. They reported that issues such as the individual's dangerousness to himself or others, his need for treatment, or his ability to care for himself outside an institution were seldom inquired into at the hearing. Significantly, more than half of the judges perceived their role in the commitment process as that of a rubber stamp ratifying the desires of the parents. Fewer than 25 percent viewed their primary role as that of active decisionmaker guarding the rights and interests of the patient.

Although 36 to 40 judges surveyed said they felt free to refuse to commit an individual, none had ever actually done so (30). Real judicial review would recognize that the parents' interests are not identical to those of the child in all cases. And even in the cases of capable and compassionate parents, the system ought to encourage them to engage early in legal planning for the protection of the retarded child. As the California study reported:

> One of the most obvious findings of the study is that parents do not perceive mental retardation as a legal problem . . . None of the parents in the northern hospital sample had ever consulted an attorney . . . (31).

Parents had generally not thought of trying to enforce the child's rights while institutionalized, or of providing by will for the appointment of a guardian to look after noninstitutionalized retarded persons after the parents' death. Some form of legislative encouragement to legal planning for the mentally retarded, such as has been provided by the development in California of Regional Centers (described below) is a prerequisite to effective enforcement of the rights which comprise the subject matter of the next two sections.

The California study does not deal with the situation of the child under 21 whose parents are alive and are by law the decisionmakers for their children. In many States there are waiting lists for entry into the dreadful institutions provided by the States. Thus a report at Willowbrook State School for the mentally retarded in New York revealed that an experimental study of infectious hepatitis was made possible by parents being presented with the following option: There are no beds now available except on the experimental ward studying infectious hepatitis. Infectious hepatitis is endemic in Willowbrook and your child will probably be infected when eventually admitted. If you allow the child to be admitted to the experimental ward where he will be infected as part of the study, the child can be admitted immediately. Many parents, under those circumstances, chose to submit their child to the experimental ward.

In Massachusetts political leverage is often exerted, and State legislators dispense admission to institutions as a form of patronage to their more demanding constituents.

It is clear that in such a context the possible interests of the patient, particularly his interest in remaining in the community or the family despite his burdensomeness, will not be given real inspection. Of course it is not certain that grafting rigid, legalistic, due process paraphernalia onto this process would ease the difficult human choices which have to be made—but it might increase the chances that adverse interests would be addressed and examined.

Reforming the Total Institution: The Institutionalized Retarded Person's Right to Habilitation

Increasing attention has been given lately to the right-to-treatment cases involving mental patients (*32*), and there has been a widespread recognition that the conditions in public institutions for the mentally retarded are, in general, far worse even than those which obtain in institutions for the mentally ill. For example, although a substantial number of State and county institutions for the mentally ill are accredited by national review organizations, only a small fraction of retardate institutions are so accredited (*33*). Despite this situation, perhaps because retardate institutions are perceived as providing but an accomodation service for the welfare of parents, because a high percentage of first admissions are young children, or because few residents are thought to be curable or potentially releasable, the potential deprivations of liberty involved in institutionalization of the mentally retarded person have not been so widely seen as giving rise to enforceable rights to habilitation as in the right-to-treatment cases involving the mentally ill.

The case of *New .York Association for Retarded Children* v. *Rockefeller* (*34*) (hereinafter referred to as the *NYARC* case) provides an instructive example. That case was a class action brought on behalf of the more than 5,000 residents of New York's Willowbrook State School for the Mentally Retarded (the largest retardate facility in North America). The District Court (*Judd, J.*) found that because of

> overcrowding and inadequate staffing at Willowbrook, conditions are . . . inhumane . . . (Testimony of parents) showed failure to protect the physical safety of their children, and deterioration rather than improvement after they were placed in Willowbrook School. (*35*).

The institution was found to fail to conform to minimal accreditation standards of various national accreditation organizations (*36*). In spite of these humane realizations, the Court refused to "impose" upon the defendants the "ideals" of national standards. It distinguished the right-to-treatment cases involving those involuntarily civilly committed or committed after diversion from the original process on the ground that "a large, part of the residents at Willowbrook entered because they had no alternative, and none have been denied a right to release," and it rejected the alternative of ordering mass releases because "the residents . . . are for the most part incapable of existing independently unless successfully habilitated" (37).

Despite some broader comments to the effect that the Constitution does not impose upon the States a duty to provide a given type, or, absent invidious discrimination, a given level or distribution of services, the real thrust of the NYARC decision is that there are "significant difficulties" in extending the rationale of the right-to-treatment cases to the mentally retarded. Significantly, however, the NYARC opinion is a strange legal hybrid, which seems, at least in part, to accomplish precisely what it gainsays. Judge Judd went on to declare that there is a constitutional right to protection from harm and to a tolerable institutional living environment—particularly since "Willowbrook residents are for the most part confined behind locked gates and are held without the possibility of a meaningful waiver of their right to freedom" (38). The court felt it unnecessary to choose which specific constitutional provision was controlling in establishing such rights, but it went on to firíd that a Federal court need not abstain in such a case, and is not barred by the 11th amendment from entering an order requiring the expenditure of State funds (39). On the contrary, the court proceeded to enter a forceful decree mandating immediate hiring of attendants, nurses, physicians, therapy and recreational staff, ordering affiliation of Willowbrook with an accredited medical hospital to insure provision of adequate physical medical care of its residents, prohibiting seclusion of the patients, and requiring the defendants to file progress reports on these measures (40).

NYARC is by no means the strongest legal decision. In Wyatt v. Stickney (41), a Federal District Court in Alabama found that "(in) the context of the right to adequate care for people civilly confined to public mental institutions, no viable distinction can be made between the mentally ill and the mentally retarded" (42). It therefore declared that conditions in the State's retardate institutions (as it had previously found conditions in the mental hospitals) violated constitutional rights to habilitation. Judge Johnson's order set forth detailed minimum standards for physical facilities, procedures, and staffing—and declared that the State would have to find the funds to satisfy the order (*43*). The case has been argued before the Court of Appeals and has been upheld.

Recently another constitutional assault on institutions for the mentally retarded has been successful. It argues that when conditions in such institutions are worse than those which the courts have held are cruel and unusual punishment in a prison setting, a valid constitutional question has been reached. The Court wrote: " . . . I am convinced that plaintiffs have stated at least one claim which is cognizable for review under the Civil Rights Act. The allegations that the conditions of confinement at the . . . Home are violative of the Eighth Amendment's ban on cruel and unusual punishment would appear to fall within the purview of the Civil Rights Act. It must be noted that the ban on cruel and unusual punishment applies not only to sentences imposed in judicial proceedings, but to conditions of confinement as well . . . ." *Horacek* v. *Exon*, 375 F. Supp. 71, (Nebraska); U.S. District Court, D. Nebraska, March 22, 1973. Conditions in many of our State institutions designed to care for the mentally retarded are well below the standard of cruel and unusual punishment for convicted criminals. It is ironic that States who exercise the power of removing children from their parents because of neglect will expose children whom they accept responsibility for to even greater depths of neglect.

The growing judicial recognition of a right to habilitation—or at least to a decent and possibly therapeutic environment for the mentally retarded is encouraging. But, as the court in *NYARC* noted, an even more powerful lever than occasional judicial decisions is the fact that States must ultimately meet the standards of HEW (and soon of the local PSRO), or lose the substantial Federal funding provided to institutions for the retarded. In either case, it is significant that the interests of the mentally retarded will be seen as sufficiently important and ascertainable to be judicially guaranteed.

The legal decisions in these cases suggest that at last there is to be some minimal legal standard to be applied to the living situation of the institutionalized mentally retarded individual. However, unlike the situation addressed in the consideration of the mentally ill, it is much more difficult to describe optimal standards for the diverse group of disorders which constitute the mentally retarded.

If one had unlimited resources, it is clear that any retarded child could show significant progress. Indeed, heavily funded demonstration programs make it clear how much can be done to normalize even the least promising child. The current situation of those institutions, however, given the numbers of such patients and the amount of care required, suggests that professional and para-professional staff, space, equipment, medical attention, etc., would have to be increased at least tenfold. Indeed, given the nature of the problems of the mentally retarded, there is no obvious limit on what would be optimal to achieve normalization of those who already suffer the profound impact of prolonged institutional-ization. Thus the appropriate legal goal would seem to be to make it extremely difficult for mentally retarded individuals to be com-mitted to such institutions, and that such institutionalization should not be triggered and achieved by the voluntary request of the parents and the clinicians' acquiescence.

Roughly, the procedural policies which might be followed in admitting to total long-term institutions, including intermediate care facilities, are: (1) No child should be admitted simply on the voluntary request of his parents or guardians or the decision of a clinician. (2) No child should be admitted who does not have some compelling need for medical and nursing care which cannot be provided on an outpatient, day care, or at home basis. Appropriate PSRO regulations could insure this result. (3) The committing authority should require the articulation of the kind of treatment the child requires and the facility must indicate its ability to provide the care which is alleged to be necessary. These criteria might also be shaped in concert with PSRO in the future. (4) No mentally retarded person should be admitted to any total institu-tion simply "for the welfare of others or for the welfare of the community" (44). (5) A mentally retarded adult who is not in need of hospitalization for urgent medical treatment should not be confined unless standards and procedures for involuntary confine-ment similiar to those for the mentally ill in that State are met.

Other Rights of the Mentally Retarded

The Right to Education

A second major thrust toward betterment of the lot of the mentally retarded has been the development of an enforceable right to a decent publically supported education. The Supreme Court recognized (45), as early as 1954, that

> Today education is perhaps the most important function of State and local government . . . . In these days it is doubtful that any child may reasonably be expected to succeed in life if he is denied the opportunity for an education. Such an opportunity, where the State has

undertaken to provide it, is a right which must be made available to all on equal terms.

And Federal courts have, correspondingly, prohibited the denial of equal educational opportunities to particular groups, such as resident aliens (46), pregnant students (47), or those excluded for medical (48) or behavioral reason (49).

Of course the argument that all children should be provided with roughly equal educational opportunities applies with special force in the case of the mentally retarded, because without special attention they may never learn (50). Perhaps for this reason, an increasing number of courts are recognizing the rights of retarded children to equal education. The starting point for such reforms is the present disastrous state of retardate education. In 48 States, although education is deemed so important as to be compulsory for normal children for 10 years, mentally retarded (as well as mentally ill, physiologically impaired, and learning disabled) children are routinely excluded from public schools either by law or by dint of informal but officially sanctioned processes. Often such statutory provisions are so vague as to render them legally suspect. For example, Alaska permits the exclusion of children with bodily or mental conditions rendering attendance "impractical" (51) while Nevada authorizes exclusion if the "child's physical or mental condition or attitude is such as to . . . render inadvisable his attendance at school" (52). One frequent estimate is that about 60 percent of the estimated 7 million children with mental, physical, emotional, or learning disabilities requiring special training never get any at any time during their educational careers (53). One major survey found that only 36 percent of the nation's retarded children were in educational programs of any kind in 1971 (54).

In the first landmark case in this area, *Pennsylvania Association for Retarded Children* v. *Pennsylvania* (hereinafter referred to as the *PARC* case), a three-judge District Court approved a consent decree prohibiting State officials from denying or delaying the provision of free public education to mentally retarded children. Although these children had long been excluded from public schools as "uneducable," or "unable to profit from schools" (56), the court declared that every child can profit from some form of education or training (57).

Other provisions of the order were that the mentally retarded would be provided with equivalent preschool services if the State decides to establish such for normal children, that mentally retarded children shall be eligible for private (home) education grants on the same basis as such grants are now given to physically disabled children who cannot attend school, and that since classification as mentally retarded carries both onerous effects and a social stigma, due process requires that parents be given notice and a right to be heard before their child is assigned to a "special education" facility (58). Finally, the court said that there is "serious doubt" whether, under equal protection analysis, mental retardation is a rational classification for the purposes of providing education.

This last point was forcefully addressed in another case, *Mills* v. *Department of Education of the District of Columbia* (59). In that case, the District Court (*Waddy, J.*) was faced with a system in which advice, coercion, fabricated suspensions, delays in diagnosis, home assignments, and other means were employed so as to exclude the mentally retarded (as well as disciplinary problems and other children) from public schools. In declaring the primary duty of the school systems to provide equal education for such children, the court made three arguments, which are worth noting in detail because of their implications for future litigation.

Legal regulation of the labeling process. First, the court found that the diagnosis and assignment process posed grave dangers of violating elemental notions of due process. Therefore, it ordered notice, hearing, review, and a record of the deliberations—basic indicia of legal accountability. These requirements are particularly important in light of both the imprecision of the IQ testing by which children are classified, and the loose correlation between even verified IQ and social adaptation (60). As we have already indicated, there are a variety of disabilities, mental subnormality, social incompetence, developmental retardation, learning disabilities, and a variety of physical or neurological problems which may result in a classification of "mental retardation" (61). The perils of the arbitrary IQ classification in the education process are legion: the self-fulfilling prophecy of diagnosis as uneducable, given the human needs for reinforcement among teachers (62), the rigid allocation of social services according to such subsequent classifications (so that a mentally retarded blind child may be shunted from one agency to another without relief), the isolation of the subnormal from normal contacts which might be highly therapeutic, and so on. The law may well have done something if it at least constrains us to be more cautious and to articulate the considerations which operate in such powerful processes as result from such indiscriminate labeling of noninstitutionalized children.

Enforcing parens patriae. Second, the *Mills* court found that there is a special obligation incumbent upon the State to provide adequate education when the State has assumed custody of the child (63). Whether because of parens patriae—a doctrine quite readily invoked when the State seeks to work its will on an unwilling but burdensome individual—or merely because of the interest of the State in maximizing the habilitative potential of its institutions in order to return as expeditiously as possible as many persons as possible to productive lives in the community, the State does have a duty to provide adequate education for institutionalized retardates.

Equality. Finally, the *Mills* court forthrightly based its opinion on the doctrine of equal protection, suggesting that with respect to provision of other services as well, mental retardation may not be a rational classification.

Right-to-education cases similar to *PARC* and *Mills* have now been brought in California, Delaware, Maryland, Massachusetts and about 10 other States (*64*). And there is every indication that such litigation will be increasingly common. Alternatively, however, such litigation may become unnecessary if other States follow the recent actions of Michigan and Tennessee in enacting legislation providing for mandatory publicly supported educational facilities for all handicapped children (*65*).

The educational implications of mental retardation have taken on powerful political overtones. The logic of the *Mills* case, seeking to scrutinize entry into the class of the mentally retarded, and at the same time to insure educational opportunity, reflects the optimum judicial approach endorsed throughout this monograph.

Again, however, the question will arise as to how effectively a court can mandate the many programs necessary for the many disorders contained within the category of mental retardation. Each category requires different kinds of educational opportunity, and no solution can be hammered out by the rough instrument of judicial opinion. This will require continuing legislative and administrative development of appropriate facilities. Furthermore, the technical problem of teaching these children will never be solved unless that teaching takes place in an environment in which enough human care is provided to sustain the developing human spirit. That means that each such child needs adult attention, and thus there is an enormous need for volunteers willing to provide this care and to supplement the skills of the teacher.

Sexual Activity of the Mentally Retarded

The sexual needs and activity of the mentally retarded seem to be a problem that our society is incapable of facing. Gebhard of the Kinsey group has produced data which, no matter how unreliable they may be, make clear what everyone who has worked with the retarded knows, namely, that "there is a great deal of sexual activity among the retarded" (66). This finding is reiterated here simply to puncture the lingering myth that the retarded are asexual "holy innocents" (67).

It also seems clear that there is no socially acceptable sexual outlet for the retarded except masturbation or the homosexual activity that takes place in institutions. Indeed, my own study of the group of males labeled as mentally retarded habitual criminals in Massachusetts suggested that it was their fumbling inappropriate attempts at sexual activity which led to their incarceration.

The following questions arise: (a) Whether there should be sex education, (b) whether there should be contraception, (c) whether the mentally retarded should be allowed to have heterosexual experience, (d) whether the retarded should be allowed to reproduce, (e) whether surgical sterilization should be sanctioned.

The last two of these questions are the only ones which have received significant attention from the law. The eugenic concerns of the first four decades of the 20th century led to the enactment of sterilization laws in many States. Burt (68) reports that in 1966, 23 States still had statutes providing for compulsory sterilization of mental retardates, but these laws are rarely applied at present. The usual point in the life of a retardate when sterilization is suggested is when he, or more often she, has been "rehabilitated" and is eligible for discharge from an institution.

Some States have tried to draw a sharper line in their compulsory sterilization statutes. Thus, Utah allows it only for those who are "probably incurable and unlikely to be able to perform properly the functions of parenthood" (69). Burt believes that even these restricted sterilization laws will be found unconstitutional (70). But as he points out, if the retarded are then allowed to reproduce, it is possible that the State will intervene and remove the children on grounds of neglect. He therefore urges that intensive child rearing services be provided in the sheltered communities organized for the retarded (71). This is the ultimate extension of the concept of normalization and it raises the question of how realistic that goal is. Certainly such policies will evoke once again the question of eugenics. This will be particularly the case if the sheltered community encourages mating between retardates where data indicate such interbreeding substantially increases the likelihood of retardation and low intelligence among offspring (72).

As we have already suggested, there is a general inclination to turn all of these problems over to guardians who would take the responsibility for making these difficult decisions. However, based on the writing available in this area, it is clear that a host of value conflicts are involved. It is my own view that no clear resolution of these conflicts is imminent; indeed, if anything, public awareness and scrutiny heightens the conflict.

Within the law there can be no resolution of the substantive questions. The approach of appointing guardians does no more than decide who shall have the role of deciding (73). The general conclusion reached here is that the parents have that role as long as they retain actual custody, the principle being that the actual caretaker be the decisionmaker. That principle is less convincing when applied within the current institutional complex. But it might well be applied at some future point if it can be demonstrated that good care in all other respects is being provided.

There is something to be said for the proposition that the mentally retarded ought to be given the opportunity to enjoy every human satisfaction available to others except when it is likely to increase the total number of mentally retarded. Thus, if conception can be avoided, they should be provided sex education, the opportunity for heterosexual experience, and lasting relationships including marriage.

Guardianship and Protection of the Interests of the Mentally Retarded

As early as 1963 the President's Commission on Mental Retardation pointed out that:

> Most States' provisions for guardianship of the retarded are relics of a time when the mentally retarded individual was considered an incompetent who had to be kept away from normal social contacts. They largely consider or assume the retarded person to be without rights, deny him due process or the equal protection of the laws, and often encumber his family's estate for years as the price of the State's assuming his care. The damage done to retarded individuals who are capable of self-support and self-reliance, to those who have become caught up in the judicial process, and to families who can in effect be held responsible for a retarded individual into a second generation is incalculable (74).

This report recommended, as have numerous studies since, that there be developed a range of possible guardianship plans so as to accommodate the degree of incapacity of the retarded person and the condition of his family life. There could be limited guardianship for the mentally retarded adult, with the scope of the guardian's

authority carefully defined by a court order, more plenary guardianship for those retarded persons unable to conduct their everyday
affairs, conservatorship for those competent as to everyday affairs
but unable prudently to manage their property interests, and public
guardianship for those persons for whom an adequate private
guardian is not available.

Naturally, the most difficult and novel of these goals is the
development of an adequate system of public guardianship. Among
the threshold questions in such an endeavor are: Should such
guardianship be available only upon the retarded person's parents'
death? Should the hospitalized person be eligible? Should the
guardian's authority extend to the property as well as the personal
welfare of the retarded person? Who should the public guardian
be? Should he have any official or quasiofficial relation to the
governmental service agencies? What should be the procedures for
initiating and terminating his authority?

In my view, there are a variety of possible guardianship models
which would have a salutary effect; nor does their implementation
seem mutually exclusive. But as a preliminary response to the
aforementioned questions, I believe the following principles have
application to any guardianship plan which is to be maximally
effective.

*Public guardianship should be available to all retarded persons
who need it, regardless of age, degree of retardation, or family
situation.* It is essential to perceive that the family's interests and
those of the child may diverge, and that therefore the existence of
a parent or relative willing to serve as guardian does not guarantee
representation of the retarded person's best interests. It is precisely
a recognition of, rather than an insensitivity to, the burdens on a
retarded person's family that compels us to realize the variety of
reasons, besides the child's interests, which the family may have for
wishing, for example, to commit the child to an institution.

These reasons may include the interests of other siblings, mental
and physical exhaustion, economic stress, hostility toward the
child, social stigma, etc. And the needs of a retarded person may
change during his lifetime. Therefore, public guardianship should be
open to all retarded persons at that point at which a major conflict
of interest develops, e.g., at the point of institutionalization, or
when parental negligence or abuse is established, etc.

Hospitalized retarded persons should be eligible for guardianship.
The need for a guardian for all retarded persons now in institutions
should be considered. In addition to monitoring the retarded

person's growing array of rights within the institution, the guardian can give attention to the retarded person's property interests, can investigate and arrange interfacility transfers which may be advantageous to the ward, can pass on experimental procedures, elective surgery, and so on; all of which may involve conflicts of interest with the family and the institution.

The public guardian should have plenary authority with respect to the ward's personal welfare, but more circumscribed power over his property. There is a vital need for a social institution which is primarily interested in the needs and not the estate of the retarded person. Although there is no need arbitrarily to exclude from the guardian's duties the conservation of the retarded person's property, still, in light of recent exposes concerning abuse of such guardianship authority, and so as to insure that the public guardian will not develop conflicts of interest, some form of judicial supervision of such property management may be appropriate.

The public guardian may be an institution, a lay citizen, or a professional licensed by the State and having some relation to the judiciary or service agencies. However, an essential qualification upon this suggestion is this: it is crucial that the guardian be independent—both personally and in terms of hiring—from the agencies and institutions which directly serve the retarded. Otherwise, it is unlikely that such guardians will consistently be able to espouse the retarded individual's interests when they challenge institutional or departmental preference, policy or prestige. One model worth considering is a group of paraprofessionals or volunteers, or both, with some law and social work training attached to a legal aid office.

The procedure for appointment and removal of public guardians should be promulgated by statute so as to assure a concrete and reviewable process. The procedure should require consultation with the retarded person or his family, or both, should be attentive to due process, should allow for appointment either by judicial order or will codicil, and should provide for some meaningful review of the capacities and performance of the guardian.

Perhaps the most promising model of public guardianship, and one which embodies most of the above principles, is the program of regional centers now operating in California (75). Following the 1963 suggestions of the President's Panel, California in 1968 enacted legislation creating regional diagnosis, counseling and service centers for the purpose of carrying out guardianship plans. Services provided by such centers include:

diagnosis, counseling, maintainance of a registry and case record, followup procedures, assistance in hospital placement where necessary, calling attention to unmet needs in community care and services for the retarded, maintaining appropriate staff, and—most innovative of all— providing State funds to vendors of service to the retarded when failure to provide such services would result in State hospitalization (76).

The regional center program has gained extraordinary public acceptance; by 1971 the centers had an annual caseload of more than 5,000 (77). Currently, the centers refuse appointments while the parents of the retarded person are alive, except in cases of incompetence or malice. But an additional salutary effect of the centers has been their influence in getting parents to plan ahead, by will, economic arrangement, etc., for the future of the retarded child.

A second major change has been that the regional centers have come to handle admissions to and referrals from the State institutions for the retarded. It was the clear intent of the original legislation (78) to reduce the excessive reliance on commitment to State hospitals, and to create a forceful mechanism for searching for alternative contexts and dispositions of the retarded persons. Thus, the regional center "follows" the person into the State or other institution, and if his program there is deemed inadequate after consultation with staff and the family, the center takes charge of arranging a more suitable placement.

Since California law also prohibits direct court commitments of nondangerous persons to retardate institutions (79) and prohibits the Department of Mental Health which operates those institutions from being appointed guardian (80), the effect of all the new laws is to move the regional centers into the center of the admission-release process, and to move the courts to the periphery. Given the professional expertise of the centers' staffs and their close contact with the family and community, this ought to make the entire process better informed and less rigid. It exemplifies a system in which guardianship is merely one of the elements in a comprehensive linked system of providing services to the retarded.

A second model, possibly complementary to the California program, would be a separate legal advocacy or legal guardian apparatus. Such programs for the mentally retarded have already been established (81). Their drawback, of course, is that the legal problems of the retarded are not readily separable from their other interests, especially when assertion of rights within the institutional context often requires a subtle mixture of legal and informal measures.

A third useful model is that of citizen or volunteer advocacy. The supposed advantages of this structure are the independence of the advocate, and the willingness and ability of the unofficial advocate to organize political and community support for programs on behalf of the retarded (*82*).

Finally, there has been growing interest in the role of the professional ombudsman (*83*). He could operate both within and outside institutions for the retarded and would have added potency by virtue of his quasiofficial role as liaison to the courts or social agencies. Obviously the role of the guardian will become less significant if the other measures suggested come to pass. If families are given the assistance and incentives to maintain the mentally retarded at home, the State can adopt a policy of nonintervention. It will be offering services, not controlling decisions through appointed guardians.

References

1. See e.g., *Me. Rev. Stat. Ann.* ch. 34 sec.2562(3) (1964), MD. *Ann. Code* 41 sec.322(7) (1965). *See generally,* S. Brakel and R. Rock, *The Mentally Disabled And The Law* (Chicago: University of Chicago Press, 1971) pp. 98-102.

2. See, e.g., J. Mercer, *Labeling The Mentally Retarded* (Berkeley: University of California Press, 1973); Brabner, The myth of mental retardation, 63 *Training Sch. Bull.* 149 (1967).

3. *American Psychiatric Association, Diagnostic and Statistical Manual II* (1969) p. 14.

4. *See generally, Mercer, supra* note 2; C. Jencks, *Inequality* (New York: Basic Books, 1972) p. 192.

5. Stadolsky and Lesser, Learning patterns in the disadvantaged, 37 *Harv. Ed. Rev.* 546 (1967).

6. *Id.*

7. World Health Organization, Technical report No. 392, Organization of Services for the Mentally Retarded, 15th report of the Expert Committee on Mental Health *(Geneva: WHO, 1968).*

8. American Association on Mental Deficiency (H. J. Grossman, ed.), Manual on terminology and classification in mental retardation *(Washington: AAMD, 1973)* p. 18.

9. American Medical Association, Mental Retardation: A handbook for the primary physician, 191 *JAMA* 183 (1965).

10. American Psychiatric Association, psychiatry and mental retardation, 122 *Am. J. Psychiat.* 1302 (1966).

11. National Institute of Child Health and Human Development, Optimal care for mothers and children (NIH publication No. 127) (Washington: NIH, 1968).

12. See, e.g. Powers, The retarded child and his family: A challenge to pediatric practice, research and education, 12 *Pediatrics* 217 (1953).

13. Dybwad, Psychiatry's role in mental retardation, In: N. Bernstein, *Diminished People* (Boston: Little, Brown & Co., 1970) p. 127; *see also* Bohan, The child psychiatrist and the mental retardation "team": A problem of role definition, 18 *Arch. Gen. Psychiat.* 360 (1963).

14. *See generally Practicing Law Institute* (B. Ennis and P. Friedman, eds.) *Legal Rights Of The Mentally Handicapped* (New York: Practising Law Institute, 1973) vol. I, pp. 15-101. Because of the scope of the present work, I focus on the constitutional rights of the mentally retarded, and the statutory provisions bearing on hospitalization. Of course, in the lives of many mentally retarded (and their families) and particularly those not institutionalized, the matrix of private or civil law rights may be of greater importance. *See generally,* R. Allen et al., *Mental Impairment and Legal Incompetency* (Englewood Cliffs: Prentice Hall, 1968).

15. *E.g.,* R. I. *Gen. Laws Ann.* sec.26-6-1 (art. II9g) 1968.

16. E.g., N.C. *Gen. Stat.* sec. 122-136 (1964).

17. *See generally,* A Deutsch, *The Mentally Ill In America,* (New York: Columbia University Press, 1949); E. Goffman, *Asylums* (Garden City, N.Y.: Doubleday and Co., 1961); L. Kanner, *A History Of The Care*

And Study Of The Mentally Retarded (Springfield, Ill.,: Thomas, 1964); R. Rugel and W. Wolfensberger, (ed.) *Changing Patterns of Residental Services For The Mentally Retarded* (Washington: Government Printing Office, 1969).

18. See *New York Association for Retarded Children* v. *Rockefeller*, 357 F. SUPP. 752 (E.D.N.Y. 1973) (Judd, J.); *Wyatt* v. *Stickney*, 344 F. SUPP. 387 (M.D. ALA. 1972) (Johnson, J.), *appeal docketed sub nom Wyatt* v. *Aderholt*, no. 72-2634, 5th Cir.; Aug. 1, 1972; *Ricci et al* v. *Greenblatt et al* Civil Action No. 72- 469F (D. Mass. 1972).

19. See, e.g., Kanner, *supra* note 17; C. H. S. Davis, *Manual For The Training And Education Of The Feeble-Minded, Imbecile And Idiotic* (New York: E. Steiger and Co., 1883); Brown, B., *The Treatment And Cure Of Cretins And Idiots* (1847); S. G. Howe, *Report To The Legislature Of Massachusetts Upon Idiocy* (1848). *But see* S. Davies and F. Williams, *Social Control Of The Mentally Deficient* (New York: T. Crowell Co., 1937).

20. E. Seguin, *New Facts And Remarks Concerning Idiocy* (New York: W. Wood and Co., 1870) p. 12.

21. Willowbrook, for example, suffers from endemic hepatitis. See cases cited at note 18, *supra*.

22. *See* The Fernald League Policy, p. 5 (1974, unpublished).

23. R. Koch and J. C. Dobson, *The Mentally Retarded Child And Its Family* (New York: Brunner/Mazel, 1971) pp. 130-131; Centerwell and Centerwell, A study of children with mongolism reared in the home compared with those reared away from home, 25 *Pediatrics* 678 (1960).

24. See, e.g., D. Klein, *Community Dynamics And Mental Health* (New York: J. Wiley and Sons, 1968).

25. *See generally* S. Brakel and R. Rock, *supra* note 1, pp. 226-341.

26. See, e.g., Proceedings of the Conference of the American Association on Mental Deficiency, IX, Sexual rights and responsibilities of the mentally retarded, Oct. 12-14, 1972; J. B. Lehane, *The Morality of American Civil Legislation Concerning Eugenic Sterilization* (Washington: Catholic University Press, 1944).

27. See, e.g., W. Wolfensberger, Normalization: *The Principle Of Normalization In Human Services* (Toronto: National Institution on Mental Retardation, 1972).

28. The information in the following summary is drawn almost exclusively from Kay, et al, Legal planning for the mentally retarded: The California experience, 60 *Cal. L. Rev.* 438 (1972).

29. *Id.* at 460-461.

30. *Id.*

31. *Id.* at 491.

32. See chapter 5 (The right to treatment), *supra*.

33. *National Association State Mental Health Program Directors Study* No.217, 1971.

34. *New York Association for Retarded Children* v. *Rockefeller, supra* note 18.

35. *Id.* at 756.

36. *Id.* at 756.

37. *Id.* at 759-762.

38. *Id.* at 764.

39. *Id.* at 765-768.

40. *Id.* at 768-770.

41. *Wyatt* v. *Stickney, supra* note 18.
42. *Id.*, at 390.
43. *Id.* at 392, 395-407.
44. S. Brakel and R. Rock, *supra* note 1.
45. *Brown* v. *Board of Education,* 347 U.S. 483, 493 (1954).
46. *Hosier* v. *Evans,* 314 F. Supp. 316 (D.V.I. 1970).
47. *Ordway* v. *Hargraves,* 323 F. Supp. 1155 (D. Mass. 1971).
48. *Margega* v. *Board of School Dirs.,* C.A. No. 70-C-8 (E.D. Wisc. 1970).
49. *Knight* v. *Board of Education* 48 F.R.D. 108 (E.D.N.Y. (1969).
50. *See generally,* Herr, Retarded children and the law. In: Symposium: Legal rights of the mentally retarded, 23 *Syr. L. Rev.* 991, 1002 (1972).
51. *Ala. Stat.,* Tit. 14, ch. 30 (1971).
52. *Nev. Rev. Stat.* sec.392.050 (1962).
53. State-Federal clearinghouse for exceptional children, summary statistics on children (1972); Comments of U.S. Committee of Education, Sidney Marland, 117 *Cong. Rec.* 6749 (May 12, 1971).
54. Roos, The mentally retarded citizen. In: Symposium, *supra* note 50 at 1053.
55. *Pennsylvania Association for Retarded Children* v. *Pennsylvania,* 334 F. Supp. 1257; 343 F. Supp. 279 (E.D. Pa. 1972).
56. *See, Pa. Stat. Ann.* Tit. 24 sec.13-1375 (Purdon Supp. 1972).
57. 343 F. Supp., *supra* note 55 at 296.
58. 334 F. Supp., *supra* note 55 at 1262-1263.
59. *Mills* v. *Board of Education of the District of Columbia* 348 F. Supp. 866 (D.D.C. 1972).
60. *See generally,* Mercer, *supra* note 2.
61. *Id.*, chapter 5.
62. R. Rosenthal and L. Jacobson, *Pygmalion In The Classroom,* (New York: Holt Rinehart and Winston, 1968).
63. See, 5 *Clearinghouse Rev.* 419, 463; *Cch Pov. L. Rep.* sec. 4460 (1971).
64. Herr, *supra* note 50 at 995 n. 17.
65. See, e.g., *Mich. Stat. Ann.* sec.15.3771(1) (Supp. 1974); Trudeau (ed), *Digest Of State And Federal Laws: Education Of Handicapped Children* (Arlington, Va.: Council for Exceptional Children, 1971).
66. W. R. Johnson, Sex education of the mentally retarded. In: F. De La Cruz and F. D. Laveck, eds., *Human Sexuality And The Mentally Retarded,* (New York: Brunner/Mazel, Inc., 1973) p. 59.
67. *Id.* p. 159; Morgenstern.
68. *Id.* p. 206; Burt.
69. *Utah Code Ann.* sec.64-10-7 (1968).
70. Burt, *supra* note 68, p. 1. note 3, p. 210
71. *Id.*, p. 212.
72. Reed and Anderson, Effects of changing sexuality on the gene pool, In: De La Cruz and Laveck, *supra* note 66, p. 114.
73. Tribe, Foreword; Toward a model of roles in the due process of life and law, 87 *Harv. L. Rev.* 1 (1973).
74. *The President's Commission on the Mentally Retarded,* The crucial decade (Washington, 1963) p. 22.
75. *See* Kay, et al., Legal planning for the mentally retarded: The California experience, 60 *Cal. L. Rev.* 438 (1972).
76. *Id.* at 508.
77. *Id.* at 509.
78. *Id.* at 512.

79. *See Cal. Ann. Welf. and Instns. Code* sec.6500.1 *et seq.* (West Supp. 1971); Kay, et al., *supra* note 75, at 1, 514-516.
80. *Cal. Ann. Health and Safety Code* sec. 416.19 (West 1970).
81. *See* Murdock, Civil rights of the mentally retarded: Some critical issues, 7 *Fam. L. Rev.* 1, 16n.35 (1973).
82. *See* B. Kugel and W. Wolfensberger, eds., *Changing Patterns Of Residential Services For The Mentally Retarded* (Washington, D.C.,: President's Commission on the Mentally Retarded, 1969) p. 400.
83. See, e.g., Cheng, The emergence and spread of the ombudsman institution, 377 *Annals* 20 (May 1968).

Chapter 9

The Juvenile System

In its final report issued in 1967, the President's Commission on Law Enforcement and Administration of Justice said this of the juvenile court system:

> It has not succeeded significantly in rehabilitating delin-quent youth, in reducing or even stemming the tide of juvenile criminality, or in bringing justice and compassion to the child offender (1).

Most of the voluminous commentary on the subject catalogues the paradoxes, ills, and brutalities of the juvenile process, and reaches a similar conclusion. The significance of this conclusion becomes overwhelming when one recognizes that by the time males reach the age of 18, one in five will have been referred to the juvenile courts (2).

The Department of Health, Education, and Welfare estimates (3) that 1,125,000 delinquency cases (excluding traffic offenses) were handled by all juvenile courts in 1971. The numbers have increased every year since 1960, and the rate of increase has been greater in each succeeding year except for 1970. Between 1960 and 1971 serious crimes (homicide, forcible rape, aggravated assault, and robbery) increased 193 percent. Delinquency among girls is rising faster than among boys, and the ratio of boys to girls has dropped from 4 to 1 to 3 to 1. Between 1960 and 1971, violent crimes by girls increased by 341 percent. Although serious and violent crimes constitute only 3 percent of delinquency cases, they are rising. And, of course, all these figures represent only the cases which get into the civil system.

The reaction to this situation typifies the patterns cited earlier. On the one hand, there are legal efforts to tighten procedures within the court, and on the other hand, reform efforts to divert youngsters from the court through various administrative processes (4). The motto is: Divert if you can and make it tougher to confine if you cannot. This requires both more alternative dispositions and more lawyers; both require more economic and human resources.

The tortured path of progress is exemplified in one jurisdiction where the juvenile confinement facility was closed because of the view that it was counterproductive. Except for the gravest offenses which may lead to legal treatment as an adult, juveniles, not diverted initially, now proceed through the court with the required procedural safeguards and are then ordered to identical rehabilitation programs. Since none of these facilities provide security measures, and none can claim great success in rehabilitation, the result is that the community has no protection against crime by juveniles. This, of course, is the dilemma we have encountered repeatedly. Absent effective alternatives, the choice is between warehousing and abdication of authority and responsibility.

It is this dilemma which breeds the demand for selective confinement predicated on identifying those who are dangerous; but as indicated earlier, that demand cannot be met. It is my view that the solution to this dilemma cannot be found within the medical model of the mental health profession because: (a) Inpatient psychiatric facilities for children with rare exception have been horrendous. (b) Whatever the value of traditional diagnostic criteria may be they are not readily applicable to children, except in the case of profound illness. (c) Psychotherapeutic methods that do exist are geared to the intact family, and that is rarely the target group of the juvenile courts. (d) Finally, as Justine Wise Polier points out, the dollar and resource cost of the medical model approach is totally unrealistic (5).

The reform alternatives are the massive development of children's services, preventive intervention, the community mental health approach, etc. Clearly the Federal Government is disenchanted with all of these because they lead to massive and expensive bureaucracies. The prevailing philosophy of the new Federalism is to leave the solution of this and other similar problems to local government. Since universal solutions to juvenile problems are an unlikely possibility, this may be wise, given adequate fiscal resources and responsive local government. There is one strong exception to the view that no universal solutions exist; it comes from the advocates of behavior modification. Whatever the merits of that treatment modality, it presents overwhelming political and ideological questions. These have been carefully analyzed by Schwitzgebel (6).

It has been the thesis of this monograph that any deprivation of freedom under the doctrine of parens patriae must carry a firm promise of benefit to the person confined. Based on what now exists in the area of treatment services for juveniles, no such benefit is likely to be forthcoming. Furthermore, I have emphasized that the treatment modality by which the benefit is provided must be acceptable in the light of social values and legal principles. Behavior modification is by that standard unacceptable if it utilizes illegal deprivations or aversive techniques. (See Chapter 6, The Right to Refuse Treatment.)

Therefore, if there is to be a legal justification for retaining the State's posture as a "parent" in the juvenile court, it must be found elsewhere than the Thank You Theory. Perhaps the parental role the State has in reality been playing is best described as the "erratic parent": "inconsistent, unreasonable, and vacillating." This is the kind of parent said by Glueck to create juvenile delinquency (7).

There are, however, a few juveniles who come before the courts who at least arguably are sick within the traditional medical model. I shall, in what follows, discuss that single aspect of the system, one which particularly meshes with the theme of this monograph: the referral of young sick persons by juvenile courts to inpatient treatment facilities.

Fortunately, we can be informed here by two remarkable, empirical studies: "Juvenile Justice Confounded" (8) and "Desperate Situation-Disparate Service" (9). Both studies deal with New York, and illustrate in powerful detail the failure of collaboration between the legal and mental health systems. They highlight the mental health profession's decisionmaking process by which a very few juveniles, usually the least troubled, are routed into genuinely therapeutic facilities, while a far greater number are sent to barely custodial institutions. This practice, and the paucity and poverty of dispositional options is seen to distort, corrupt, and betray the whole system. Without effective therapeutic services, the juvenile system becomes just another bureaucratic torment to disordered youths.

Anyone who sits for a few days in a juvenile court will conclude that nothing could be more difficult than the task of the court—which is expected to find an appropriate disposition for each child. The courts, of course, look to the mental health system for possible dispositions whenever the child's psychiatric condition is at issue. And the hospitals, in turn, have their own priorities (treatability, good teaching cases, research interests, etc.) and are unwilling to become the repositories for court-sent long-term patients. Charge and countercharge result:

> The charge raised by the hospitals [is] that the Court abuses their services with inappropriate remands; and the counterclaim raised by the Court [is] that the hospitals are unresponsive to the Court's needs (10).

At issue is more than simply who shall decide which children are sent where. That question is important only insofar as there really are alternative types of facilities available. Here, as elsewhere in the mental health system, the gut issue is resources. If we assume a base rate of 0.5 percent of children with serious mental illness, of New York City's 2 million children there would be 10,000 youngsters seriously disturbed mentally. This postulated rate is well below the usual estimate; indeed, "Desperate Situation" places the figure at between 20,000 and 40,000 (11). And there are likely an additional 160,000 to 200,000 less seriously disturbed children (12). To deal with them, the city has available about 189 beds for emergency short-term care (13).

Ironically, the pattern of reforms favoring deinstitutionalization described in earlier sections of this monograph has intensified this basic problem. It would be perverse, as well as morally and factually mistaken, to place the primary blame for the lack of resources on those who have consistently demanded more and urged reform, rather than upon those who have slashed budgets and stalled reform. However, it is true that the old days of warehousing allowed for more facile juvenile court dispositions. The growth in awareness of civil rights or the dangers of institutionalization, or both, has led to a drastic cutback in the number of available beds for children and an unwillingness by psychiatrists to retain children for long periods of time. Almost as important is that mental health professionals are increasingly unwilling to utilize coercive modalities within institutions. There are fewer locked wards, greater reluctance to restrict freedoms; and all this leads to an increase in what are called in institutionalese elopements. Thus, many psychiatric institutions are no longer as secure as the courts might like.

And on the other hand, the right-to-treatment movement, though perhaps a latent or informal force, has not yet gone so far as to make the promise of adequate treatment a reality for juveniles. The Supreme Court's significant recent concern with the juvenile process in such cases as *Kent, Gault,* and *Winship* (14) has extended only to procedural protections during adjudication, and not to preadjudicatory or postadjudicatory decisions; i.e., to the process of entry and exit from the system. There have been some court-inspired advances: recently, courts have barred the use of solitary confinement in State juvenile facilities (15), prohibited juvenile courts from committing male felons to the same institutions as adult offenders (16), limited corporal punishment and non-medically supervised use of tranquilizers (17), and suggested that lack of adequate treatment for civil commitants violates due process (18). But for the most part, courts still limit themselves to the precatory observation that the juvenile process is justified only if treatment of some kind is given.

A recent case, *Nelson et al.* v. *Heyne*, indicates the crucial sticking point in right-to-treatment cases. A U.S. Court of Appeals dealing with a suit brought in Indiana, held that individual treatment programs and individual counseling were constitutionally required for confined delinquents, but remanded the case to the trial court to decide what minimal treatment must be provided to satisfy constitutional due process (*19*). In light of what is known about effective treatment, that will be a challenging task indeed.

The right-to-treatment approach could have a major impact on the juvenile system. But enthusiasm should not impair our vision as to what it will and will not do (*20*). Clearly it will not clarify the vague criteria for legal intervention in disfavored or antisocial juvenile behavior, or resolve the problems of racial discrimination in the utilization of the juvenile courts, or enforce procedural rights in the process, or improve the biased and unscientific disposition process. Nor will it necessarily disentangle and redefine the roles of legal and mental health workers in the system. Finally, and most important here, the right-to-treatment approach, per se, does not stimulate the development of noninstitutional alternatives. It does not raise the questions of whether juveniles are best changed by inpatient care, and why the courts should have inpatient facilities at their disposal at all. The studies of the New York experience reveal the practices which develop when the courts have such power.

The New York Family Court Act sets up four categories of children who may be brought before the court: (a) those whose parents are alleged to be abusive or neglectful, (b) those who have been abandoned, (c) persons in need of supervision (PINS), and (d) delinquents (*21*). The first two groups theoretically have committed no antisocial act, and the court's jurisdiction and power to refer them to institutions rests purely on the parens patriae doctrine. As to these nondelinquent children, the court can, given certain conditions, release the child to the custody of his parent, guardian, or another suitable person, or issue an order to such person to act in a certain way, or place him under the supervision of the Department of Social Services or place him on probation (*22*). In practice, the distinction between abused and abandoned children is disregarded, and in many cases the aforementioned milder remedies are not resorted to. Of the more than 5,000 such cases each year, a significant number are placed in public institutions with few treatment opportunities (*23*). Another group of cases are sent to foster care, but the value of that disposition is increasingly under fire (*24*).

The third category, PINS, are those boys under 16 or girls under 18 who are truant, incorrigible, or habitually disobedient, and beyond the control of parents or guardians (25). They are distinguished from delinquents in that they have committed acts which would not be crimes if committed by adults. Again, the court may take actions ranging from home supervision, to probation, to institutionalization. The 1962 New York legislature, which enacted the Family Court Act, apparently realized that existing facilities were unable to provide effective treatment to delinquents, and that adding the nondelinquents would merely compound the problem. They specifically refused to authorize placement of PINS in facilities of the division of youth, i.e., maximum security facilities. Indeed, a primary purpose of creating a new category called PINS was to prevent the placement of nondelinquents in the State training schools. Nevertheless, the failure of that and succeeding legislatures to provide any alternatives resulted in a 1968 amendment permitting the very evil originally sought to be avoided (26).

The fourth category is delinquents, those who have committed acts which would be criminal if done by an adult.

The New York law, it should be noted, provides for institutionalization for purposes of supervision or treatment for PINS, and for supervision, treatment, or confinement for delinquents. Thus, the promise of treatment is central to the rationale for both types of confinement. This is reasonable to the extent that at least some of such youngsters are disturbed in the perspective of the medical model.

For diagnosis, the court can send the child to a clinic affiliated with it, to the inpatient service of a city hospital, or to a new project, the Rapid Intervention Project (27). Time limits for the (preliminary) and dispositional hearings for each category are set by law, but these limits are apparently often ignored (28). Although the National Council on Crime and Delinquency strongly recommends preadjudication detention with foster families under agency supervision, in New York they are generally unavailable, as are any other alternative, nonjail facilities (29). Hence, though the estimate is that just 10 percent require it, New York confines 31 percent in high security facilities (30).

These are the detention centers which have all the same problems that adult jails in large cities demonstrate. Conditions in these centers have been denounced by a series of commissions, and there has been substantial litigation (31).

As to long-term detention, theoretically none but delinquents can be "committed." However, in the usual jabberwocky fashion, the other categories may be "placed," and a judge may effect long-term commitment via successive 1-year extensions after the initial 18-month "placement" (32).

Theoretically available to the Family Court for disposition of a given juvenile are the following: (a) voluntary child care agencies, (b) New York City shelters, (c) New York State training schools, (d) New York City psychiatric hospitals, (e) State hospitals for the mentally ill, (f) State training schools, and (g) State institutions for the retarded. In 1970 the Family Court placed 1,396 children with public or private agencies, and another large number with the State institutions for the mentally ill or retarded (*33*). But in 1970 the slow move toward decent facilities was dramatically reversed. There followed a series of job freezes, budget cuts, and tightenings of the boundaries between bureaucracies which have greatly augmented the obstacles faced by the Family Court in placing children. In order to appreciate the chaotic, arbitrary, and often exclusionary system here at work, it is worth looking at each type of institution or dispositional option in some detail.

Voluntary child care agencies. These private or publicly funded agencies, or both, are the major initial conduit, handling a majority of the children placed by the Family Court or Bureau of Child Welfare (*34*). However, the major study reports that between 1963 and 1970 there was

> a slow but steady decrease in the total number of delinquent and PINS children accepted by the agencies and a dramatic shift in the categories of children for whom they provide care (*35*).

As one reviews the data, what emerges is that these agencies use traditional psychiatric diagnostic criteria and indices of treatability. The latter include such variables as intelligence, literacy, intact family, lack of dangerous acting out, etc. The result of these criteria generated by the traditional approach is a failure to accept youths of minority background.

Of one study sample, the agencies accepted for placement 78 percent of the white children, and just 27 percent of the minority group children (*36*). Some of the agencies have absolute IQ minima for accepting children. Where a child's record showed drug abuse, "efforts to secure private agency placement . . . were minimal"; these children often seem not even to have been evaluated for any underlying psychiatric diagnosis which might make them appropriate for consideration by the agencies. As might be expected, the exclusionary biases are mutually reinforcing. Thus, even those private agencies specifically dedicated to dealing with children with drug problems accepted 67 percent of the white applicants and just 14 percent of the minority children (*37*).

There was similarly dramatic evidence of bias against youths with tougher records (43 percent of the PINS boys were accepted while just 21 percent of the delinquents were accepted—and none of the female delinquents), and against the older children (just 29 percent of the male PINS and delinquents over 14 were accepted (*38*). Probably these exclusionary biases are due to more than individual prejudices. In a contracting budgetary system, each agency has its own priorities and is eager to develop as successful a record as possible. Perhaps the expectation as to which children are likely to be rehabilitated is influenced by racial or psychiatric stereotypes, but overall institutional pressures to select a treatable group may be even more important. In any case, the results are clear. Litigation seeking to remedy this de facto discrimination is now under way.

Ironically, "little is known about the quality of care provided by any of the voluntary agencies." Although State agencies are supposed to investigate the delivery of services, many institutions have not been surveyed in many years (*39*). However, since the agencies are funded at a higher rate than other programs such as the training centers and usually provide care to smaller numbers in smaller units, it is assumed that they provide somewhat better care. Unfortunately, however, just 26 percent of the children placed with the agencies go to residential centers (5 percent) or special treatment-oriented units (21 percent) which provide the best therapy. The remainder receive less good care.

In sum, the agencies have

> for the most part ceased to serve those children with the fewest resources in their homes, schools, and communities and those with the most severe . . . problems (*40*).

When the children are rejected by the voluntary agencies, the court's only recourse is placement in the training schools or with the Commissioner of Social Services. The former, as we shall see, is a bleak prospect, while placement with the latter leads to long stays in one of the city's doleful shelters—during which stay Social Services, rather circularly, tries to place the child with the very same voluntary agencies which have rejected the court referral.

New York City shelters. Because of the long wait for admission to other facilities, including State mental hospitals, many of the children in the shelters are mentally ill or retarded; yet they remain in primarily detention facilities with no treatment programs. And though the PINS and delinquent children are supposed to remain

152

there only for a short time, many must linger on; recently a suit was brought by a child who had remained for 2 years (*41*). A director of the Children's Center has called the population of these shelters the most deprived of the deprived (*42*).

Originally, the shelters accepted only the abused or neglected children, rejecting the more disturbed or troublesome PINS. And since 1970 when PINS were first accepted, the difficulties in securing placement with the Department of Social Services have grown increasingly grave. One study found that of a sample which had been placed with Social Services for a full 9 months, just 19 percent had been transferred to voluntary agencies, while 41 percent remained in shelter care and 25 percent had been returned to court (*43*).

As for conditions at the shelters, New York State Attorney General Lefkowitz has termed them "disgraceful," "dreadful," and "inadequate" (*44*). Overcrowding has converted virtually all potentially therapeutic space—classrooms, crafts rooms, lounges, etc.—into dormitories (*45*). Psychiatric care and drug.abuse help is said to be virtually nonexistent (*46*). Staffing is chronically thin; one shelter with an average population of 121 girls was budgeted in 1970 for 21 psychiatric man-hours and 31½ psychological man-hours per week, including diagnosis and consultations (*47*). Despite an occasional rash of election time promises for reform and new appropriations (*48*), conditions in the shelters show no hope of improvement in the foreseeable future.

New York State training schools. New York has 14 training schools with a combined capacity of about 2,400 (*49*). These are institutions conceived as a last resort for delinquents, and now used as a primary repository for many other categories as well. PINS are routinely sent there—despite the fact that it was one of the major legislative purposes of designing the new category of PINS to avoid sending nondelinquent children to such institutions (*50*). The Family Court Act still prohibits sending abused or neglected children to the training schools but such placements may occur anyway. This is illustrated by the recent case of *In Re Lloyd*. A family court judge, frustrated at the choice of sending a boy back to inebriated, neglectful parents, to a shelter where he had remained with minimal care for a long period, or futilely seeking placement with voluntary agencies, decided to dub the boy a PINS and send him to a training school for 18 months. The State Supreme Court reversed, saying that although it sympathized with the "impossible situation" of the judge, the legislature has long recognized that the State training schools are hardly a beneficial haven for young people in need of supervision and such disposition was first indicated . . . and then allowed as a stopgap measure for three years . . . until it was finally made permanent (51).

But the high court was rather impotent too; noting that it could not create an institution where none existed, it remanded merely in the "hope" that a private agency placement could now be found. Again, the discriminatory structure of the system reveals itself. Those placed in the last-resort training schools included, in one study, 20 percent of the white delinquent boys, but 84 percent of the Puerto Rican and 91 percent of the black delinquent boys (52).

Most of the training schools are located in small rural communities far from most children's families, who live in New York City and are often too poor to be able ever to visit the schools. The schools vary as to age, sex, racial character, and degree of troublesomeness of the residents, as well as the security, amenities, and per capita expenditures of the institution. The only apparent constant is that

Not one school is equipped to provide even minimal mental health treatment for the seriously disturbed children it receives (53).

The trained mental health personnel available in the small communities (and with the inadequate funding levels) is limited; they are often part-time employees who work full time at nearby State hospitals for the mentally disabled. Civil Service bumping may replace specially qualified younger employees with less qualified, more senior ones. Usually there is one full-time or part-time psychiatrist, and an inadequate number of social workers. Only one school has a real drug program. The educational programs have been termed "token affairs of little use" (54), and little effort is made to arrange for instruction in local public schools or to coordinate training school instruction with that in public schools (55). Recreation is, for the most part, limited to a few games and watching television (56). Medical and mental health care are grossly deficient, and apparently many children are on tranquilizers for control rather than therapeutic purposes (57).

Finally, since release from the schools depends on factors other than the seriousness of an offense, nondelinquent children may be confined in this unsuitable environment even longer than the delinquent ones! As one study put it:

Length of stay is more likely to be determined by the adjustment to institutional rules and routine, the receptivity of parents or guardians to receiving the children back home, available bed space in cottages and the current treatment ideology. Juvenile status offenders tend to have more family troubles and may actually have greater difficulty in meeting the criteria for release than their delinquent peers. The result is that the delinquents without crimes probably spend more time in institutions designed for delinquent youth than "real" delinquents (58).

This is a typical distortion of a system which is coming apart at the seams. The training schools have to accept the children rejected elsewhere, often those with the most serious personal and family problems; yet they are totally unequipped to provide the needed treatment. In light of these findings, one can readily understand the familiar suggestion of a recent study that all but a few of the schools should be closed (59).

New York City psychiatric hospitals. In New York there are four municipal hospitals with psychiatric facilities for children. They perform two primary court-related functions: they diagnose children referred by the court, and on occasion they accept children for somewhat longer term care. The hospitals have a total of 189 beds for children. About half are taken by severely disturbed children remanded by the court and remaining for a rather long time. Other beds are taken up by retarded children awaiting admission to State institutions for retardates (60).

Thus, the spaces available for short-term intensive care which, theoretically these facilities should be especially able to provide, are quite limited. The hospital is placed in a bind: while it may reject applicants from other institutions, it must accept all those referred by the court. But since the State hospitals for the mentally ill have of late refused, quite rightly I believe, to accept all but the most extreme cases, an expanded demand for care confronts the city hospitals. Other obstacles to placement in the State hospitals include the requirements that the patient be from the right geographic catchment area and not have been diagnosed for long-term care (61). In response to these rigid standards by State institutions, at least one city hospital has joined in the escalatory spiral by refusing admission to former State patients, and asking the court to deal directly with the State hospital (62).

These open skirmishes between beleaguered bureaucracies can only further distort the delivery of already scant mental health resources. They, too, are the costs of the tortured road to reform.

State Hospitals for the mentally ill. In New York, seven new hospitals for the mentally ill, each with a separate children's unit, had been opened or were anticipated to open during the 1971-72 fiscal year. But then the massive State budget cutbacks previously described were effected. More than a third of the Department of Mental Hygiene jobs were eliminated. When a subsequent bond issue failed, the hiring freeze was tightened, admissions at some hospitals were closed, and it was announced that some institutions might have to be closed entirely. As I have indicated in the chapter on civil commitment, I do not regard closing such institutions as necessarily a disaster. But what is disastrous is that it is unaccompanied by any plans for alternative, community facilities, and that the cutbacks have been more on staff than buildings. Vacancy rates in the highly qualified caretaker positions have been 30-50 percent in many institutions. This perpetuates a bad situation without in any way spurring its improvement.

Thus, since 1970 the number of children served by the State hospitals has declined to the point that they are now 25 percent underutilized, at least as to space. Hospitals have quite rightly refused dull children, disciplinary problems, and those who are acting out. Thus, they demonstrate a strict adherence to the kind of reliable criteria urged in the earlier chapter. However, many children who are refused are instead sent for longer periods to the even bleaker training schools. Thus, although there seems to have been a reversal of the pattern of the sixties when all sorts of children were sent to State hospitals for lack of alternative facilities, the overall result is no less tragic.

When we examine this result it is once again quite clear that those who were warehoused in the megainstitutions of psychiatry were not political prisoners. Rather, as with these unfortunate children, they are a group who have been abandoned by their parents, by their community, and by the elected officials of the State and Federal Government.

Conclusion

The use of courts to deal with noncriminal social problems (the abused, the abandoned, and the PINS), is part of America's monomania for legalistic solutions. The juvenile courts demonstrate the total inadequacy of that legal approach. The court's only function in many instances is to funnel children from unsuitable homes to unsuitable placements. As to those who are sick, the few good treatment facilities are discriminatory in their exclusion of minority children. Thus, the courts are participating in a system which to the limited extent it does provide benefits, may well be operating unconstitutionally.

The State hospitals have at least defined their proper role, and this has helped to expose the masquerade of treatment. In New York the confinement of juvenile delinquents is now nothing more than that. Certainly the training schools do not meet any right-to-treatment standard, and the shelters seem even more destructive, if that is possible.

Here, as elsewhere, the subjects of this bankrupt system are disproportionately minority children and the caretakers are not. The bitter harvest of this tragic planting will be reaped by generations to come.

Solutions?

When Judge Polier, whose judicial career has been devoted to these problems, surveyed the prospects for the future in 1968, she looked with some optimism to the community mental health movement then in its ascendancy (63). That optimism must now be muted by the experience of the intervening years. Kittrie (64), writing in 1971, called for

> epidemiological approaches—addressed to the social causes and settings of delinquency rather than solely to the affected juvenile himself.

This substitutes the public health model for the medical model and is as little help. Practitioners of the public health approach have, for example, identified smoking and obesity as critical epidemiological factors in heart disease. Yet, if anything, smoking and obesity have increased rather than diminished. Lack of opportunities, poverty, racism, and broken homes, though perhaps not as convincingly demonstrated, are significant epidemiological factors in juvenile delinquency. They cannot be ameliorated by courts, by physicians, or by public health expertise. Even the hope of a solution requires massive social change and political effort. Meanwhile the chaos will mount as the megainstitutions disgorge their subjects under the new pressures of constitutional litigation and administrative reform.

References

1. Task force on juvenile delinquency, president's commission on law enforcement and administration of justice, *Juvenile Delinquency And Youth Crime* (Washington: Government Printing Office, 1967) p. 7.
2. Blumstein, Systems analysis and the juvenile courts, 374 *Annals* 92, 99 (1967).
3. Department of Health, Education, and Welfare, *Juvenile Court Statistics* (DHEW pub. No.SRS 73-03452) (1971).
4. *See* Lemert, Instead of court: Diversion in juvenile justice (NIMH monograph; DHEW No.(HSM) 72-9093) (Rockville, Md.: National Institute of Mental Health, 1971).
5. J. W. Polier, *The Rule Of Law And The Rule Of Psychiatry* (Baltimore: Johns Hopkins Press, 1968) p. 107.
6. *See* R. Schwitzgebel, *Development and legal regulation of coercive behavior modification techniques with offenders* (DHEW pub. No. (HSM) 73-9015) (Rockville, Md.: NIMH, 1971), C. M. Franks and T. G. Wilson (eds.) *Annual Review Of Behavior Therapy Theory And Practice* (New York: (Brunner/Mazel, Inc., 1973).
7. Quoted In: J. Katz et al., *Psychoanalysis, Psychiatry And Law* (New York: The Free Press, 1967) p. 396.
8. National Council on Crime and Delinquency, *Juvenile Justice Confounded* (Washington, 1972) [hereinafter cited as Juvenile Justice Confounded].
9. Office of children's services, judicial conference of New York, *Desperate Situation-Disparate Service* (New York, 1973) [hereinafter cited as Desperate Situation].
10. *Id.* at 1.
11. *Id.* at 13.
12. *Id. See also Joint Commission on Mental Health of Children and Youth,* Crisis in child mental health: crisis for the 1970's (1972) p.2
13. *Juvenile Justice Confounded* p. 68.
14. *In re Gault,* 387 U.S. 1 (1967); *Kent v. United States,* 383 U.S. 541 (1966); *In re Winship,* 397 U.S. 358 (1970).
15. *Lollis v. New York State Department of Social Services,* 322 F. Supp. 473 (S.D.N.Y. 1970).
16. *State v. Fisher,* 245 N.E. 2d 358 (Ohio 1969).
17. *Nelson v. Heyne,* 491 F. 2d 352 (7th Cir. 1974).
18. *Creek v. Stone,* 379 F. 2d 106 (D.C. Circ. 1966); *Stockton v. Alabama Industrial School for Negro Children,* C.A. No. 2834-N (M.D. Ala. July 23, 1971); *Martarella v. Kelly,* 349 F. Supp. 575 (S.D.N.Y. 1972).
19. *Poverty Law Reports* No. 47 (Feb. 18, 1974).
20. For an optimistic view, see Kittrie, Can the right to treatment remedy the ills of the juvenile process? 57 *Geo. L. J.* 845 (1967).
21. *See New York Family Court Act* sec.1013, 1058 (McKinney Supp. 1971).
22. *Id.* sec.1052.
23. *See* Note, Nondelinquent children in New York 1972 *Col. J. Law and Soc. Probs.* 249.
24. See, e.g., Mnookin, Foster care: In whose best interest, 43 *Harv. Educ. Rev.* 599 (1973).

25. *New York Family Court Act* sec.712(b) (McKinney Supp. 1971).
26. *Laws Of New York*, ch. 874 at 2654 (1968).
27. Note, *supra* note 23 at 258.
28. *Citizens Commission for Children of New York, Inc.*, Juvenile detention problems in New York City (1970) at 3. *See* Note, *supra* note 23 at n. 58.
29. Note, *supra* note 23 at n. 59.
30. *Id.*
31. *Id.* at 261-264.
32. *Id.* at 259.
33. *Juvenile Justice Confounded* at 4.
34. Id. at 22-23. Other studies have placed the figure as high as 80 percent, see, e.g., Note, *supra* note 23 at 265 n. 110.
35. *Juvenile Justice Confounded* at 53.
36. *Id.* at 24.
37. *Id.* at 26.
38. *Id.* at 27-29.
39. *Id.* at 58.
40. *Id.* at 53.
41. *In re Lloyd*, 33 App. Div. 2d 385 (1970).
42. *The New York Times*, July 26, 1970 at 26, col. 1.
43. *Juvenile Justice Confounded* at 61.
44. *The New York Times*, July 27, 1970, at 56, col. 7; July 30, 1970, at 30, col. 4.
45. *The New York Times*, July 26, 1970 at 26, col. 1.
46. *Juvenile Justice Confounded* at 63.
47. *Id.*
48. See, e.g., Statements by Governor Rockefeller and other State officials cited in Note, *supra* note 23 at 264-266.
49. *Id.* at 268.
50. *See* New York State Legislature, second report of the joint legislative committee on court reorganization (1966), *Sess. Laws of New York* 3428, 3434-3436 (McKinney 1966).
51. *In re Lloyd*, *supra* note 41, at 387.
52. *Juvenile Justice Confounded* at 24.
53. *Id.* at 37.
54. Citizens committee for children of New York, the New York training school system (1967) p. 5.
55. *Id.*
56. *Id.*
57. *Id.* at 4.
58. Note, *supra* note 23 at 267.
59. Citizens' Committee, *supra* note 54.
60. *Juvenile Justice Confounded* at 67-69.
61. *Id.* at 69.
62. *Id.*
63. Polier, *supra* note 5.
64. N. Kittrie, *The Right To Be Different* (Baltimore: Johns Hopkins Press, 1971) p. 168.

Chapter 10

The Aging

One tenth of the American population — 21 million people — are aged 65 and older. And this fraction, which has increased so markedly since 1900, will grow to greater proportions in the future(1). As a group, older Americans are caught between fixed incomes and rising prices, depleting resources and longer lifetimes.

Eighty-one percent of the aged manage on their own. But 86 percent have chronic conditions, diseases, or physical impairments of some kind. They are in poorer health, need more care, pay more for it and can afford it less than other groups. Despite medicare-medicaid, old persons' per capita out-of-pocket health costs have actually increased since 1966! In 1972, these per capita health care costs were $981, of which medicare paid just 42 percent. Other sources paid an additional 30 percent — still leaving an aged individual with an average of $276 in out-of-pocket health costs.

Only one-third of aged persons have what the government optimistically terms a moderate income on which to live. The median income of aged persons living alone or with nonrelatives is $2,199. This is less than half the median for the rest of us. Aged women and minority group members are even poorer.

Many of the aged not in institutions live in poor housing; yet, on average they pay 34 percent of their income for housing. Most nursing homes, State hospitals, and like institutions are bleak. The aged are rarely employed. They have relinquished most occupational and personal roles. They are often detached from family and former friends, lonely, depressed, and without hope. One of every four suicides in America is committed by a person over 65.

In sum, the aged are a huge and growing group, and one with problems which are both special and especially grave. Solutions to these problems, or even marginal improvements, depend on coordinated policies in all the areas mentioned—income, health, housing, and human relations. As with most social problems based in part on denial and inequity, greater expenditures are one prerequisite to amelioration. But programs for the aged already cost some $50 billion(2). Now this is vastly different than defense expenditures, since a large part of it is not budget outlays but payroll deductions in trust funds, e.g., in Social Security. But from a political standpoint, the answer cannot simply be more money expended. And the problems of human isolation and personal obsolescence cannot be solved with money alone.

This chapter cannot attempt to survey all the problems of the aged. This is a monograph on the law and mental health systems, and I shall confine myself to three topics: guardianship, confinement, and intervention. My perspective is based on the premise that programs for the aged should have as a prime object the creation of incentives for maintaining and regenerating family-connected life for old people, and that fostering such family relations will increase the welfare yield of many current expenditures for the aged.

Twenty-two percent of the aged live alone. Seventy percent live with a family—most with just a spouse. There may be relatively little contact with other family members. Three percent of the aged live with some nonrelative, and 4 or 5 percent are institution-alized(3). When aged people become ill, or senile, or difficult, we observe in yet another context how the modern family externalizes its problems. And most often with the aged, the mental health system is called on at one time or another. Indeed, for several decades, the problem of finding a decent living context for the aged was perceived as primarily a medical and mental health problem. Thus, beginning in the heyday of institutional warehousing and continuing until the past few years, about 40 percent of the State hospital population has been over age 65 (4).

The sociological reasons for this tendency to abandon the aged to nonfamily or institutional contexts have been repeatedly cata-logued: the rise of the nuclear family, the postwar baby boom, and the ideal of the independence and privacy of the detached suburban house, the society's fascination with youth, occupational obso-lescence, and the increasing skill and productivity demands of industry and so on. As one commentator has put it:

(Our society) accords status to work over leisure . . .
prizes youth over seniority . . . venerates knowledge more
than experience and (above all) abhors death (5).

Whatever the causes, the family that cares for its aged parents is an endangered if not yet extinct species. Families may not dump their elderly with pleasure; but the social norms and to some degree the facilities exist which permit it. And the mental health profes-sions have contributed to this by defining the care of the aged as a technical problem. I do not vainly lament the passing of the caretaking family, nor urge its resuscitation unaware of its costs. Nor do I challenge, at this juncture, why the State should lend its force at all to the externalization of family problems. I assume for the present argument that in dealing with the aged, there is a role for the State as a direct provider of services. This is so if for no other reason than that there are those with no family, or families psychologically unable to help them. My point really is that the basic instruments of the law-mental health system have permitted and encouraged the further disintegration of family-connected life—without really being able to otherwise satisfy the needs of the aged. This will be made apparent in each of the sections which follow.

Competency and Guardianship

How does the process of determining the incompetency of an aged—or other—person work? An exhaustive study sums it up thus :

> Proceedings are instituted by petition, usually by a close relative. Most cases are uncontested and the hearings are brief. In large cities, with their crowded court dockets, the average case may take only a minute or two. If incompetency is found, the court appoints a guardian, often the petitioning relative, and sets the amount of the guardian's bond (6).

Elsewhere it is said that a hearing "sometimes takes place, sometimes does not take place, and sometimes, though it occurs, is so perfunctory as not to be a hearing. . ."(7). Often the proposed ward is not present. Very few jurisdictions provide for appointed counsel for the alleged incompetent. If counsel is asked for, the court may suggest one from a rotating list of attorneys. The attorneys provide service to the court on nonlucrative cases, and in turn are granted fees on large estates. If the attorney views his role as neutral fact-finder for the court rather than as advocate for the alleged incompetent, the court may approve this role (8). Evidence is minimal, usually just consisting of a physician's letter along with the petitioner's testimony. Evidence is not strictly limited and free use of hearsay is permitted. Jury trial, which though often provided by statute, is actually granted at the discretion of the judge, and is quite rare (9). By this vague and summary process, aged individuals lose the right to control property they have worked all their lives to acquire. What then is the rationale? And is it sufficient?

The incompetency procedure is a venerable one. But it was designed to deal with a few men of wealth who might become unable to run the affairs of their (literal) estates. Today, on the other hand, people live longer and, thus, there are more people likely to become senile. There is a huge middle class of persons who may need guardianship of some kind, but whose estates are too small to support the costs of administration.

In bygone days, the appointed guardian was usually also a man of wealth, experienced in managing property, known in the community, and thus socially as well as legally accountable. Relative to the need, there are fewer such people today. Property was then quite simple; today, coordinating receipt of Federal and local program benefits, pensions, and expenditures for taxes, and institutional care is a complicated task. For all these reasons, the incompetency process has become depersonalized, harsh, often abused, and inadequate to the need to protect the (aged) individual. This is not really surprising, for the incompetency procedure was developed to protect property—it had little to do with the non-economic welfare of the individual. It far predates the development of hospitalization procedures or institutional care for the mentally ill(10). And though competency has acquired ancillary usages— competency to contract, execute a will, marry, have a driver's license—the proper disposition of property has remained the prime concern of the competency process. As to the aged, therefore, the real problem is to devise a guardianship procedure which will care for the person as well as for his property.

All 50 States and the District of Columbia have incompetency statutes — ranging from a single paragraph in some States to detailed codes in others. But the statutes define as indicia of incompetency no less than 55 conditions, states or characteristics, from "vicious habits," to "idleness," to "unsound mind," to "insanity." Twenty-six statutes specifically mention old age, and five more mention senility (11). As in many mental health contexts, there is a facile slide from the proper focus on competency to manage the property to the shorthand mentally ill label. But the medical terminology seems to misdirect the focus rather than clarify it, and has the added cost of stigmatizing needlessly. Even from a mental health perspective, the statutory criteria are a "heterogeneous collection of archaisms, nosological classifications, symptoms, and colloquial descriptions of behavior. . ." (12). A very common standard, "mental weakness not amounting to unsoundness of mind", is rejected by many psychiatrists as uselessly vague, if not meaningless (13). Each of these criteria, alone or combined with others, together with the often routine inference that "by reason of" the given condition the person is unable to manage his affairs "properly" or is likely to be imposed on by others, provides the legal basis for incompetency (14). The person thereby loses his right to control various aspects of his personal life (e.g., the right to marry) as well as power over the disposition of his property.

The purposes of property guardianship are to protect against the dissipation of wealth by an incompetent person—to protect him, his family, and the State whose charge he might become. But each of these goals raises distinct considerations. Especially when applied to an older person with no prospect of recovery of full competency, who has worked his whole life to accumulate some funds, the parens patriae doctrine of protecting a person against himself should be very strictly limited. Middle-aged veneration of saving should not be allowed to prevent people in old age from doing what may bring them happiness.

A now famous example is posed by the case of *In re Tyrell* (*15*). An 85-year-old man had assured his personal security by contracting with a rest home for care until his death, and his burial expenses were prepaid. He had no living children nor a spouse. During the course of a few years, he spent about $9,000, or 40 percent of his remaining assets. He gave $2,000 to a widow whom he felt needed it. He had entrusted his remaining estate—about $12,000 in stocks— to his sister-in-law. When he asked for its return, she initiated incompetency proceedings. A brief hearing ensued. No court-ordered examination was held. The court conceded that Mr. Tyrell had a keen mind, and had lucidly conducted a number of recent transactions. The evidence of incompetency consisted of Mr. Tyrell's physician's testimony following a 15-minute examination in the jury room, and the court's own observations. Mr. Tyrell's wishes were overruled and a guardian was appointed to "conserve" his estate, for purposes not stated (*16*).

It is difficult to estimate the numbers of these cases compared to those in which judges with the help of careful medical and psychiatric testimony make prudent decisions. These are decisions not to husband resources for the benefit of relatives but to make sure that the aged person will benefit from his own limited funds and not be exploited by his relatives.

As to society's interest in preventing sharp practices at the expense of the aged, and the consequent shifting of burdens of care onto the State, a number of things may be said. First, legal doctrines already permit the voiding of coerced or unconscionable contracts or bequests, without the need to preemptively nullify the aged person's wishes. This is just to replace a private predator with the State; the victim is the same. Second, people are permitted to do lots of things—have more children, loaf on the job, or blow up at the boss and thereby become unemployed, speculate, deal, lose, and go bankrupt, or just refuse to save — which may ultimately place burdens of support on the State. Now surely an aged person who just does not know what he is doing should be protected. But the mere fact of age, or of some medically-predicated inference of inability to manage properly, should not justify preemptive State intervention. If a man can still hear at 85, who has a better right to walk to a different drummer?

The *Tyrell* case mentioned above poses what I take to be a critical fact situation. If the account of the case in the *Maryland Law Review* is accurate, Tyrell had made certain that he would be secure until his death. What the litigation concerned was the surplus and who would decide how it was to be spent or rather conserved. That decision is apparently contradictory to the general thesis of this monograph that State intervention in a citizen's life must be in the interest of the citizen.

Perhaps the wiser solution in this conflict of interests would be a more refined two-step procedure. If a relative believed that an aged person was being imprudent with his funds, he could petition to have incompetence declared. But there would be two levels of incompetence and two quantities of the estate considered.

If the court found that an aged person was merely unable to cope with calculations, became forgetful etc., but was not irrational or disoriented, it could take the following steps. It would appoint a guardian whose responsibility would be mainly for bookkeeping purposes. The court would evaluate the aged person's current estate and his life expectancy on an actuarial basis. An amount would be set aside which would be sufficient to permit the aged person to continue to live in the style and with the comforts he then enjoys—as a minimum. If funds beyond that are available, then the court would allow the alleged incompetent to expend it as he wished unless a greater degree of incapacity could be demonstrated.

The purpose of this first step incompetency is to provide the aged person with financial supervision and protect him against his own improvidence. Petitioner would have to prove that the aged person's faculties were such that he could not manage his own affairs by reason of memory loss, inability to calculate, etc. — the signs of early senility. But such a finding would still permit the aged person control over any funds in excess of those needed to sustain him.

The second level of incapacity could only be reached by proving that the aged person's judgment was impaired such that he no longer recognized his friends and relatives, was confused and disoriented, was influenced in his financial decisions by delusions or mistaken perceptions—substantial evidence of senility and/or senile psychosis. Here the court would again calculate what was necessary to sustain the aged person and appoint a guardian to conserve both that and the surplus.

Obviously all of these difficulties could be avoided if the legal profession helped guard against this eventuality by proper estate planning. The aging should be encouraged to select an acceptable arrangement before their competency is put in question. Even people with very small estates should be encouraged to designate in some valid legal instrument (17) a person whom they trust to be their guardian in the event of their becoming incapacitated.

Because for the vast majority of the aged, with moderate or very low incomes, the problem is not what to do with their property, but how to live, a self-selected guardian is the most sensible approach to meet this need. Of the 41 jurisdictions which provide for some court appointed guardianship, 35 have guardianship of the person as well as of property. And of the 17 jurisdictions with conservatorship for the aged, eight have conservatorship of the person (18). Lamentably, while in theory, fiduciary responsibility for the welfare of a person and surrogate management of his property are quite different, in practice they often become merged in the same person, and even the same state of mind. One major study concludes that separate guardianship of the person is unknown (19). The consequences of this fusing of functions can be anticipated. A recent national conference concluded:

> Guardianship, as it is practiced in most states, does not adequately protect most impaired elderly persons in need of protection. When it is used, it safeguards property not the person (20).

Of course, in some cases, these two roles might best be served by the same person. But the law-mental health system should be alert to financial interests and personal stresses or conflicting loyalties which may impair a person's ability to perform what ought to be the guardian's role. Generally, banks and other financial institutions have declined to serve as guardians of the person. As to family members, who pose both advantages and disadvantages, a wise approach is posed by the Uniform Probate Code which gives priority to family members but permits the court, at its discretion, to appoint others (21). The related problem, of course, is that judges view competency determinations and guardianship review as the lowliest of their tasks, and have generally been unwilling to spend much time on it (22).

The guardian of the person should perceive his role as that of safeguarding the interest of the ward as the ward, were he competent, would wish them to be served. Though often facilely construed thus, this is not a reasonable-man test. On the contrary, it presumed a fairly solid human relation to the ward, at least deep enough to have a sense of his values and priorities among the choices open. The guardian, if he also has charge of the estate, should especially avoid ritually applying frugal norms to negate the elder person's desires. The requirement of many statutes (23) that the guardian spend from the estate "frugally," is an inflexible one which ignores the size of the corpus, the style of living of the aged person, and the pleasure he derives from various types of gifts or expenditures.

Public Guardianship

Guardianship of the person and of property have not been civil rights; they are available only if a willing person may be found, or if the estate can bear the costs of administration. In this light, far too much of the discussion of guardianship for the aged has focused on that small minority with wealth, friends, and qualified advisors. Increasingly, therefore, it has been suggested that decent care for the aged really requires a system of public guardianship and assistance, available on request or need, to all.

Something like public guardianship is purported to exist in a number of States. Minnesota has a State guardianship plan, but it is limited to mentally retarded persons, does not seek out those who need aid, and has very few safeguards against the personal risks of those liable to the discretionary power of State officials (24). California has a more sensitive plan, but again limited to the retarded (25). North Carolina, Ohio, Colorado, and Texas have statutes providing for public-official guardians, but their activity is largely limited to distribution of estate assets, not investigating the welfare of the individual. The same can be said of the New York law, which focuses on payment of institutional costs. Both the Social Security and Veterans' Administration have provisions for special guardians to handle disbursements under their aegis to incompetent recipients of their beneficiaries (26). None of these satisfies the need for a guardian of the person's welfare. A broad proposal for a public guardian with wide powers (although also stressing property matters) has been formulated by the National Council of Senior Citizens (27). It stresses that such a public guardian is necessary to help those with too little money for a private guardian and no friends or relations in the vicinity. And it provides that the impaired elder citizen may himself request such a guardian.

Of course the goal of guardianship of the person is to provide the semicompetent person with supportive services so as to enable him to function in the community and avoid institutionalization. Thus the goal should be to preserve the autonomy of the aged individual as much as possible. Thus, the enlightened California law provides that those found to be "mentally disordered and bordering on mentally ill" should ordinarily be permitted to remain at home "subject to the visitation of the counselor in mental health" (28). Note that the counselors are not guardians (the disordered person is technically a ward of the court) but helpers. And they are backed up by the Department of Mental Hygiene, which performs various direct field services of a financial and personal nature and coordinates relations with relevant institutions. Despite this hopeful counselor model in California, a recent survey of the guardianship program concludes:

> Guardianship of the person is not well utilized, and it is not well understood. Supervision by the courts of such guardians is not only inadequate, it does not seem to exist (29).

Clearly there is a need for closer supervision of the work of personal guardians. Some have suggested that an administrative agency can do this job better than the courts, though this view too has been challenged (30). While State guardianship has, no doubt, provided some useful protective services, its primary accomplishment seems to have been saving the costs of private guardianship.

A true public guardianship system would be available to anyone substantially deprived of his capacity to manage his affairs, without the stigma of mental illness criteria. It would seek out private guardians, and where necessary, itself provide such services. It would view its role as, at the least, that of aiding the individual in personal and financial matters, seeking benefits, investigating service alternatives and supervising the delivery of institutional, outpatient, or home care. It should not view the problem of the marginally competent or incompetent aged person as just a mental health problem. Rather, it should serve to coordinate available services with respect to income, housing, health care, nutrition, companionship, and so on.

Hospitalization

We have already said that a finding of incompetency should never itself be the reason for civil commitment. But of course there will be those aged persons who need help and cannot function in the community even with the aid of a guardian. The aged as a group suffer a higher incidence of mental illness than most other groups (31). Frequent disorders include chronic brain syndrome, depression as well as psychoneurotic illnesses. My view on the proper criteria of civil commitment has been set forth in a separate section. The current, vague statutes permit commitment for mere behavioral oddity rather than proven mental disease—and the aged are particularly apt to strike us as acting strangely. Danger to others is rarely a factor; but danger to self has often been used as an umbrella rubric by means of which to confine those thought unable to live alone properly.

Clearly some very delicate balance must be struck between protection under parens patriae and individual autonomy. But it seems to me that a number of considerations warrant greater deference to the aged person's desires than is normally given in civil commitment proceedings. The aged person is experienced. He will rarely have dependent children whom he may harm or neglect. His problem is likely to be physical rather than mental; his disorder, though capable of being attenuated, is unlikely to be cured. The rationale of coercively protecting him now for his future welfare is weak. And, a person with but a few years to live may indeed have some reason to live in ways which strike the rest of us as foolish.

In another sense, however, the entire question of the aged patient's volition is deceptive. With admirable clarity, some recent statutes have distinguished voluntary from nonprotesting hospitalization. In the District of Columbia, for example, the former requires the patient's own request, while the latter requires only an acknowledgment by him at the time of admission that he does not protest (32). But for a disoriented aged person with nowhere to go, this distinction is an irrelevant nicety. An understanding of this reality is succinctly expressed by one New York judge in "Application of Certification of _____" (33). He criticized New York's system of administrative transfer and commitment, without judicial hearing, of senile aged "who do not make positive objection"—a practice which had effected the confinement of more than 1,000 aged in a 9-month period. After first decrying the lack of a judicial hearing, he noted that such hearing would be spurious in any case, since "grounded on a fictitious consent given by one who concededly is confused and disoriented." He continued:

> ... the senile is not likely to understand that the institution is a mental institution .... Often he is chagrined and humiliated following family rejection and has neither the will nor the capacity to object even if he be carefully advised (34). ... In short, the ... procedure, in my view, is little less than a ruse designed to circumvent the need for judicial consideration or review of the transfer of a senile to a mental institution. Thus unknowingly certified, without opportunity to secure private

custodial care, we have assembly line incarceration, depriving the aged of their liberty of person . . . .

It is contended by those who favor it that it is applied only where relatives or friends petition for certification. But generally relatives are all too eager to rid themselves of the senile . . . .

The diagnosis is the usual one, namely, chronic brain syndrome associated with cerebral arteriosclerosis. The added phrase "with psychotic reaction, mild" is the diagnostic phrase currently used to insure qualification for admission to a State mental institution. Yet all that the senile concededly needs is custodial attention in a hospital for the aged which is unavailable because the State and local governments have thus far failed to adequately supply such facilities.

The basic question is, of course, what good institutionalization is anyway. Another poignant example of a system twisted by lack of alternatives is posed by the now famous case of *Lake* v. *Cameron* (35). A 60-year-old woman was committed to St. Elizabeth's Hospital when police found her wandering. She was admittedly harmless, not manifestly mentally ill, and there was scant evidence of the likelihood of her harming herself by wandering. But the committing court found that her organic brain syndrome rendered her "of unsound mind" and therefore committable. Ms. Lake wished to be released. Her long absent husband returned and, along with her sister, offered to make a home for her. The court refused to permit this, deeming these persons "unable to give the patient the necessary care and supervision."

On appeal, the D.C. Circuit Court reversed and remanded the case (36), declaring that the intent of the D.C. statute was that:

the entire spectrum of services should be made available, including out-patient treatment, foster care, halfway houses, day hospitals, nursing homes, etc. [citation omitted] The alternative course of treatment or care should be fashioned as the interest of the person and of the public require . . . . Deprivations of liberty solely because of the dangers to the ill persons themselves should not go beyond what is necessary for their protection.

The majority openly declared that it was the duty of the court to explore alternatives, especially in the case of an indigent who could not retain counsel to do so. The court suggested that any potential harm from Ms. Lake's wandering should be abated by the least drastic means possible, e.g., by carrying an identification card, by home health care, etc. The superintendent of St. Elizabeth's at the time testified that "only 50 percent of the patients . . . require hospitalization in a mental institution," and that "for many older patients, the primary need was found to be for physical rather than psychiatric care" (37). Nor was this need well met at the hospital. The court recognized that long-term hospitalization debilitates patients, and that the last thing an aged person needs is the depersonalization of a large institution, further isolation, loss of dignity, and boredom.

Unfortunately, though this view carried the day, it lost the battle. On remand, the lower court decided that there were no alternative facilities, and Ms. Lake was sent back to St. Elizabeths (38). And since *Lake*, the prevailing view has generally been that of then Judge Burger who protested in dissent that "Neither this court nor the District Court is equipped to carry out the broad geriatric inquiry proposed or to resolve the social and economic issues involved" (38a).

However insensitive this dissent may be, it is instructive on a number of points. Burger is surely right that courts are not set up to make inquiries—or even to get followup feedback on the real effects of their dispositions. He is also correct that "a person's freedom is no less arrested . . . if he is confined in a rest home with a euphemistic name rather than at St. Elizabeth's Hospital" (39). This was true since little treatment was available at either place, and little dignity either.

The real fault, of course, is that the Burger view hardly inquires into the patient's needs and desires. He says it would be "unmitigated folly" to release Ms. Lake, but does not say why she is foolish to prefer taking her chances to commitment to a huge institution, the superintendent of which says it will not do her any good. And the Burger view perpetuates the misplaced reliance on the mental health system in the disposition of the aged.

Courts have long seen the basic problem. In 1954, the New York Supreme Court reluctantly committed senile elderly persons despite its awareness that they were merely physically impaired. The Court said, "Since denial of custodial care and hospitalization to these people would probably result in their death, I find myself compelled to certify them as mentally ill"(40). In 1957, however, the same court inclined the other way, saying, ". . . mental deterioration due to old age should not serve as an excuse for bundling off to a mental institution an aged hospital patient suffering from a multitude of physical ailments"(41). But most often since then, courts have been willing to pass over the solecism involved in committing the aged as mentally ill—with no inquiry into alternatives and no faith in the existing facilities.

The trend of involuntarily committing the aged to mental hospitals has declined in recent years. Most of these persons will now be voluntary residents of nursing homes rather than civilly committed. Their legal status will be small comfort against the hardships of the social isolation and neglect which occur in all but the best of these facilities. When one contemplates the fate of the aged American the fact that only 5 percent are institutionalized may seem reassuring. But examined from a longitudinal perspective it is likely that one out of every five aged persons will end up in an institution(42).

The quality of life in those institutions is affected by administrative practices in the mental health system as indicated in the concluding section of the chapter on right-to-treatment. The problem once more is the manipulation of labels for administrative purposes. But in this case it is being done in the name of progress.

State hospitals over the past several decades built up a backlog of patients who are process schizophrenics and retardates over 65. Many of these patients had spent all of their lives in the State hospital. Some geriatric wards consisted entirely of such patients. The integration of such aged mental patients into nursing homes, intermediate care facilities, locked nursing homes, boarding houses, etc., is a problem of quite major proportions. There have been notable successes but there have been tragic failures in this regard as well. A major ethical question must be faced with these patients: Will they be written off as the failures of a past era and be the last residuum in the State hospital system? Or will we run the risk that their presence will lead to deterioration of alternative facilities and resentment and rejection by the communities to which they are sent?

Protective Intervention Services

A major thrust of recent thinking about the problems of the disabled is how to avoid institutionalization through the provision of partial or protective services. Thus, a recent statement unanimously agreed to by the National Conference of Lawyers and Social Workers, and later approved by the Board of Governors of the American Bar Association states:

> What must be provided is the means by which assistance may be rendered to these persons to the end that they may remain in the community as long as possible, living as full lives as possible—and that others like them

may be returned to the community from the institutions
in which they are now to be found (*43*).

Though it seeks to avoid the coerciveness of (often involuntary or
at best, resigned) hospitalization, the concept of protective services
cannot avoid the basic dilemma of parens patriae vs. autonomy.
Beneficence is not costless; at some point the helping hand becomes
coercive.

Of course there are simple cases where deference to the elder
person's idiosyncracies is proper or where emergency hospitalization is necessary and will soon be appreciated. But at some point
we must face the difficult case of the little old lady who just will
not leave her decrepit, infested apartment, and prefers peanut
butter and pet foods to charity meals, or the eccentric who is
convinced that if he goes to the hospital, he will die. Protective
services are proactive—they go out and find people in need. They
raise problems for those who might both want to intervene, and
who are aware that there has already been too much projection of
middle-age lifestyles onto older people. It is particularly perplexing
to mental health professionals whose ego-image is of one assuaging
the pain of a desperate patient who seeks out help. And working
with the aged is frustrating, and always in danger of being declined
because they

> defy our omnipotence, rip holes in our omniscience,
> show no promise of being grateful, do not stimulate or
> excite us, and constantly threaten to dirty our clean
> skins, clothing, bill of health, and our own record of
> treatment successes (*44*).

At numerous points throughout this monograph, I have criticized
the abusive paternalism of the law-mental health system. However,
paternalism is not an epithet which neutralizes all competing values
in its path. The reality of the situation·is that few older people are
able to choose their way of life; they are condemned to it. They are
likely to welcome any attention, kindness, or assistance—especially
if it is provided not by an imperious, scrutinizing commitment
system, but by a flexible agency sensitive to their changing needs.
The conflict between paternalism and autonomy cannot be facilely
resolved. But it is essential to a sustained commitment to protective
services to realize that this basic moral paradox—or, better, moral
tension—is an ineradicable element and not an abuse or flaw of any
social welfare system. Indeed an acceptance of this moral burden is
reflected in the lawyer-social worker accord previously described
(*45*). That statement makes a further crucial point:

174

> While recognizing that protective service—involving as it does an act of intervention under color of legal authority—must be based on law, it must also be acknowledged that in the absence of an interrelated program and network of preventive, supportive, and rehabilitative services and facilities, the law which confers the authority to act for and on behalf of an incapacitated person is of limited value and significance (46).

And it has been suggested that, especially when dealing with the aged, the law-mental health professions should not overestimate the purely medical aspect of their purpose. Rather, rehabilitation should be construed in its original meaning, "to invest or clothe again with some right, authority, or dignity" (47). Under these principles, protective services could only be welcomed.

Under most conceptions, protective services would not mainly provide primary want-satisfactions, such as housing, but rather, would provide supportive and coordinating services. More specifically, protective services involve three types of activity:

(a) *Preventive services*—helping older persons avoid debilitation of their capacities by contact and information, referral to physical and mental health clinics (e.g., assuring maintenance of eyeglasses, hearing aids, or drug therapy), followup care, counseling, and fostering of social relations; (b) *supportive services*—such as legal aid, lobbying, fiscal management, investigating hospital care, home delivery of meals, homemaking, foster home care, visiting, etc. A primary object of the protective services agency would be to serve as a central responsible organ coordinating all society's fractionated services; (c) *surrogate services*—providing a new decisionmaker in areas where the elderly person cannot function well.

Above all, the protective services agency should give the elderly person a sense of continuity and security.

There are few real-world models of how a going protective services program would work. One, the Benjamin Rose Institute in Cleveland, seems to have compiled a mixed record, including on the good side a large variety of services performed and a reduction of stress on other agencies, but also on the bad side, an increase in institutionalization and of death rates (48).

Other data confirm the impression of the Cleveland study that institutionalization may lead to premature death for the aged. Thus statistics for State and County Mental Hospitals in 1970, after criteria for confinement of the aged had been made more rigorous, demonstrated an alarmingly high death rate shortly after admission. Of those over 65 at the time of mental hospitalization, more than one in 10 died within 30 days of admission (*49*).

Once again we witness the dangers of misguided paternalism. This surely suggests that protective services must not be allowed to rely on institutionalization as a remedy. The Cleveland study concluded "these are discouraging facts that should not deter us from further attempts to help. We should, however, question our present prescriptions and strategies of treatment" (*50*). That conclusion applies to every aspect of our society's treatment of the aged.

References·

1. This and the other statistics set forth below are drawn from Developments in Aging: 1972 and January-March 1973, A Report of the Senate special committee on aging, *Sen. Rep.* No. 93-14 7 (hereinafter 1972 report); Developments in Aging 1970, A Report of the Senate special committee on aging, *Sen. Rep.* No. 92-46 (hereinafter 1970 report).
2. 1972 report at 9.
3. E. Brody, Aging, in National Association of Social Workers, 1 *Encyclopedia Of Social Work 51* (1971).
4. *See* Morris, In: Symposium on the aging poor, 23 *Syr. L. Rev.* 45, 48 (1972). As to recent changes, see the discussion below on hospitalization of the aged.
5. Simmons, Aging in primitive societies: A comparative study of family life and relations, 27 *Law and Contemp. Probs.* 36, 49 (1962).
6. R. C. Allen, et al., *Mental Impairment And Legal Incompetency* (Englewood Cliffs: Prentice Hall, 1968) p. IX.
7. *Id.* at 82.
8. See, e.g., *Mazza* v. *Pechacek*, 233 F.2d 666 (D.C. Circ. 1956).
9. *See also* Alexander, et al., Surrogate management of the property of the aged, 21 *Syr. L. Rev.* 97, 132 (1969-1970); Zenoff, Civil incompetency in the District of Columbia, 32 *Geo. Wash. L. Rev.* 243, 252 (1963).
10. *See generally* R. C. Allen, et al., *supra*, note 6 at 2-3.
11 *Id.* at 32-33.
12. *Id.* at 34.
13. *Id.* at 38-40.
14. For a detailed catalogue of statutory provisions, see S. Brakel and R. Rock, *The Mentally Disabled And The Law* (Chicago: University of Chicago Press, 1971) pp. 266-302.
15. *In re Tyrell*, 92 *Ohio L. Abs.* 253, appeal dis. 174 Ohio St. 552, 554 (1963).
16. For a full account of a similar case, see Substitution of Judgment for Mentally Incompetent, *In re DuPont*, 24 *Md. L. Rev.* 332 (1964).
17. As to the various legal devices for this purpose, see R. C. Allen *supra*, note 6, pp. 144-196.
18. Alexander, et al., *supra*, note 9, pp. 138, 145-147.
19. R. C. Allen, et al., *supra*, note 6 at 95.
20. *National Council on the Aging*, Overcoming Barriers to Protective Services for the Aged 37 (1968).
21. Uniform Probate Code, sec. 5-410.
22. See, e.g., Kay, et al., Legal planning for the mentally retarded: The California experience, 60 *Cal. L. Rev.* 438 (1972).
23. See, e.g., *Mass. Laws Ann.*, Ch. 20, sec. 38 (supp. 1972).
24. *See* Levy, Protecting the mentally retarded: An empirical survey and evaluation of state guardianship in Minnesota, 49 *Minn. L. Rev.* 821 (1965).
25. *See* Kay, et al., *supra*, note 22.

26. *See* R. C. Allen, et al., *supra,* note 6, at 97-112.
27. *See* Legal Research and services for the elderly, *A Handbook Of Model State Statutes* 153 (1971).
28. *Cal. Welf. and Inst. Code* sec. 5206 (1972).
29. R. C. Allen et al., *supra,* note 6 at 96.
30. *See* Levy, *supra,* note 24.
31. *See* The Aged and community mental health, G.A.P. report at 81 (1971).
32. D.C. Code Ch. 21, sec. 503 (1966).
33. 172 N.Y.S. 2d 869 (Sup. Ct. 1958) (per Brenner, J.).
34. As to other reasons for not protesting, *see* Goldfarb, In: Symposium on the aging poor, *supra,* note 4.
34a. *Supra,* note 33 at 870-1.
35. *Lake* v. *Cameron,* 364 F.2d 657 (D.C. Cir. 1966).
36. *Id.* at 659-660.
37. *Id.* at 660 n.9.
38. *Lake* v. *Cameron,* 267 F. Supp. 155 (D.C.C. 1967).
38a. *Supra,* note 35 at 663.
39. *Id.* at 664.
40. Application for the certification of anon. No. 1 to No. 12, 138 N.Y.S. 2d 30 (1954).
41. Application for the certification of anon. No. 3, 159 N.Y.S. 2d 842 (1957).
42. Kastenbaum, *Medical World News,* Geriatrics issue p. 76 (1973).
43. *See* Policy statement 2 *Family Law Q.* 107, 108 (1968).
44. Bennett, Protective services for the aged, In: DHEW, 3 *Working With Older People 52 (Public Health Service Publication No. 1459, 1970).*
45. *See* Policy Statement, *supra,* note 43 at 108.
46. *Id.* at 109.
47. *See* Symposium, *supra,* note 34 at 45,53.
48. *See* Blenker, Bloom and Nielson, A Research and demonstration project of protective services, 52 *Social Case Work* 483, 484 (1971).
49. Based on statistical Note 74 DHEW Pub. No. (HSM)73-9005, (1973).
50. *Supra,* note 48 at 498.

Chapter 11

Quasi-Criminal Confinement:
Sex Psychopaths and
Defective Delinquents

The law-mental health system includes a variety of noncriminal procedures for the indefinite confinement of persons thought to be both criminals and mentally ill. These forms of civil incarceration, the majority of which aim at deviant sexual behavior, illustrate all of the problems exposed by the preventive confinement analysis. Presumably the standard for such confinement should be the prediction of dangerous acts (1). However, the legislative history and the language of the statutes suggest that the distinction between abnormal sexual behavior and dangerous sexual behavior was never clearly delineated. Virginia, for example, requires only that the person be convicted of a crime that indicates sexual abnormality (2).

Since none of the statutes seems to have parsed out the meaning of dangerousness in terms of objective measures of harm, considerable leeway in decisionmaking was left to the court and to the mental health profession. The latter became the arbiter of what is abnormal and, therefore, by definition dangerous.

The typical problematic cases created by this ambiguity are a variety of consensual sexual acts and compulsive exhibitionism where society, with or without the help of the psychiatrist, posits some psychic harm.

These examples suggest once again the ideological nature of society's definition of harm. The offense of exhibitionism is behavior which exemplifies all of the controversial aspects of quasi-criminal confinement. The exhibitionist is easily caught, is often a recidivist, is often untreatable, and is perhaps the least dangerous of the sex criminals who end up in preventive confinement. The incarceration of such persons might be justified on two grounds: first, protecting society, particularly children, against alleged psychic harm; and second, preventing behavior which is simply repugnant to society.

Whatever the merits of that reasoning may be, it is clear that exhibitionism under the criminal law carries modest penalties (e.g., the Model Penal Code classifies indecent exposure as a misdemeanor) (3), whereas civil confinement will permit indefinite incarceration for the identical behavior. However, for many sex "crimes" between consenting adults the various State criminal codes provide lengthy sentences (e.g., Massachusetts law provides sentences up to 20 years for sodomy and buggery) (4). Thus, civil confinement may sometimes be considered a humane alternative by the court. But whatever the courts' reasoning may be, it is clear that by adding the vague notion of mental illness, the State acquires broader discretionary powers than are otherwise available.

If one examines the way such discretionary use of quasi-criminal confinement has been invoked, it becomes clear that it sometimes is a means of confining persons whom the prosecutor strongly believes belong in prison but, for technical or procedural reasons, cannot convict. The recent case of *Hamrick* v. *Alabama* (5) dramatically illustrates the nature of this legal tactic. Two female victims had apparently consented to sexual intercourse but instead had been subjected to anal sodomy. At the trial of the first victim it became clear that her consent technically vitiated the legal charge of rape. Hamrick was found innocent. Instead of proceeding to the second case, the prosecuting attorney simply used "a transcript of the testimony of the complaining witnesses in each of the preliminary hearings on the rape charge" (6) to have Hamrick found a sexual psychopath. He was subsequently committed to the standard term of 1 day to life. The U.S. Supreme Court dismissed Hamrick's appeal. It may well be that the Alabama legislature believes persons who behave like Hamrick should be confined and that justice was done in this case. But clearly what happened was that the technical constraints with which the criminal law is hedged about were bypassed because this was a sexual offense, and the quasi-criminal alternative was available. Had Hamrick murdered, robbed, or maimed, and had the only competent evidence been excluded, he would have gone free on the basis of some such technical flaw.

Dershowitz cites the *Hamrick* case as an example of "imprisonment on suspicion of an unproven or unprovable past offense." What he means is unproved or unprovable under the existing criminal law—thus he considers the *Hamrick* result an illustration of abuse. Perhaps Hamrick's incarceration is an abuse, but surely it offends the legal mind more than the popular sense of justice. For example, in Sweden, it is apparently impossible for a defendant to be acquitted for a procedural error alone (7). Its value as an example is in demonstrating the discrepancy between the criminal law's procedural and substantive constraints, and the looser framework of sexual psychopath statutes which are civil proceedings typical of what I have called quasi-criminal confinement.

Given the differences between the criminal and civil process, the legal criteria which allow a defendant to be transferred from one category to the other become central. If, as I shall attempt to demonstrate, those criteria are vague and ambiguous, and the conditions of civil confinement offer little prospect of treatment, then there is reason to believe that all quasi-criminal confinement is an abuse.

The question is why was this marginal man, the quasi-criminal, carved out as an exceptional case in the criminal law? In the late 1930's, largely in response to celebrated and grisly sex crimes (8), sexual psychopath statutes were first enacted in about six States (9). The avowed goal was two-pronged: first and most important, to impose longer sentences for sexually motivated crimes, and second, to provide treatment (10). In the first legal test the Michigan statute was struck down by the Michigan Supreme Court. But shortly thereafter the U.S. Supreme Court upheld a Minnesota law against challenges that its statutory definition of sex psychopath was unconstitutionally vague, and that in defining a class of special offenders the statute violated equal protection (11). Much of the constitutional difficulty was avoided by the assertion that these were civil rather than criminal proceedings.

Legislation is now in effect in about 31 jurisdictions dealing specially with "sexual psychopaths," "sexually dangerous persons," "mentally disordered sex offenders," "defective delinquents," or a similar category (12). Really, these laws represent two approaches. The first deals exclusively with sexually motivated, disordered offenders. A typical statute provides for the commitment for an indeterminate term of 1 day to life of any sexually dangerous person; that is:

> Any person whose misconduct in sexual matters indicates a general lack of power to control his sexual impulses, as evidenced by repetitive or compulsive behavior and either violence, or aggression of an adult against a victim under the age of 16 years, and who as a result is likely to attack or otherwise inflict injury upon the objects of his uncontrolled or uncontrollable desires (13).

The second model broadens the category to include all mentally abnormal repeat offenders deemed dangerous. The paradigm statute of this type is Maryland's defective delinquent law, which permits the incarceration of

An individual who, by the demonstration of persistent, aggravated antisocial or criminal behavior, evidences a propensity toward criminal activity, and who is found to have either such intellectual deficiency or emotional unbalance, or both, as to clearly demonstrate an actual danger to society so as to require such confinement and treatment . . . (*16*).

I will deal primarily with the first type because it is more common and its rationales underlie the second type of law, which will be dealt with only occasionally.

A different sort of defective delinquent statute once was in force in Massachusetts. It was aimed at persons who were both mentally retarded and habitual criminals. Its legislative history reflects a strong conviction that this combination of characteristics was a genetic entity. At first its major function was to transfer trouble-makers from the institutions for the mentally retarded to a more secure institution. A study I did shortly before that special institution was closed, suggested that no treatment existed at all. Many of the inmates were by no standard habitual criminals. Indeed most of them were incarcerated when they made their first sexual advances to children. By the time the institution was finally closed many of the inmates were at an age where they could be transferred to old age homes. (Stone, unpublished study of defective delinquents Mass. 1972.)

Most fundamentally, the statutes vary as to whether they are activated by conviction ("post-conviction statutes") or by mere filing of a criminal indictment or information ("preconviction statutes"). But there is much variance, indeed murkiness, as to the other elements necessary to come within the statutes.

The Mental Illness Criterion

As to the criterion of mental condition, some statutes require a finding of not "committable" or not "insane" (*15*); most require mental illness not so great as to result in criminal irresponsibility (*16*). Others require one of an array of conditions, from mental illness of a year's duration (*17*), to just present mental illness (*18*), to disorders which only some would classify as mental illiness at all—"lack of power to control his sexual impulses" (*19*), emotional instability or impulsiveness of behavior, or lack of customary standards of good judgment (*20*), or still more vague definitions (*21*). Even the Maryland statute previously discussed fails to specify the degree of mental illness, except dependently, by reference to past and predicted dangerous acts.

Clearly none of these definitions of mental illness are posed in terms of treatability; indeed, some of the legislative history candidly suggests an awareness of the impossibility of treating such persons (22). Nor is there any familiar psychiatric diagnostic language; in fact, influential psychiatrists urged that diagnostic labels be avoided because they were apt to become antiquated in the face of the developing science of psychiatry (23). Several decades later, despite some interesting genetic and psychophysiological findings, it is fair to suggest that psychiatric science has contributed minimally, if at all, to the treatment or definitive diagnosis of this group of persons. Despite advocates such as Cleckley (24), who insist there is a specific syndrome including antisocial behavior, there is a strong and growing current of opinion that what was called in turn hereditary moral insanity, constitutional psychopathy, psychopathic personality, and now sociopathic personality, is little more than a psychiatric label for what other people call the criminal element. Placing the word sexual in front of psychopath only adds to the ambiguity.

As one respected commentator points out, "the concept of sexual psychopath is too vague for judicial or administrative use" (25). It is also too vague for use by the mental health professions (26). If it is to have any purpose at all, dubbing a man a "sexually dangerous person" must mean more than just: "Since he committed a sex act, he might do so again." If it does not, then the quasi-criminal law merely brings with it a lot of obfuscatory psychiatric baggage, and accomplishes no refinement either of prediction or protection, or of treatment decisions.

Even Kozol, who has for many years taken part in the administration of an institution for sex psychopaths concedes that "No such entity exists in the nosology of psychiatry" (27). Presumably he experiences no cognitive dissonance on this point because he believes he knows who the proper subjects for confinement are. This may be sound practice for an experienced physician in choosing his patients, but it is surely bad law for a legislative purpose of screening those likely to commit dangerous, sexually motivated acts; the difficulties, in sum, are these:

> All sex offenders are not sexually deviated; all sex deviations do not become sexual offenses; some non-sexual offenses are motivated by sexual conflict; there are nonsexual conflicts that stimulate sexual deviance or offense; there are a variety of psychiatric conditions and

dynamic factors which go into producing any one of the sex offenses (*28*).

Thus, if the legislature asks the psychiatrist a question he can answer, such as who is sexually deviated, it gets no solution to its real concern; i.e., whose deviation will result in a sexually motivated act and an antisocial or violent one. And if asked the critical question, "Is he a dangerous person?" the psychiatrist must either confess his incapacity, or conceal it behind his conviction that someone has to make these difficult decisions for society.

If I were to characterize the method used by those who have taken most seriously the challenge of diagnosing dangerousness, it is a combination of police investigation, clinical psychiatry and psychology, intuition and experience. Kozol, for example, emphasizes that a careful interrogation of the victim is an essential element in the diagnostic process. From the mental health perspective this makes excellent sense. The description by the victim of the crime may suggest the motive of the crime and this may provide insight into the specific compulsive element, which may, for example, be sadistic. The victim may be able to give some impression of whether the attacker was drunk, a claim made by many offenders. But from the legal perspective the clinician is involved in fact determinations which would ordinarily be subject to cross examination.

After all, the victim may be giving a false depiction; fear and panic may have distorted the original perceptions; shame and guilt may have transformed memory. What I mean to suggest is that to the extent psychiatrists have wisely focused on the actual behavior rather than the offender's personality, they have assumed a legal role of investigator without the legal constraints usually deemed essential to assure accuracy. The same may be said (and will be below) about interviewing technics with the offender which often attempt to extract a confession, again without the legal safeguards. It is as though in civil proceedings against quasi-criminals, we forego our traditional Anglo-American adversary system of criminal justice and replace it with the European inquisitional system—with the mental health professional playing the role of the European magistrate.

As to the potentially beneficent purpose of the statutes, I have earlier alluded to the general paucity of active treatment programs in many public mental hospitals; with some exceptions this is even more true in the hospitals for the criminally insane. And as to knowledge, the fact is that less rather than more is known about treating the mentally ill person who is a sex offender. A decade after the first rash of quasi-criminal statutes were enacted, it was still widely felt that "an underlying difficulty is the lack of psychiatric knowledge of methods that can be employed to deal with psychopathic offenders" (29). Despite some progress a more recent study in a State known for innovations in the mental health field concluded that "(though various studies) claim varying levels of success . . . there has been no single method of treatment, with or without custody, which has been demonstrated to be any more successful than any other " (30). A still more recent study says that the results from various States can be regarded at best as inconsistent, and at worst as warranting the conclusion that there has been no success at all in treating sex offenders (31).

Nonetheless, some institutions do claim success and recent reports suggest that length of stay has been reduced to proportions that many would deem reasonable. California claims an average stay of 18 months (32). Massachusetts claims to rehabilitate many in less than 5 years; however, an independent retrospective study claims that 49.8 percent of those committed in Massachusetts were still confined after 13 years (7). Since in all of these situations the offender knows that violation may mean lifetime incarceration, it is difficult to isolate the punitive element from the therapeutic. Indeed, punitive-therapeutic approaches are increasingly endorsed by those who work with the quasi-criminal offender.

One of the most outstanding claims of success has come from the Patuxent Institution in Maryland, which reports extremely low recidivism rates for its released patients. Patuxent uses a graded tier system which is in my view a mixture of rewards and punishments in a rudimentary type of behavior modification.

Good behavior leads to better living conditions and bad behavior leads to remaining in unpleasant, or as some would suggest, dreadful living conditions. Though its results are suggestive and potentially impressive, they are questionable because of the failure to provide precise statistical data on the released group, because much of the release appears to be partial and enforced by threat of lifelong incarceration for any infractions, and because there appears to be little or no effect of treatment on the recidivism rate for the most serious crimes. (33).

There have been some claims of success abroad, notably in Denmark, but these writers (unlike those of the Patuxent report) acknowledge the special numbers, conditions, and resources which made such success possible—conditions which have not generally been replicated in American institutions (34). Despite the fact that Denmark's institutions for the quasi-criminal are by all accounts superior to the best American institutions, the Danes have recently decided to phase them out.

Few American institutions for such offenders have full or active treatment programs. One comprehensive survey (35) found that all three types of facilities—prisons, security hospitals, and mental health facilities—were primarily security conscious. They were understaffed and had few programs. Where treatment was available, it was usually not with a psychiatrist because that profession has largely ignored these problems and avoided these institutions. And ironically, the panoply of new treatments for the quasi-criminal, e.g., hormones, stereotaxic psychosurgery, behavior modification, etc., some of which may have considerable potential, all present grave constitutional questions. (See Chapter 6, The Right to Refuse Treatment.)

I have already presented the evidence suggesting the profound limitations on psychiatric predictions of dangerousness. To the extent these statutes require a psychiatric prediction of dangerousness, they are likely to be faulty. Unlike the situation in civil commitment of the mentally ill, most of these persons neither have reliably diagnosable mental illness, nor are they incompetent to refuse treatment. Thus, there are serious questions not only about the validity of psychiatric participation, but also about the ethics of such participation. It is in light of these conclusions that I turn to a consideration of the current procedures for quasi-criminal confinement and in particular the privilege against self-incrimination.

Procedures

The procedural aspects of the quasi-criminal commitment process are rife with ambiguities, with stretch points linked together by precious few carefully tooled hinges. Many postconviction statutes did not even provide for a separate hearing on psychopathy, which was the basis for transfer from the limited criminal sentence to the unlimited civil sentence. Such a hearing was required by the Supreme Court's 1967 ruling in *Specht* v. *Patterson* (36). Both preconviction and postconviction laws provide for a medical examination, usually by two court-appointed physicians. However, in a number of States these need not be psychiatrists. In some States, hospitalization and observation is required, while in others brief interviews suffice to justify commitment.

Confinement for observation alone may continue for up to 2 months in many States. And a number of studies have noted that this period may be extended by various administrative delays, and that both for the released subject and the declared psychopath, this is dead time, not counted as part of the eventual term (37). Until recently the prevailing view that sex psychopathy proceedings were civil was regarded as justifying denial of most of the procedural requisites of the criminal process. For example, and perhaps especially important, as of 1971, just three States provided for appointed counsel (38).

The quasi-criminal statutes provide generally for indeterminate terms of 1 day to life, leaving full, and in large part, unreviewable discretion as to release in the hands of institutional staff. Release requires a finding that the person is "fully recovered," is no longer "dangerous," that release is in the "interests of justice," etc. Besides their apparent vagueness, it is clear that these standards are, in practice, higher than the standard needed to avoid original commitment (39). And review of releasability may not be very expeditious. In Massachusetts, for example, review is mandated once during the first year of confinement and once every 3 years thereafter.

One study has found that since release shall be "upon such terms or conditions as [the board] shall prescribe," outright release is rare (40).

Many of these vague standards and lack of procedural safeguards recur throughout the law-mental health system and are dealt with in the chapter on civil commitment. However, there is a particularly thorny procedural question which is especially relevant here. This is the problem of the protection the fifth amendment affords persons in quasi-criminal commitment; more explicitly, what sources of information should in fairness serve as inputs to the quasi-criminal decisionmaking process?

In recent years, courts have extended more and more of the procedural rights or safeguards of the criminal process to the mentally ill. But the fifth amendment privilege has not been among these, even though it has been extended to other nominally civil proceedings (41). Statutes in most States provide for a court-ordered psychiatric examination in specified cases, and the courts have disagreed as to the rights of refusal and exclusion of matter disclosed (42). The fourth circuit, for example, has rejected the contention of a fifth amendment privilege in a quasi-criminal commitment on the ground that to permit the patient (advised by his attorney) to pick and choose which questions to answer would "stultify" the diagnostic process and prevent the State from ever meeting its burden of proof (43). The lower court, and one dissenting justice disagreed, holding that if little or no treatment was provided at the quasi-criminal institutions, then commitment to them was penal not civil, and the panoply of safeguards should come into play. This is consistent with the views of other courts, including the Supreme Court, that it is the nature of the penalty, incarceration, or "exposure" possible which determines which label should apply (44). The Supreme Court has twice avoided directly confronting the issue—though in one case it held that if a person does refuse to cooperate in a psychiatric diagnosis, he cannot be held indefinitely (45).

A frequently stated recent view is that the question of the fifth amendment privilege in relation to psychiatric examinations is contextual; that is, that it depends on the specific type of mental-health proceeding, and the weight which each of the rationales for and critiques of the privilege merits in that given context.

Since in this context the diagnosis to be established is usually not a treatable condition (as I have defined that term in the chapter on civil commitment), and its impact is usually destructive in the eyes of the person to whom it is applied, one can only conclude that the psychiatrist is acting not as an agent of the patient, but as an agent of the court. In the quasi-criminal context, the psychiatrist can most realistically be viewed as an inquisitorial magistrate with mental health training. As indicated, Kozol's group suggests that one of the most important diagnostic keys is a detailed reconstruction of the crime including interviews with the victim(s).

Thus, the rationales supporting the privilege in this context are compelling. Recent commentary has identified four basic rationales for the privilege, all of which apply here:

1. Our legal system has preserved itself in many ways as an accusatorial rather than an inquisitorial system. Thus, courts exclude illegally seized evidence and uninformed or incompletely voluntary confessions—even in some situations where the invasion of privacy or the coercion is relatively minor and the relevance of the evidence great. The theory is that, overall, permitting such evidence will tempt law enforcement agencies to conduct less exhaustive investigations and to rely more and more on coercing statements from the defendant himself (46). Although the question is somewhat different, similar policies support the exclusion of hearsay evidence—both because it is inherently unreliable and because it tempts a lazy proof of facts by uninvestigated rumor.

It had been contended that the hearsay exclusion did not apply to civil proceedings to determine the best disposition of an individual over whom the State exercises a parens patriae power. But the Supreme Court indirectly rejected this view in In Re Gault (47), and at least one lower court has done so directly (48). And since I believe the State has no legitimate parens patriae role in quasi-criminal confinement, that contention against the fifth amendment privilege has no relevance. The procedure may be nominally civil, but the State is by no means acting as a helpful parent.

2. The fifth amendment privilege significantly enforces a right to a private enclave in one's life (49). Despite the increasing judicial concern with privacy rights in our centralized-information society (50), this argument is inconclusive insofar as it has always been recognized that such rights are qualified and not absolute. But again the question is contextual; it seems only right that a person who raises the insanity defense should waive privacy objections to inquiry into his mental condition. But the same cannot be said of quasi-criminal commitment in which the State raises the claim and seeks to exercise extraordinary power over the individual, indeed, to impose a longer sentence than would be possible were the person criminally convicted. The invasion of privacy is particularly great here since the psychiatric examinations may pry into all aspects of one's prior acts, thoughts, and dreams, may ask incriminating true or false questions, and may be supplemented by interviews and inquiries of past friends, employers, and so on.

3. The privilege prevents the subjection of persons to the cruel dilemma of deceit, facilitating his own incarceration, or incurring penalties for refusing to answer. Nowhere is this argument more convincingly made than in the area of quasi-criminal evaluation. The typical patient either cons his psychiatrist or mistakenly condemns himself by a misplaced trust.

4. The privilege against self-incrimination primarily serves to protect the defendant from coercion, physical or psychological. The latter type is particularly relevant to a mentally disordered offender. In some institutions like Patuxent, the nature of his communication to his psychiatrists determines the condition of his confinement.

A number of compromises have been suggested to provide a partial privilege. The quasi-criminal defendant may have counsel present to restrain coercion, or may engage his own psychiatrists if he prefers to be examined by someone not employed by the State, or the privilege may be transmuted into a less drastic means notion whereby the State can overcome his objections only if there is no other way to gain the information needed to evaluate dangerousness and mental state (51). But each of these will bring its own problems and will sacrifice some degree of rights for what I take to be an illusory gain.

Few persons are coerced physically in psychiatric examinations, although sodium amytal and hypnosis verge on it. The real questions are whether psychological pressure is employed or the defendant is immediately informed of his right to passivity, and whether those who refuse to cooperate are held indefinitely, or are released after some period, such as the criminal sentence maximum. Whatever the resolution of the argument in civil commitment (where the duration of permissible confinement, the release standard, the treatment available, etc., may be decisive), it is my belief that the fifth amendment privilege should be respected in the quasi-criminal process.

Because the penalty of indefinite commitment is so great, because the safeguards and standard of proof are less than in the criminal process (through which these persons would otherwise be conducted), because the manifest lack of institutional care falsifies any benevolent purpose to the laws, and because the psychiatrist is an agent of the State rather than the patient, the privilege is especially necessary in this context. If such privilege prevents quasi-criminal commitments, society will not be endangered; it will simply mean that the criminal process used for similarly dangerous offenders must be used.

Psychiatric Discretion

What the legislature seems to be saying to the psychiatrists in the sexual psychopath statutes is: "You know what we're looking for; find it!"

A concomitant evil of asking psychiatrists to assign patients to such a vague category, neither medically nor legally specific, is that they are unsure which authority or which imperative to serve. Some will be overly deferential to what they perceive as the legal goals, and will make dispositional rather than psychiatric diagnoses.

In one State it was found that the department routinely recommended commitment if it believed the subject's behavior was due to a treatable mental disorder (52)—even if he was not regarded as dangerous in any way! And judges, in turn, faced with vague judgments seemingly beyond their expertise, and impressed with the idea that treatment "can't do any harm" may rely overmuch on the psychiatric staff's recommendation. Thus one major study found that the court ordered observational commitment in every case where a psychiatrist suggested it (53), and ordered intermediate commitment in all but 8 of 397 cases! Indeed, in their zeal to defer to psychiatric judgment, courts have sometimes asked the wrong questions, casting them not in terms of

190

psychopathy, but sanity, mental illness, competency, etc. And some conservative judges likely still cling to the view that the statute's civil label and ostensibly helpful purpose render unseemly too much caviling about its substance or safeguards. Thus one judge was heard to say: "Having invoked the beneficent provisions of the . . . law . . . appellant cannot question [its] constitutionality" (54).

This is a waning view, and the leading edge of change is directed at the lack of procedural safeguards in the quasi-criminal process. Though some courts still hold such proceedings civil (55), the trend is away from that view (56), and recent decisions, first by the third circuit (57), and then by the Supreme Court (58) have rendered the mere label less important. In Specht v. Patterson (59) the Supreme Court held that a separate hearing on psychopathy was required, and that the defendant has the right to counsel, confrontation with witnesses against him, presentation of evidence, and preparation of a record sufficient to permit appeal.

In Millard v. Cameron (60), the D.C. Circuit Court reversed a commitment based merely on the trial judge's ratification of the conclusory diagnosis of the examining psychiatrist. In Cross v. Harris (61), the same court, though pointing out that it decided no constitutional questions, construed the D.C. statute to require very careful findings of mental illness, dangerousness, magnitude, and likelihood of harm. It went on to stress the danger of quasi-criminal laws becoming excuses for the confinement of all disliked or strange persons, reiterated its grave doubts about the constitutionality of preventive confinement statutes, and essentially suggested that they be used only where no alternative forms of restraint or treatment are possible. Other courts have required that treatability be a criterion of commitment (62). And working with a worse statute, a three judge Federal court in Alabama went beyond Cross v. Harris. It openly declared that the Alabama statute unconstitutionally imposed double jeopardy by permitting postcommitment transfer to a nontherapeutic facility, and by failing to inquire into treatability and the actual delivery of therapy (63).

Other courts have criticized quasi-criminal statutes for being unconstitutionally vague, for punishing for a "mere status" in contravention of the Supreme Court's holding in Robinson v. California (64), and on other grounds. A series of cases testing the validity of the Maryland defective delinquent law have rejected many of the arguments of the cases previously cited (65). But the special conditions obtaining in Maryland (66), the fact that the Supreme Court decision in that series did not pass on most of the major issues (67), and the contrary implications of a number of other Supreme Court decisions at the same time (68), all reduce the significance of any lessons to be drawn from that line of cases. There can be little doubt that the future will see even more hostile judicial scrutiny of quasi-criminal laws.

A final, and extremely practical criticism is suggested by McGarry's study of the Massachusetts law (69). We start out with a vague, hard-to-define or administer law. The law requires for its effective use the coordinated and reinforcing efforts of the departments of mental health, corrections, and parole, as well as psychiatrists, the courts, and perhaps private facilities. None of these agencies really feels that the alleged sexually dangerous person is really its subject matter, and none likes to work with him. Given our experience in other realms—such as welfare or civil commitment— where the subject population is far more attractive and where interagency coordination is still sorely lacking, is there any reason to wonder at the disastrous results in quasi-criminal commitment?

Abolishing the Quasi-criminal Confinement System

Even beyond these procedural ills, erratic applications, abuses, and constitutional infirmities, I believe the quasi-criminal statutes are unjustified. They are based on erroneous assumptions, fail to serve their ostensible purposes, and should be abolished, remitting their subjects to the normal criminal process.

The overarching intent of the quasi-criminal commitment statutes was to provide greater security for society than is achieved by use of the criminal process alone. It is occasionally asserted that the laws were primarily humane enactments to provide treatment to mentally agonized offenders; and it may be true that such reformist sentiment did aid in generating such laws. If so, this goal has been sorely betrayed, for a great deal of warehousing and precious little treatment was provided. But commentators are in agreement that by far the dominating purpose of such laws was safety, not treatment. The baldness with which this was stated may be shocking to even the most cynical. For example, the commission which originally drafted the much admired Maryland law stated: "The fundamental approach to the problems considered has not been primarily on behalf of the criminal and/or mentally defective person who has run afoul of the law. On the contrary, the paramount interest is and must always be the welfare of the community as a whole. The interests of the individual must ever be subjugated to the interests of the community where the two are in irreconcilable conflict . . . (70).

And the final report to the legislature went on:

"A secondary purpose is more effectively and humanely to handle them, which aids in the cure, where possible . . . . If they cannot be cured, such indeterminate sentence accomplishes their confinement for life (71), which the protection of society demands . . . ."

The intention of other States' legislatures was usually similar (72). Given these goals, the statutes were based on three major premises, each of which I believe has been shown to be false.

"Sex offenders ought to be dealt with differently"

The first and most basic question is, of course, why sex offenders should be singled out for special statutory treatment. The Supreme Court alluded to a possible reason for upholding one of the first such laws: "The legislature is free to recognize degrees of harm, and it may confine its restrictions to those classes of cases where the need is deemed to be clearest" (73). But of course courts may hold legislatures to certain standards of reasonableness based on all the information—including scientific data. And the fact is that sex offenders are not a unique, dangerous group apart from the bulk of offenders. Only a small percentage—probably under 5 percent of sex offenders are dangerous or assaultive (74). As one major study concludes, "Most of the deviates are mild and submissive, more an annoyance than a menace to the community" (75). This has been recognized in practice and now confinement is usually based on a more stringent criterion of dangerousness.

Second, there is no evidence that sex offenders have higher recidivism rates than other offenders. Of course any study merely of those to whom the special statutes are actually applied is deceptive, because the laws often require recurrent crime as a prerequisite, and, as noted below, these persons are often guilty of minor offenses for which the recidivism rates are relatively high. But as to those about whom the public is principally concerned and whom the statutes were ostensibly enacted to restrain—the assaultive sexual criminal—all the evidence indicates they have lower rates of prior conviction and parole violation than any other type of prisoner (76). One commentator has summarized his research saying: "Our sex offenders are among the least recidivous of all types of criminals" (77). A California study found that only 7 percent of sex offenders, but 16 percent of other offenders had been imprisoned two or more previous times, and that fewer than 10 percent of sex offenders commit new serious crimes while paroled. Including all offenses, serious and minor, sex offenders had a 32 percent parole violation rate compared with a 52 percent rate for all other offenders (78). Also, studies have shown that sex offenders do not progress from minor to serious or assaultive crimes to the same degree as other criminals (79).

Third, given the purported statutory purpose of achieving greater protection against dangerous acts with sexual motives, it is ironic that the statutes are not routinely applied to those who have committed the most threatening acts. Some. States remove major offenders from the coverage of the quasi-criminal statute by law. And numerous studies have found that even where this is not done, the practice is that when a major crime is committed, the criminal process is usually relied on (unless the prosecutor lacks a strong case), and the quasi-criminal law has in the past been primarily applied to sex offenders of a passive or nonviolent sort (80). This practice has been condoned by some courts and condemned by others (81).

The point of all this is not that sex offenders are all nice people, or harmless people, or that their offenses do not carry great pain, or do not repel, and in some ineffable way frighten us all. Rather, the point is that the criminal process has been designed to deal with such acts; and if society wants to buy more protection, it may make the sentences for such acts much longer. But when the State singles out a group to be dealt with differently and invokes parens patriae, it ought to have rational and convincing reasons. It ought to know what needs to be done, and it ought to do it.

If there is any good reason to isolate sex offenders it is, ironically, to protect them from the rest of the prison population. The prison population in its own way reflects society's specially hostile attitudes toward those who are sexually deviant.

Sex offenders are often meek and physically timid. When these factors are combined with the stigma attached to their crimes, it is easy to understand the dangers of imprisonment. But that problem can be dealt with by a separate cell block as is common practice for homosexuals in many correctional facilities, and if there does exist treatment for the sex offender, why can it not be provided in prison?

References

1. *See*, Dershowitz, Preventive confinement: A suggested framework for constitutional analysis, 51 *Texas L. Rev.* 1277, 1311-1313 (1973).
2. *Va. Code Ann.* sec.53-278.2 (1958).
3. *Model Penal Code* sec.149 (Proposed Official Draft, May 4, 1964).
4. *Mass. Ann. Laws* ch.272 sec.34 (1970).
5. *Hamrick* v. *State of Alabama*, 199 So. 2d 849 (Ala. 1966), *appeal dismissed*, 389 U.S. 10 (1967).
6. Quoted in Dershowitz, note 1 *supra* at 1289.
7. *See*, Moyer, The Mentally abnormal offender in Sweden, 22 *Am. J. Of Comp. Law* 71 (1974).
8. S. Brakel and R. Rock, *The Mentally Disabled And The Law* (Chicago: University of Chicago Press, 1971) p. 341.
9. These states were Illinois, Massachusetts, Michigan, Minnesota, Ohio and Wisconsin. *See generally*, Hacker and Frym, The sexual psychopath act in practice: A critical discussion, 43 *Cal. L. Rev.* 766 (1955).
10. S. Brakel and R. Rock, *supra* note 8, at 341-343.
11. *See, People* v. *Frontczak*, 281 N.W. 534 (Mich. 1938); Minnesota *ex rel. Pearson* v. *Probate Ct.*, 309 U.S. 270 (1940).
12. *See*, Brakel and Rock, *supra* note 8, tables 10.1-10.2.
13. *Mass. Ann. Laws* ch. 123A sec.1 (1965).
14. *Md. Ann. Code* art. 31B sec.5 (1967).
15. See, e.g., *D.C. Code Ann.* ch. 22-3503 (1) (1967); Iowa Code Ann sec.225A.1 (1969).
16. See, e.g., *Ala. Code* tit.15 sec.434 (Supp. 1967); S. Brakel .nd R. Rock, supra note 8, tables 10.1-10.2.
17. See, e.g., *Ill. Ann. Stat.* ch. 38 sec.105-1.01 (Smith-Hurd 1964); *Mo. Rev. Stat.* ch. 202.700 (1959).
18. See, e.g., *Pa. Stat. Ann.* ch. 11 sec.1166 (1964); *Utah Code Ann.* 77-49-5 (Supp. 1967).
19. *Mass. Ann. Laws* ch. 123A sec.1 (1965); *Neb. Rev. Stat.* 29-2901 (1964).
20. *Minn. Stat. Ann.* sec.526.09 (1969).
21. See, e.g., *Ohio Rev. Code* 2947.24B (Baldwin 1964).
22. See, e.g., *New Jersey, Report Of The Commission On The Habitual Sex Offender* 47 (1950). *See* also, Note, The plight of the sexual psychopath: A legislative blunder and judicial acquiescence, 41 *Not. Dame Lawyer* 527 (1966).
23. Group for the Advancement of Psychiatry, report: Psychiatrically deviated sex offenders, report No. 9 (1950).
24. H. Cleckley, *The Mask Of Sanity* (St. Louis: Mosby, 1955).
25. Sutherland, The sexual psychopath laws, 40 *J. Crim. L. C. and P. S.* 543; *see also* authorities cited in S. Brakel and R. Rock, supra note 8 at 350; *Wolfe* v. *State*, 219 N.E. 2d 807, 809 (Ind., 1966).
26. M. Ploscowe, *Sex And The Law* 216-217 (New York: Prentice Hall, 1951). Sadoff, Sexually deviated offenders, 40 *Temp. L. O.* 305 (1967).
27. Kozol, et al., The criminally dangerous sex offender, 275 *N. E. J. Med.* 79,80 (1966).
28. Fisher, The legacy of Freud, 40 *U. Colo. L. Rev.* 242, 313 (1968).

29. *New Jersey, Report Of The Commission On The Habitual Sex Offender* 32 (1950).
30. Frisbie, Recidivism among treated sex offenders, Cal. dept. of mental hygiene (1963). *But see,* Field and Williams, The hormonal treatment of sex offenders, 10 *Med. Science and The Law* 27 (1970); Anderson, Neurosurgery for the paedophiliac homosexual 6 *World Medicine* 42 (1970); The exchange of tape recordings as a catalyst in group psychotherapy with sex offenders, 19 *Intern. J. Of Group Psychother.* 214 (1969).
31. Bowman and Engle, Sexual psychopath laws, In: *Sexual Behavior And The Law* 757, 769 (R. Slovenko, ed.) (Springfield, Ill.: C. C. Thomas, 1965).
32. *Id.*
33. *See,* Stone, Letter, *Psychiatric News* (APA Newspaper) Sept. 1, 1971.
34. See, e.g., Stürup, Will this man be dangerous? In: *The Mentally Abnormal Offender* (A. V. S. Reuck and R. Porter, eds.) 5, 16 (Boston: Little, Brown and Co., 1968).
35. W. C. Eckerman, *A nationwide survey of mental health and correctional institutions for adult mentally disordered offenders* (Rockville, Md.: NIMH, 1972).
36. *Specht v. Patterson,* 386 U.S. 605 (1967).
37. *See,* S. Brakel and R. Rock, *supra* note at 343-346 and sources cited therein.
38. The states were Iowa, Minnesota, and Nebraska. *Id.* at 345.
39. See, e.g., Cohen, Administration of the criminal psychopath statute in Indiana, 32 *Ind. L. Rev.* 450 (1957).
40. McGarry and Cotton, A study in civil commitment: The Massachusetts sexually dangerous persons act, 6 *Harv. J. Legis.* 263, 286 (1969).
41. See, e.g., *In re Gault,* 387 U.S. 1 (1967) (juvenile proceedings). *See generally,* Aronson, Should the privilege against self-incrimination apply to compelled psychiatric examinations? 26 *Stan. L. Rev.* 55 (1973).
42. *Compare, e.g., Shepard v. Bowe,* 443 P. 2d 238 (Ore. 1968), *State v. Olson,* 143 N.W. 2d 69 (Minn. 1966), *and French v. Dist. Ct.,* 384 P. 2d 268 (Colo. 1963), *with Lee v. County Ct.,* 267 N.E. 2d 452, *cert. denied,* 404 U.S. 823 (1971), *and Parkin v. State,* 238 So. 2d 817 (Fla. 1970), *cert. denied,* 401 U.S. 974 (1971).
43. *Tippett v. Maryland,* 436 F. 2d 1153 (4th Cir. 1971).
44. See, e.g., *In re Gault, supra* note 41 at 49-50. *Kennedy v. Mendoza-Martinez,* 372 U.S. 144, 168-169 (1963).
45. *McNeil v. Director, Patuxent Inst.,* 407 U.S. 245 (1972); *see also, Murel v. Baltimore City Crim. Ct.,* 407 U.S. 355 (1972). *See also* Lefelt, Pretrial mental examinations: Compelled cooperation and the fifth amendment, 10 *Am. Crim. L. Rev.* 431 (1972).
46. *See, Miranda v. Arizona,* 384 U.S. 436, 460 (1966); *Rollerson v. United States,* 343 F. 2d 269, 271 (D.C. Circ. 1964); Note, Requiring a criminal defendant to submit to a government psychiatric examination: An invasion of the privilege against self-incrimination, 83 *Harv. L. Rev.* 648, 660 (1970).
47. *In re Gault,* supra note 41. *See also,* In re Winship, 397 U.S. 358 (1970).
48. *Lessard v. Schmidt,* 349 F. Supp. 1078 (E. D. Wis. 1972).
49. *See* Aronson, *supra* note 41 at 64-65. See also the fourth and fifth amendment cases discussed in Greenwalt, The right to privacy, In: *The*

Rights Of Americans (N. Dorsen, ed.) (New York: Random House, 1971) pp. 299-325.

50. See, e.g., *Griswold* v. *Connecticut*, 381 U.S. 479 (1965); *Katz* v. *United States*, 389 U.S. 347 (1967); *Chimel* v. *California* 395 U.S. 752 (1969). *See also*, Miller, Personal privacy in the computer age: The challenge of a new technology in an information-oriented society, 67 *Mich. L. Rev.* 1089 (1969).

51. See Aronson, *supra* note 41 at 90-91.

52. Pacht *et al.*, Diagnosis and treatment of the sexual offender: A 9-year study, 118 *Am. J. Psychiat.* 802 (1962) (Wisconsin).

53. Granucci and Granucci, Indiana's sexual psychopath act in operation, 44 *Ind. L. Rev.* 555-572 (1969).

54. *People* v. *Hymes*, 327 P. 2d 219, 222 (Cal. App., 2nd Dist. 1958) (Herndon, J.).

55. See, e.g., *Commonwealth* v. *Ackers*, 175 N.E. 2d 677 (Mass. 1969).

56. See, e.g., *Baxstrom* v. *Herold*, 383 U.S. 107 (1967); *Specht* v. *Patterson*, 386 U.S. 605 (1967).

57. *Gerchman* v. *Maroney*, 355 F. 2d 302 (3rd Cir. 1966).

58. *See* cases cited at note 56, *supra*.

59. *Specht* v. *Patterson*, *supra* note 56.

60. *Millard* v. *Cameron*, 373 F. 2d 468 (D.C. Cir. 1966).

61. *Cross* v. *Harris*, 418 F. 2d 1095 (D.C. Cir. 1969).

62. See, e.g., *Millard* v. *Cameron*, *supra*, note 60; *Huebner* v. *State*, 147 N.W. 2d 646 (Wis. 1967); *People* v. *Succop*, 433 P. 2d 473 (Calif. 1967). *See also, Cal. Welf. and Instns Code* sec. 6308 (West 1972).

63. *Davy* v. *Sullivan*, 354 F. Supp. 1320 (M. D. Ala. 1973) (three-judge-court); *but see Cullins* v. *Crouse*, 348 F. 2d 887 (10th Cir. 1965).

64. *Robinson* v. *California*, 370 U.S. 660 (1962).

65. *Sas* v. *Maryland*, 334 F. 2d 506 (4th Cir.), *aff'd* sub. nom. *Tippett* v. *Maryland*, 436 F. 2d 1153 (4th Cir. 1970); *cert. dismissed as improv. granted, Murel* v. *Baltimore Crim. Ct.*, 407 U.S. 355 (1972).

66. *See* State of Maryland, Dept. of Public Safety and Correctional Services, Maryland's defective delinquent statute – a progress report (1973).

67. *Murel* v. *Baltimore Crim. Ct.*, 407 U.S. 355 (1972) (dismissing certiorari as improvidently granted).

68. *Cf. McNeil* v. *Director, Patuxent Inst.*, 407 U.S. 245 (1972); *Jackson* v. *Indiana*, 406 U.S. 715 (1972); *Humphrey* v. *Cady*, 405 U.S. 504 (1972).

69. McGarry and Cotton, *supra*, note 40.

70. Maryland Commission to Study Medico-Legal Psychiatry, Report to General Assembly and Governor, p. 11 (1948).

71. Md. Legis. Council Res. Div. Res. Rept. No. 29 (Dec. 1950).

72. Sutherland, The diffusion of sexual psychopath laws, in W. Chambliss, ed., *Crime And The Legal Process* (New York: McGraw Hill, 1969) pp. 74-81. Hacker, The sexual psychopath act in practice: A critical discussion, 43 *Cal. L. Rev.* 766 (1955); Bradley and Margolin, The Oregon sexually dangerous persons act, 8 *Will. L. J.* 341, 349-350 (1972) and sources cited at 349-350 n.42.

73. *Minnesota ex rel. Pearson* v. *Probate Court*, 309 U.S. 270, 275 (1940), citing *Lindsley* v. *Natural Carbonic Gas Co.*, 220 U.S. 61, 78-79 (1911).

74. See, e.g., Illinois, Report of the Illinois Commission on Sex Offenders to the sixty-eighth General Assembly of the State of Illinois 11 (1953); A. Ellis and R. Brancale, *The Psychology Of Sex Offenders* (Springfield, Ill.: C. C. Thomas, 1956) pp. 32-33.

75. Tappan, Sentences for sex criminals, 42 *J. Crim. L. C. and P. S.* 332, 336 (1961).
76. *Id. See also* S. Brakel and R. Rock, *supra* note 8 at 348-350; Gigeroff, Mohr and Turner, Sex offenders on probation; heterosexual pedophiles, 32 *Fed. Prob.* 17, 21 (December 1968).
77. *Id.*
78. California Department of Mental Hygiene, California sexual deviate research 15, 21 (1953).
79. M. Guttmacher and H. Weihofen, *Psychiatry And The Law* (New York: W. W. Norton and Co., 1952) p. 11; Tappan, Some myths about the sex offender, 19 *Fed. Prob.* 7, 9 (June 1955); Michigan, Report of the Governor's Study Commission on the deviated criminal sex offender 131 (1951).
80. *See* Burick, An analysis of the Illinois sexually dangerous persons act, 59 *J. Crim. L. C. and P. S.* 254, sec. (1968); P. Tappan, *Crime, justice and correction* (New York: McGraw-Hill, 1960), p. 414; *Ind. Ann. Stat.* sec.9-3401 (Burns 1956).
81. *Compare* opinions in *Cross* v. *Harris:* 418 F. 2d 1095 (D.C. Cir 1969), *see* Note, Indiana's sexual psychopath statute, 44 *Ind. L. R.* 242 (1969).

Chapter 12

Competency to Stand Trial

Introduction

Many socially deviant acts can be labeled either as sick or criminal or both. The particular label chosen often depends on the social class of the actor, the value system of those designated to control or remedy deviant acts, and the choice of community resources made by those responding to the deviant act. The same domestic battle which brings the police to an inner city tenement and results in a jail sentence for resisting an officer will bring to the suburban home a general practitioner with sedatives and a referral to a family therapist.

Thus whether identical acts in the course of social events become defined in their salient aspects as criminal or symptomatic is often determined by extrinsic social factors unrelated to the criminal code or the courts. Law enforcement officials are often expected to deal with deviant acts which they consider both criminal and symptomatic of mental illness. These deviant acts range from bizarre and ghastly crimes to public drunkenness. At the end of the continuum where crimes are less serious, considerable police discretion exists. A drunken college student who provokes a brawl may be brought by police to the college infirmary, while a drunken laborer who provokes a brawl may spend the night in jail. The social class and status of the deviant, the available social resources, and police discretion may all affect the label the offending behavior is eventually given (1).

Where the deviant act is initially treated by the police as criminal and an arrest is made, the court and the attorneys retain the option of raising the possibility of mental illness at the arraignment, the indictment, or at any point thereafter.

Given the overwhelming numbers of criminal cases, the enormous expense of criminal trials, and the general dissatisfaction with the results of incarceration, there exists both judicial and prosecutorial interest in diversion from the criminal process. When it is possible to raise the question of mental illness and divert the actor to some mental health facility, the courts will often seize upon it even as a temporary alternative.

Critics of the mental health system create the impression that being labeled as mentally ill by the courts is always a bad result for the offender. This is certainly not the case; in fact, in the lower criminal courts the judge is often willing to accept outpatient treatment, day care, even once-a-week group therapy as an alternative for criminal sanctions which carry a high penalty. Whatever stigma the label may carry, many defendants gladly accept it rather than a prison sentence.

Indeed, the effective criminal lawyer in these courts is often the one who is an access specialist to good mental health facilities. Here again the label is less significant to the person than the results which flow from the label. But the mental illness label is clearly meretricious when it leads to an indeterminate sentence in a total institution. The chapter on mental retardation revealed the result when the mental health profession controls entry into such facilities. This chapter will indicate the obverse problem; namely, the results of allowing the criminal court and its officers, merely by raising the question of mental illness, to commit defendants to inpatient facilities for the criminally insane.

The law of the United States as interpreted by the Supreme Court, *Pate* v. *Robinson* (2), requires the defense attorney, the prosecutor, and the judge to raise the question of mental illness whenever they believe that it may interfere with the defendant's capacity to participate in the trial. That question of competency can and must be raised at any point in the criminal process, as illustrated in figure 2. This figure also emphasizes competency to serve a sentence. This is a complex and separate legal question not considered here. But see the Supreme Court's discussion of competency to be executed! *Solesbee* v. *Balkom* 339 U.S. 9 (1950).

There is no standard in law for raising this threshold question; it is entirely discretionary. This is extraordinary given the consequences to the defendant. Yet few lawyers or mental health professionals recognize the importance or understand the standard of "competency to stand trial." It is, in fact, the most significant mental health inquiry pursued in the system of criminal law. Its significance derives from the numbers of persons to whom it is applied, the many points in the criminal trial process at which it can be applied, the ease of its being invoked, and the consequences of its application.

The potential consequences for the defendant are: (a) he may be denied bail, (b) he may be incarcerated for a period longer than the maximum sentence for the crime he is alleged to have committed, (c) he may be placed in an institution that combines the worst

Figure 2. Psychiatric interventions (*) within the criminal process (highly schematic)

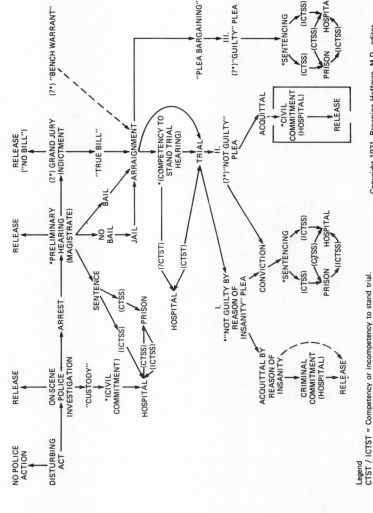

Copyright 1971, Browning Hoffman, M.D., editor
(unpublished syllabus, Psychiatry and the Criminal Process).
Reprinted by permission of the author.

Legend
CTST / ICTST = Competency or incompetency to stand trial.
CTSS / ICTSS = Competency or incompetency to serve sentence.

elements of jails and hospitals, and (d) any pretrial mental examination poses serious questions about the fifth amendment rights of the defendant (cf. the quasi-criminal defendant).

The significance of the competency question has been typically obscured by confusing it with the insanity defense. Consider the case of an obviously mentally ill person who commits some criminal act. Such an offender is typically arrested shortly after the crime. Since mental illness is apparent to everyone, two important legal questions arise. First, if this person is to be tried, will he be able to consult with his lawyers and participate in his defense? Second, was he responsible for the crime with which he is charged? The first is the question of competency to stand trial, the second is the question of insanity. Before a criminal trial can be held to answer the second question, the defendant must be restored to competency. Thus, in the typical case it is the question of competency that arises first, and its resolution often determines the fate of the defendant.

In practice, however, these legal issues are often not faced directly either by the courts or the mental health professionals consulted by the courts. The reason this is so is partly the result of the ambiguity of legal procedures, and partly because the courts are eager to dispose of cases by any reasonable disposition (3).

The judge, if the crime is not serious, may simply commit the mentally ill defendant and drop the charges. Thus, the only responsibility of the psychiatric facility may be to treat and discharge. Alternatively, the judge may commit and file the criminal charges awaiting the outcome of mental examination and treatment. These are court dispositions available in some jurisdictions which exist separate from the court's capacity to refer for an evaluation of competency to stand trial. Given the complexity and expense of a trial on the issue of not guilty by reason of insanity, and the congestion of the courts, a judge will often prefer to divert the patient from the criminal process in this way, particularly if he believes the hospital will provide either treatment or secure confinement (4).

Separate from this type of commitment, but often combined with it, is referral by the court to determine both competency and criminal responsibility while the criminal charges remain pending. Competency commitment of this sort is available in every jurisdiction because a competent defendant is an essential legal requirement for a trial.

Unfortunately few psychiatrists understand the distinction between competency and criminal responsibility. In fact, most psychiatrists equate psychosis with insane (not criminally responsible) and they assume insane includes incompetent to stand trial. In fact, the American Psychiatric Association's glossary perpetuates this error:

> Insanity: A vague legal term for psychosis, now obsolete in psychiatric usage. Generally connotes: (a) a mental incompetence, (b) inability to distinguish right from wrong, etc. (5).

As I shall indicate, the legal statutes are equally confused.

Since the court refers defendants in an ambiguous manner and asks both legal questions at the same time, and since the insanity defense is more familiar, it is easy to understand how psychiatrists might become confused. However, there is a vital distinction: the finding of incompetency means that the defendant will not get his day in court and will remain in limbo as to the criminal charges against him until competency is restored. Such a result should not be confused with a finding of not guilty by reason of insanity, which means the criminal charges have been permanently rejected. The relative practical significance of these issues is illustrated in Massachusetts where, during 1970, no one was committed after trial as not guilty by reason of insanity, and 2,101 were committed by the courts pretrial (6).

Data demonstrate that far more persons are confined on the basis of incompetence than because they have been found not guilty by reason of insanity. An incompetent defendant often could expect to spend his life in a hospital for the criminally insane. In 1972, 8,825 men, 5,349 of whom were nonwhite, were committed as incompetent. (Unpublished statistics provided by Taube; see table on page 44.) During the past decade a series of studies have demonstrated in painful detail the consequences of this little understood law-mental health label, and attempts have been made to educate the legal and mental health professions as to its significance. The Supreme Court of the United States has also addressed itself to the competency question in *Jackson* v. *Indiana* (7). There, a court unanimously announced principles which require drastic revision of current practices in all but a few States. Thus it would seem that the stage is set for reform that is long overdue.

Historically, the legal notion of competency has been thought to serve both ritual and justice (8). The requirement that the criminal defendant be able to understand the proceedings and aid in his defense flowed from the view that the entering of a plea at trial invoked the judgment of God, sustained the adversarial nature of the court, and aided the discovery of truth. Likewise, the derivative notion of competency to serve sentence, even competency to be executed, was premised on the fact that some aims of the criminal law, such as retribution, could only be served if the inmate understood why he was being punished.

More specifically, a determination of competency to stand trial ostensibly serves the following needs of the legal system (9):

Guaranteeing the accuracy of criminal proceedings, especially where a competent accused might provide his counsel with crucial facts, especially facts known only to the accused.

Guaranteeing the fairness of the trial. There is an ineffable sense in which it has long been felt that an accused has not been fairly convicted, no matter what the extrinsic evidence, unless he is able to understand the nature of the proceedings and the basic defense options and consequences.

Maximizing the efficacy of punishment, both in terms of individual deterrence and retributive catharsis of the rest of society.

Preserving the dignity of the judicial process. It may be argued that the judicial process is impermissibly demeaned if the defendant is incompetent, acts bizarre, or is unable to complement the rationality of the adversary process. Though there may be a kernel of truth in this assertion, I believe that unlike the aforementioned three rationales, this is a politically dangerous argument on which to base the competency procedure. The peril of this view is that it focuses on the interests of the system only, and impliedly denies that the defendant could have any rational reason for disrupting a trial. More will be said below about the interest of the allegedly incompetent accused in proceeding to trial. The central point, however, is that the incompetency procedure is rational and justifiable only insofar as, in practice, it really does advance the first three goals previously outlined.

Given these goals, it is not surprising to find that the prevailing legal criteria of the competency of the defendant are

> whether he has sufficient present ability to consult with his lawyer with a reasonable degree of rational understanding, and whether he has a rational as well as factual understanding of the proceedings against him (*10*) *Dusky v. United States.*

Unfortunately, however, in most jurisdictions:

> Statutory terminology turns out to be a source of confusion: the competency provisions. . .speak only in terms denoting other inappropriate conditions such as idiot, lunatic . . . mentally deranged, and so forth (*11*).

And although the Supreme Court promulgated the criteria cited, they have failed to define or delimit their terms; e.g., reasonable degree and rational. Consequently, lower court decisions manifest a wide divergence. For example, in Massachusetts a lobotomized defendant was deemed competent to stand trial because he was

> sufficiently a human being, though impaired, to appreciate the peril of his position . . . (*12*).

while in a leading Iowa case, a defendant was held incompetent because he was

> so mentally deranged as not to *appreciate exactly* the nature of the criminal charge against him (*13*).

While there is a consensus among judges and commentators alike that some clarification of the incompetency standards is required, no new criterion or formulation has been put forward by any of the prominent scholarly or reform-oriented legal groups (*14*). Perhaps the reason is that the real evils of the incompetency process arise not from mistaken goals or a wrong formulation, but from procedural omissions or abuses which undermine and falsify those goals.

Inconsistency and confusion aside, the real tragedy of the incompetency process is that it has, in many places, lost its distinct purpose of protecting defendants and has become merely another element in the array of techniques used by the State to effect the same result: involuntary confinement of worrisome individuals in grossly substandard facilities. As one commentator has noted:

> The incompetency procedure has become a general catch-all by which all kinds of purposes are achieved, often at the expense of genuine consideration of the competency question. The procedure has been used, among other things, for pretrial discovery, strategic delay of trial, and long term preventive detention without the necessity for trial or civil commitment (*15*).

Thus, lawyers improperly use the procedure for tactical reasons. And psychiatrists often misserve their proper function of accurately but helpfully informing the judicial system of the capacities of the accused. Too often they merely proffer ritualistic and conclusory assertions based on their own view of the proper disposition of the defendant. In so doing, they lend medical sanction to an arbitrary and summary process. Above all, the courts have permitted either hypocritical or just unrealistic use of the competency procedure. They employ an idealized notion of competence which is insensitive to the real needs of the specific trial at hand, and which prejudices the potentially competent accused's interest in proceeding to trial.

Does a defendant require the same competence to plead guilty to a charge of public drunkenness as needed to plead guilty to first degree murder? Whatever the defense, all too often a determination of incompetency leads to lifetime confinement in a hospital for the criminally insane. Individuals are blithely remitted to these institutions until "restored" to competence—with little apparent attention to the utter lack of therapeutic or restorative conditions in most such institutions.

Much of this will doubtless change as the result of the Supreme Court's ruling in *Jackson* v. *Indiana (16)*. *Jackson* involved a mentally defective deaf-mute who was clearly incompetent to stand trial, and who was unlikely ever to become competent. The Court forthrightly held that due process limits the period of observational confinement of an allegedly incompetent defendant to a reasonable time necessary to determine the likelihood of his being restored to competency in a foreseeable period of therapy. The Court concluded that if the defendant will never be competent,

> the State must either institute the customary civil commitment proceedings . . . or release the defendant (*17*).

Consistent with this ruling, new less ambiguous legislation is required based on these premises: *that institutional commitment of the incompetent accused should be a last resort, and that competency should always be evaluated with regard to the minimal real needs of the given trial.* But as I have previously indicated, I believe the difficulties of the competency procedure can be rectified only by a thoughtful reworking of each step of the competency-commitment process. The empirical data which informs such a reworking indicate that true incompetency is a rare event (*18*). Some States have already rectified the inequities described in the following pages.

How the Competency Process Works (And How It Ought To)

The police phase. The police initiate about one-fourth of all procedures which result in hospitalization for mental infirmities (*19*). Large numbers of these cases involve persons of questionable competency who were apprehended for minor crimes, quasi-offenses (e.g., loitering, following someone), or merely for odd or suspicious behavior in public. At this point the police have a critical choice whether to canalize the individual into criminal process or civil procedures, or merely to do nothing. Currently, this decision consumes much police-officer time, is capricious, and brings to bear little expertise.

Often the police seem to be interested in that alternative which will keep the person off the streets for the longest period of time. Thus, in California when reform of the civil commitment law greatly reduced the length of hospital stay, police began to route huge numbers of persons through the criminal route. They would be charged with minor crimes, found incompetent to stand trial, and thus confined for longer periods than under the noncriminal process (*20*). This finding makes it clear that piecemeal reform of the law-mental health system can produce results even more deleterious than those the reformers sought to improve. These persons now are not only involuntarily confined, they also have criminal charges; the worst of both worlds it would seem.

The prosecutorial phase. In deciding whether or not to challenge the competency of the accused to stand trial, the prosecutor may be animated by a variety of considerations unrelated to the law's primary purpose. The most important of these is bail, which has many legal implications and is discussed below. But the fact is that the prosecutor can by successfully raising the question of competency to stand trial prevent the defendant from going free on bail. Since, as I have pointed out, there is no clear threshold which must be reached for raising this question, this gives the prosecutor, if the court agrees, a wide margin of discretion.

The prosecutor in many jurisdictions has no legal procedure available to him for determining the mental status of the defendant other than a request for a competency determination. Often he may be willing not to press charges if the crime is minor, and the defendant will accept treatment. The prosecutor, like the judge, is looking for dispositions. But he may have no alternative available to him for such a disposition except raising the question of competency. Furthermore, if the prosecutor believes that the defense of insanity may be raised at trial, he will want his own evidence as to the defendant's mental condition. The only way he may be able to get it is by raising the competency question (*21*).

Finally, empirical studies reveal that prosecutors will sometimes raise the question of competence as a favor to their supposed adversary, the defense attorney. The typical situation which brings this about is when the defendant angrily and sometimes menacingly insists that he is not crazy and refuses even to discuss the question with his attorney. Fearful of his client's wrath, or unwilling to provoke him, the attorney turns in secret to the prosecutor (22).

Whatever the wisdom or the validity of these procedures may be, it is clear that even the possibility of mental illness leads to tactics which are otherwise legally and ethically unacceptable. When one realizes that before the recent reforms the outcome of being found incompetent was lifetime incarceration in an institution for the criminally insane, it is clear that this is a grave abuse of the law-mental health system.

Bail and speedy trial. Although the Federal Constitution does not provide a right to bail in all cases, there is a Federal statutory right to bail in noncapital cases (23). And the possibility of a constitutional right to bail in various circumstances has been discussed by the Supreme Court (24) and commentators (25). In addition, about 40 States provide, either in their constitutions or by statute, for bail in noncapital cases (26). The overriding factor in granting or withholding bail is supposed to be the likelihood that the defendant will appear for trial. The most glaring exception to this well-developed process is the case of persons alleged to be incompetent to stand trial; once again, the legal system seems to change all its premises when mental illness is suggested. When the competency of the defendant is challenged, setting of bail is deferred, or, if bail has been granted, it may be revoked (27). There is little case law contesting this exceptional treatment; the impression is widespread among lawyers that the entire issue of bail is ignored once the defendant's competency is brought into question. Thus, the question of imcompetence creates the possibility of unregulated preventive detention. That judges and prosecutors use it in this way is common experience (28).

Such routine denial of bail consideration to those allegedly incompetent to be tried may well violate constitutional rights. Courts have repeatedly held that due process prohibits the determination of bail based on master plans or general rules, and that consideration must be given to the cases on an individual basis (29). And in *Marcey* v. *Harris*(30) the D.C. Circuit directly held that in a case where release would otherwise be contemplated by the Bail Reform Act, pretrial commitment for examination or observation is not a sufficient reason for withholding bail. This decision reflects a number of compelling but oft-ignored facts. First, there is scant correlation between mental impairment and likelihood of flight before trial. Indeed, unlike many States, the Federal law wisely obliges the judge to consider the mental condition of the accused as it may relate to fugitivity (31). Second, all that is required to prevent bail under most current State schemes is some reasonable doubt by one of the parties as to the accused's competence. Third, the alleged offense of the accused may well be minor, the evidence to support it insufficient, or the charges already dropped (*32*). The fact that charges are dropped demonstrates that courts use competency to obtain a final disposition rather than its intended purpose. The inequity of that subterfuge is that in many jurisdictions the competency determination is carried out in the facility for the criminally insane, which is typically the worst institution in the State (*33*).

Proposal: *Those allegedly incompetent to be tried should be evaluated for bail purposes just like other defendants, using mental difficulties as merely another datum in the calculation of likelihood of appearance at trial. And if an order providing for examination and observation is deemed necessary and bail is denied, the accused should still have the right to a hearing on the least restrictive means (facility) by which he could be examined (34).* Some States now permit the incompetency evaluation of a nondangerous defendant to be carried out at any appropriate mental health facility.

One sensible suggestion is that there should be some form of pretrial conference involving prosecutor, judge, and defense counsel, which could draw on a speedy precharge screening procedure. The primary goal of these procedures would be to consider rationally the interests of all parties without routinely resorting to prolonged confinement of the defendant for psychiatric examination (*35*). McGarry's research suggests that far more care should be taken in screening before referral to a hospital for the criminally insane.

A 1971 Massachusetts Department of Mental Health study, for example, revealed that only 74 of 1,806, or 4.1 percent, of pretrial admissions to Massachusetts mental hospitals actually resulted in a finding of incompetency to stand trial (*36*). Unnecessary referrals may have traumatic antitherapeutic effects on the marginally-well, and may stigmatize those who are brought to trial. In those numerous jurisdictions where confinement for observation and examination may continue for 30, 60, 80 days or more (*37*), it may well mean loss of job, separation from family and community, and, in general, an exacerbation of the problems which likely brought the person to court in the first instance.

The use of a court-related or community clinic, or a rotating panel of local psychiatrists may render unnecessary many hospitalizations. Though some may persist in the belief that some greater expertise or certainty would be brought to bear in an inpatient examination, I believe the evidence suggests that many such

209

prolonged examination processes are unnecessary. For example, one study of persons committed for pretrial examination to the Medical Center for Federal Prisoners at Springfield, Missouri, found that the average stay was 89 days. Unless the order specifically stipulated otherwise, the staff apparently felt that a full study was warranted —including physical examinations, laboratory studies, x-rays, electroencephalograms, compilation of histories by correspondence with relatives, psychological tests, and observation of the patient's socialization over a period of time. The staff's zeal was apparently undiminished by the fact that they ultimately found two-thirds of the patients competent to stand trial (38)!

Lipsitt and co-workers have described a screening device which seems quite adequate for avoiding unnecessary competency commitment (39).

Determination of competency after screening. The quality and comprehensiveness of examinations after referral to an inpatient facility vary markedly; in some jurisdictions cursory interviews are the rule despite long stays, while in others observation and complicated testing during months of hospitalization is a common practice. The manner of examination may depend on statutory requirements, the custom of the courts, the availability of local psychiatrists, financial arrangements, and so on. But it has been observed that the most consistent, salient factor in the administration of competency examinations is the prevalence of dispositional diagnoses; i.e., the examiners' finding whatever is necessary to achieve the institutional result they favor (40).

The general question which must be asked at this point is: How can psychiatric information best be offered so as to aid the court in determining the issues which ought rightly to be addressed at this stage? There is, at this juncture, no need for elaborate psychiatric evaluations unrelated to the role the defendant plays in the trial. One commentator has outlined the questions which should be asked as follows:

> In what ways the accused's mental condition would affect his ability to understand the particular legal proceedings in prospect and to cooperate with his counsel; whether he requires immediate treatment, and if so, what kind; what problems his counsel should be aware of; what possibility there is of changes of his condition under stress of trial or during pretrial detention; how likely he is to regain competency or to recover from his illness if hospitalized; whether he might with the aid of drugs or short-term therapy be made more able to understand the proceedings and cooperate with counsel; whether, if

treatment is indicated, he requires a maximum security institution or could safely be treated in a regular State hospital as an outpatient (41).

In this context, the numerous efforts to develop competency evaluation forms and checklists will be extremely helpful. If they did nothing else, they would have value because they make it clear to both the psychiatrist and the court what the questions are (42).

A major issue is whether the current practice of commitment for long periods of psychiatric examination and treatment violates the right of the defendant to a speedy trial as provided by the sixth amendment. In general, statutory speedy trial provisions have seldom been applied in cases where incompetency was alleged (43), and the constitutional speedy trial right has been considerably attenuated in recent years (44). But as noted previously, the effect of *Jackson* v. *Indiana* will be to expedite this process markedly. And beyond this, the speedy trial analysis lends further support to the need for some procedure by which the allegedly incompetent person could raise those defenses which by challenging the sufficiency of the charges, could lead to immediate dismissal of the case (45). Perhaps other States will follow Massachusetts (46) in providing the option of a provisional trial for the defendant who is deemed incompetent. The defendant would stand acquitted just as if he had been competent; but if convicted, the trial would be deemed void. And if the accused did not want a provisional trial, he could proceed immediately to treatment in an appropriate facility. Now it may immediately be objected that this merely doubles the load on the judicial processes since many provisional trials would be voided, only to be later repeated. But it is also true that fundamental rights of the defendant, institutional resources, and judicial time would be saved by the avoidance of long-term confinement of those against whom charges could be disposed of, in spite of their partial or ample infirmities.

Final disposition. At the present time, statutes in most States provide for mandatory commitment to a mental hospital for those found incompetent to stand trial (47). Presumably they are to be restored to competence. Many jurisdictions even require that these commitments be to a maximum security facility—which is unlikely to be maximally therapeutic as well. But a judicial attitude hostile to these reflex-commitments was revealed in *Baxstrom* v. *Herold* (48), in which the Supreme Court limited the time a convicted prisoner could be held over beyond the expiration of his sentence for psychiatric reasons, but without civil commitment. And this attitude reached fruition in *Jackson*. As noted previously, the Court in *Jackson* held that both the duration and conditions of confinement must bear some reasonable relation to its purpose. Therefore, an alleged incompetent defendant may be held only long enough to determine the chances of his being restored to competency. If he cannot be so helped, he must be released; and if he is retained, "continued confinement must be justified by progress toward [competency]" *(49)*.

Many of the persons found incompetent to stand trial, of course, are not dangerous and cannot reliably be predicted to be dangerous. Operation Baxstrom suggests at least that many can be transferred to less secure surroundings *(50)*. Therefore, I would propose that incompetent defendants who would otherwise have been eligible for bail, should be civilly committed by the same standard and to the same therapeutic institutions as other mental patients in that jurisdiction. The commitment hearing should question the person's need for inpatient care, and if conducive to early restoration to competency, the treatment program should include or progress toward outpatient care. Only defendants who are not legally entitled to bail and who are in need of treatment should be remanded to high security facilities.

Two added problems remain. First, absent an extraordinary patient's initiative in bringing a habeas corpus suit, or a family's desire to assert a defendant's rights, or an overburdened hospital staff member's willingness to take a risk in recommending a patient for release, it is possible that the intent of *Jackson* will be subverted by an institution's overoptimistic estimates of therapeutic progress. A pattern of prolonged confinement, despite *Jackson*, might develop not from the malice of institutional staff, but from their response to the role they believe society wants them to play.

Proposal: *Therefore, there should be a specific statutory limit to the length of time a person may be confined for return to competency purposes.* I would suggest this period be 6 months, or the maximum sentence the accused could have received for the most serious crime for which he was charged, whichever is less. Six months is a period much longer than that shown to be necessary to treat most civilly committed patients, particularly since the advent of drug therapy. It is my belief that after 6 months, the vast majority of the alleged incompetents will be in one of two categories: those who are competent to stand trial, and those who are suffering from mental disabilities, such as mental retardation, brain damage, or chronic deteriorated states such that restoration to competency, ever, is unlikely. The first group should be brought to trial, and charges against the second group should be dropped. A small residual category of persons not clearly in either group could, under carefully reviewed procedures, be confined for another 6 months and then disposed of as previously indicated. In the case of those charged with minor offenses, the time should be even shorter, and the reviewing court should promptly consider alternatives to prolonged incarceration such as probation, outpatient care, or dismissal of the charges. Courts should, of course, be attentive to any tendency to subvert the previously discussed limits by periodic recommitments on dubious minor charges.

Perhaps the most difficult aspect of this sort of plan is that it requires the courts to shed their traditional passive role and to take the initiative in developing a process of periodic review of the fates of those they commit. A central registry and recording system might aid in keeping to a calendar of judicial review.

The Special Problem of Drug Therapy of the Defendant Awaiting Trial

If the reform of competency procedures is achieved, it is apparent that one result will be that many criminal defendants will be rapidly returned to trial, having been treated with a regimen of psychotropic drugs. These drugs will alter their courtroom demeanor as well as assisting in returning them to competency. Once again the problem of the relationship between the question of competency and insanity asserts itself. Any defense attorney will recognize that one of the best pieces of evidence for convincing a jury that a person was not responsible for his crime is a defendant who is obviously crazy at the trial. That dramatic impression is blunted by the drugs. The effect of such drugs, when unknown to the jury in its appraisal of a defendant's demeanor, has in fact led to the reversal of a conviction (51).

During the early 1960's, there was considerable judicial and correctional confusion about the facts of drug treatment and this led to tragic results. Defendants whose acute psychotic symptoms were relieved by the use of major tranquilizers would be returned to local jails to await trial. The necessary drug treatment was curtailed, and in some instances this produced a reexacerbation of acute symptoms. A Michigan study of this process reports a number of striking examples:

> One patient accused of killing her sister's children was committed to Ionia . . . . In late 1965 her condition had improved to the point where she was recommended for return to court. The Superintendent (of Ionia) advised the court by letter that the defendant required drugs and set forth the prescription. The defendant remained in jail

for over a month before being examined by a local psychiatric commission. She was given no drugs (during that month) and her condition deteriorated to the point where she began to actively hallucinate, and finally attempted suicide by pouring lighter fluid on her hair and setting fire to it. She was returned to Ionia as still incompetent (52).

Consider the institutional solution to this problem. Dr. Charles E. Smith, Medical Director of the Bureau of Federal Prisons, in 1966 writes:

> The use of tranquilizing medication has given rise to a new problem. These drugs are effective in improving the mental condition of many cases so that while receiving the drugs their condition is so improved that they may be regarded as competent. However, frequently such a patient will relapse if the medication is discontinued. Because of the problems involved in handling such cases in a trial proceeding, we have taken the position that it is undesirable to return them for further hearing so long as they required tranquilizing drugs. In all such instances thus far, the courts have supported this position (53).

Dr. Smith's judgment is, I believe a typical response of the person in a bureaucratic position. If it were the policy followed by psychiatrists in the disposition of other patients suffering from mental illness, it would negate the major revolution in psychiatric treatment accomplished by psychotropic medication. Why should defendants found incompetent to stand trial be bound to a standard of improvement which is so arbitrary and in so many cases impossible of fulfillment?

Surely the Supreme Court of Louisiana was more sensible when it concluded that:

> A defendant whose mental capability was maintained only through use of a prescribed medication was competent to stand trial, and likelihood that defendant would relapse if use of medication was interrupted did not ban defendant from proceeding to trial (54).

Nonetheless, the legally undesirable consequence of drug-induced demeanor must be minimized. The Group for the Advancement of Psychiatry has suggested the following partial remedy for this situation (55). When a defendant in such circumstances appears in court, the judge and both counsel should be told by the examining psychiatrists: (a) that the defendant is appearing under the influence of drugs, and (b) the type of drug the defendant has taken, the dosage, and the effect the drug has had on the defendant's demeanor. This information should be admissable at the discretion of the defense attorney and the judge so that the jury can take this aspect of the defendant's demeanor into account when dealing with the insanity defense (56). Excerpts from videotaped psychiatric interviews of the defendant before treatment is initiated might be a useful device for establishing a baseline in such cases.

It is important to note at this point that there may well be other psychological and psychiatric treatment and diagnostic procedures which are legally and ethically unacceptable for restoring a defendant to competency. Electroshock therapy is an obvious example because of its possible effect on memory. In a recent Detroit murder case (57) the defendant, after being found competent, was given shock treatment before his trial; surely that is an anomalous procedure. Troubling diagnostic interventions are those which trench on fifth amendment rights such as the giving of amytal before interviews and the use of hypnosis. In my view such treatment and diagnostic techniques should be used only with the consent of defense counsel and the authorization of the court.

A Final Caveat

The various reforms suggested here, those already enacted by various States, and those indicated by the Supreme Court in *Jackson* all have one important disadvantage. They create an incentive for malingering by knowledgeable defendants. A guilty defendant facing a long prison sentence in the past had little reason to feign mental illness. The psychiatric facilities were worse than the prisons and there was no limit to the length of confinement. Now if he can malinger incompetence, he may go to a community mental health center, be treated as an outpatient, and avoid trial.

The only thing that stands in the way of this evasion of the criminal process is the capacity of the mental health profession to detect malingering. If Rosenhan's study is to be given any credibility at all, it indicates that the mental health profession cannot detect malingering (58). Thus, the pendulum will have swung so that mental illness, once a weapon against the defendant, might become an impediment to the prosecution.

The court and the mental health profession must be aware of this possibility. Perhaps the prosecutor should be allowed to insist that criminal charges not be dropped in cases where malingering seems to be a possibility. But in the end malingering may simply be a cost that reform must pay.

References

1. D.R. Cressey and D.A. Ward, *Delinquency, Crime and Social Process* (New York: Harper and Row, 1969).
2. *Pate* v. *Robinson*, 383 U.S. 375 (1966).
3. Kadish, The crisis of overcriminalization, 374 *The Annals Of The Am. Acad. Polit. And Soc. Sci.* 158 (1967).
4. Misuse of psychiatry in the criminal courts: Competency to stand trial, GAP report No. 89 (New York: *Group for the Advancement of Psychiatry, 1974*).
5. A psychiatric glossary, 3rd ed. (Washington, D.C.: *American Psychiatric Association, 1969*).
6. L. McGarry, Competency to stand trial and mental illness, In: *Crime and Delinquency Issues,* an NIMH monograph series, DHEW Publication No. (HSM) 73-9105 (Rockville, Md., 1972).
7. *Jackson* v. *Indiana*, 406 U.S. 715 (1972).
8. A.J. Robertson, *The Laws Of The Kings Of England, Edward To Henry I* (Cambridge, England: Cambridge University Press, 1925); N. Walker, Crime and Insanity In England, vol. 1, *The Historical Perspective* (Edinburgh, Scotland: Edinburgh University Press, 1968).
9. An excellent review and analysis of the legal commentary (incompetency to stand trial) is to be found in 81 *Harv. L. Rev.* 454-473 (1967).
10. *Dusky* v. *United States* 362 U.S. 405 (1960) (per curiam).
11. S. Brakel and R. Rock, *The Mentally Disabled And The Law* (Chicago: University of Chicago Press, 1971).
12. *Commonwealth* v. *Harrison* 342 Mass 279, 173 N.E.2d 87 (1961).
13. *State* v. *Bruntlett* 36 N.W.2d 450, 240 Iowa 338 (1949).
14. Model penal code (proposed official draft, 1962), sec. 4.04, comment (tentative draft no. 4, 1955).
15. Leavy, The mentally ill criminal defendant, 9 *Crim. L. Bull.* 197 (1973).
16. *Jackson* v. *Indiana, supra* note 7.
17. *Id.* at 738.
18. L. McGarry, *supra* note 6.
19. R. Rock, *et al., Hospitalization And Discharge Of The Mentally Ill* (Chicago: University of Chicago Press, 1968), p. 87.
20. GAP Report No. 89, *supra* note 4.
21. *Id.*
22. J.P. Acher, R. Guzman and T.H. Lewin, *Psychiatric Evaluation In Criminal Cases* (Ann Arbor: Mich., Department of Mental Health, March 1967).
23. The Bail Reform Act, 18 U.S.C. sec 3141-52 (1970).
24. See, e.g., *Stack* v. *Boyle,* 342 U.S. 1, 4 (1951); *Carlson* v. *Landon* 342 U.S. 534, 545 (1951) (Black and Frankfurter, JJ., dissenting).
25. Mitchell, Bail reform and the constitutionality of pre-trial detention, 55 *U. Va. L. Rev.* 1223 (1969); Foote, The coming constitutional crisis in bail, 113 *U. Pa. L. Rev.* 955 (1961).
26. *See* sources cited in Kaufman, Evaluating competency; are constitutional deprivations necessary? 10 *Am. Crim. L. Rev.* 465, 471 (1972).

27. *See* 18 U.S.C. sec. 4244; Kaufman, *supra* note 26 at 471-472 and notes 24-25.
28. GAP report No. 89, *supra* note 4.
29. See, e.g., *Stack* v. *Boyle, supra* note 24 at 5-6. *Ackies* v. *Purdy*, 322 F. Supp. 38, 41 (S.D. Fla. 1970), citing *Gannis* v. *Ordean*, 234 U.S. 385, 394 (1914).
30. *Marcey* v. *Harris* 400 F.2d 772 (D.C. Cir. 1969).
31. 18 U.S.C. sec. 3146, *et seq.* (1970).
32. L. McGarry, *supra* note 6 at 73-76.
33. P.L. Scheidemandel and C.K. Kanno, The mentally ill offender: A survey of treatment programs (Washington, D.C.: Joint Information Service, APA-NIMH, 1966).
34. *See Covington* v. *Harris*, 419 F. 2d 617, 623 (D.C. Cir. 1969); *United States* v. *Klein*, 364 F.2d 657, 660 (D.C. Cir. 1966).
35. *See* Shah, The mentally disordered offender, in R.C. Allen, E.Z. Ferster and J.G. Rubin, *Readings In Law And Psychiatry* (Baltimore: Johns Hopkins Press, 1968) pp. 347, 349.
36. L. McGarry, *supra* note 6.
37. *See* S. Brakel and R. Rock, *The Mentally Disabled And The Law* (Chicago: University of Chicago Press, 1971) table 11.2.
38. *See* Settle and Oppegard, The pre-trial examination of Federal defendants, 35 F.R.D. 475, 479-481 (1964).
39. Lipsitt, Lelos, and McGarry, Competency for trial: A screening instrument, 128 *Am. J. Psychiat. 105* (1971).
40. A.R. Matthews, *Mental Disability And The Criminal Law: A Field Study* (Chicago: American Bar Foundation, 1970).
41. Leavy, *supra* note 15 at 217-218.
42. McGarry, *supra* note 6; Bukatman, Foy, and Degrazia, What is competency to stand trial? 127 *Am. J. Psychiat.* 1225-1229 (1971); A. Robey, Criteria for competency to stand trial, Presented at the 121st annual meeting of the American Psychiatric Association, 1965.
43. *See*, Kaufman, *supra* note 26 at 491 and n. 107, 495.
44. See, e.g., *United States* v. *Marion*, 406 U.S. 307 (1971); *United States* v. *Ewell*, 383 U.S. 116 (1966).
45. *See*, Association of the Bar of The City of New York, Mental illness, due process, and the criminal defendant 108, 115 (1966); American Law Institute, Model Penal Code sec. 4.06 (3) (1962).
46. McGarry, *supra* note 6.
47. Brakel and Rock, *supra* note 11.
48. *Baxstrom* v. *Herold*, 383 U.S. 107 (1966).
49. *Jackson* v. *Indiana, supra* note 7 at 738.
50. *Cf.* Chapter 2 (dangerousness).
51. *State* v. *Murphy*, 56 Wash. 2d 761, 768, 355 P 2d 323, 327 (1960).
52. Acher, Guzman, and Lewin, *supra* note 22.
53. Smith, Psychiatric approaches to the mentally ill federal offender, *Ninth Circuit Sentencing Institute* 39 F.R.D. 523, 560-561 (1966).
54. *State of Louisiana* v. *Eunice Hampton* 253 La. 399, 218 So. 2d 311 (1969).
55. GAP Report No. 89, *supra* note 4.
56. *Id.*
57. *People* v. *Arville Garland*, 44 Mich. App. 243, 205 NW 2d 195 (1973).
58. Rosenhan, On being sane in insane places 13 *Santa Clara Lawyer* 379 (1973).

Chapter 13
The Insanity Defense

A mountain of scholarly work exists on this subject, and yet, as one sensible commentator noted, the annual judicial utterances of not guilty by reason of insanity are rarer than the annual incidence of poisonous snake bites in Manhattan (*1*). In New York State during the decade of the sixties there were only 11 successful cases of not guilty by reason of insanity (*2*). Despite the rarity of the tangible event the outpouring of scholarship continues. Recently, there has been a spate of critical writings suggesting the abrogation of the insanity defense (*3*). Former President Nixon proposed that the traditional insanity defenses be done away with in the Federal courts so as to curb unconscionable abuse of the insanity defense by criminals (*4*).

Why does such a rare event achieve such academic and political significance? One important answer, I believe, is that the insanity defense touches on ultimate social values and beliefs. In its application to particular cases, it purports to draw a line between those who are morally responsible and those who are not (*5*), those who are blameworthy and those who are not (*6*), those who have free will and those who do not (*7*), those who should be punished and those who should not (*8*), and those who can be deterred and those who cannot (*9*). The nature of such distinctions has every reason to claim the attention of philosophers, lawyers, behavioral scientists, theologians, and others interested in man and law. It is more difficult to understand, however, why it should so trouble those concerned with the practical problems of administering the criminal justice system.

Perhaps it is merely the possibility of such line drawing which explains why the insanity defense, although rarely invoked and less often successful, is still a political issue which inflames the public imagination. A society which feels itself increasingly unable to cope with crime might well consider such a distinction as a crack in the dike of law, order, and justice. And a society ever less able to maintain a consensus on personal values may fear the fact that, as Lord Devlin has asserted, "the concept of illness expands continually at the expense of the concept of moral responsibility" (*10*).

Rejection of the insanity defense, however, comes from all sectors of the political spectrum. It is attacked on one side because it excuses too many (*11*), and on the other because it excuses too few (*12*). One abolitionist claims that it is unfair because it is only available to the rich (*13*). Another claims it is applied only to the poor and minorities as a stigmatizing weapon of oppression (*14*). Former President Nixon is concerned that the insanity defense allows dangerous criminals to go free (*15*), while others argue that the blameless mentally ill are confined longer than criminals (*16*). Whatever their reasons, a growing list of noteworthy persons are calling for the abolition of the insanity defense: The American Psychiatric Association (*17*), Lady Barbara Wooton (*18*), Professor H. L. A. Hart (*19*), Professor Norval Morris (*20*), Dr. Thomas Szasz (*21*), former President Richard Nixon (*22*), Dr. Karl Menninger (*23*), and Chief Justice Joseph Weintraub of New Jersey (*24*).

One of the most interesting questions now being asked, particularly by Goldstein (*25*) and Morris (*26*) is: Why do we have the insanity defense? Professor Morris and Judge Weintraub seem to agree that its historic purpose has been to avoid capital punishment. History suggests that there is some truth in that theory (*27*). After all, the 18th and 19th century Anglo-American system of law had hundreds of capital offenses, and it may well be that compassion and reason together balked at condemning to death for a mild but capital crime those who were clearly mad at the time of the offense (*28*). Hadfield, whose case was one of the turning points in the English law, for example, had a serious war injury, and the jury was encouraged to feel his exposed brain before deciding whether to execute him for shooting at and missing the King (*29*).

If one examines the cases rather than the law of insanity, one develops the impression that the function of the insanity defense in the 19th century was to exclude that minimal group of criminal offenders who were by all the prevailing standards mad; that is, mad to the man on the street. Psychiatric testimony might be necessary to do it up right, but psychiatric wisdom was not essential.

Legal formulas that would define those rare persons were introduced, but history suggests that those formulas meant different things at different times, and like the psychiatric testimony they were perhaps less important for the ultimate decision than the lawyers thought. The most famous insanity decision is *M'Naghten* (*30*) but the legal test was formulated after the trial, and of course he killed the wrong man. Had he killed the Prime Minister, his fate might well have been different no matter what the psychiatrists said, or the legal test indicated. Equally, had Hadfield killed the King, instead of missing, palpating his brain might have been less convincing to the jury.

The 20th century brought the deterministic theories of psycho-analysis and sociology into the courtroom. Efforts were made to expand the concept, broader legal tests of insanity were called for and at last arrived in full measure in the *Durham* test (*31*).

Why was the gigantic step taken? Was it because Judge David Bazelon, who announced it, had an interest in psychiatry and psychoanalysis? Certainly that is true, but the legal test of insanity was being stretched in various ways in jurisdictions all over the country (*32*).

Judge Bazelon has in retrospect suggested that his reason for expanding the test was to let the psychiatrist come into court and explain to the jury, that microcosm of the community, how this person came to commit this offense. That is, the psychiatric profession was to be given the widest possible scope for injecting their "causal" wisdom into the court's deliberation. But a painful series of Bazelon (*32*) decisions make it clear how little wisdom was thus afforded. It is too easy to suggest that this was because the particular psychiatrists were inadequate; they may well have been. It is also easy to conclude that psychiatrists have no wisdom. I think there is a more important question, however; namely, why would the court want to understand? What difference would that make?

Justice Weintraub, in a remarkable decision, deals with psychiatric testimony which meets all of Judge Bazelon's humanistic criteria. Weintraub writes about that testimony as follows:

> Now this is interesting, and I will not quarrel with any of it. But the question is whether it has anything to do with the crime of murder. I think it does not. It seems clear to me that the psychiatric view expounded by Dr. . . is simply irreconcilable with the basic thesis of our criminal law, for while the law requires proof of an evil-meaning mind, this psychiatric thesis denies there is any such thing (*34*).

Chief Justice Weintraub is quite right; indeed, none of the social or behavioral sciences of the 20th century have a theory of an evil-meaning mind (*35*). Freud, 50 years ago, recognized that a psychoanalyst could not generate a theory of responsibility. He wrote:

> The physician will leave it to the jurist to construct for social purposes a responsibility that is artificially limited to the (psychoanalytic construct of the ego). It is notorious that the greatest difficulties are encountered by the

attempts to derive from (the psychoanalytic constructs) practical consequences which are not in contradiction to human feelings (*36*).

Human feeling demands that people be held responsible for their acts. Freud thus anticipates former President Nixon's reaction to an expanded insanity defense. Nor have the jurists been able to construct anything better than the good Dr. Freud. Indeed, the limited function of the insanity defense over the centuries reflects those human feelings. Dean Abraham Goldstein of Yale Law School, author of a marvelous analysis of the insanity defense, reaches a similar conclusion:

> The real problem has been to find a formula that keeps the exception closely attuned to what the public can accept (*37*).

Professor Joseph Goldstein, in a remarkably bitter attack (*38*) on the Brawner decision (*39*), which terminated the expanded insanity defense of *Durham*, reiterates his view that:

> Neither legislative report, nor judicial opinion, nor scholarly comment criticizing or proposing formulations of the insanity defense has faced the crucial question: What is the purpose of the defense in the criminal process? or: What need for an exception to criminal liability is being met and what objectives of the criminal law are being reinforced by the defense? (*40*).

I am quite sure that many authors (Wooton (*41*), Hart (*42*), Szasz (*43*), and others), believe they have answered those questions, and one can only conclude that Goldstein finds their answers unsatisfactory. His own recommendations are, as Dershowitz points out (*44*), compatible with former President Nixon's; both believe that the findings which lead to an insanity defense should aim instead at the traditional requisite legal elements of the crime; e.g., specific intent (*45*). Former President Nixon presumably believes that will lead to less abuse, less going scot-free. Professor Goldstein believes that it would and should lead to more people for the first time going scot-free; i.e., the result would be the same as in a successful defense of self-defense (*46*). Professor Goldstein emphasizes that a finding of insanity now leads to involuntary confinement and is retributive (*47*).

My own answer to Professor Goldstein's questions is that they are misdirected. The insanity defense is critical only to the criminal law itself. Its purpose is to insure that the criminal law has moral authority.

The Brawner court states the basic premise as follows:

> The concept of "belief in freedom of the human will and a consequent ability and duty of the normal individual to choose between good and evil" is a core concept that is "universal and persistent in mature systems of law" (*Morrissette* v. *U.S.* 342 U.S. 246, 250, 1952). Criminal responsibility is assessed when through "free will" a man elects to do evil (*48*).

And a few sentences later: "The concept of lack of 'free will' is both the root of origin of the insanity defense and the line of its growth" (*49*).

Professor Goldstein, commenting on this section of the Brawner decision, states: "The court mistakenly equates the proposal to abolish the insanity defense with a proposal to eliminate free will . . . "(*50*). But the court may be inadvertently closer to the truth than is Professor Goldstein. The Brawner court recognizes that the criminal law stands or falls on the premise of free will. But what is a court to do when it confronts a case so bizarre and so incongruous that all the premises of criminal law, including free will, seem inappropriate? Should the court simply grit its teeth and go on? The court is then in that ludicrous position of the American tourist who assumes that if he speaks English loud enough, the foreigners will understand him. If so, the criminal law risks demeaning itself, risks demonstrating that its language is not universal, its moral comprehension not encompassing. How much wiser for the criminal law instead to have an escape hatch, not only to avoid embarrassment, but also because by obverse implication every other defendant does have free will. Thus, the insanity defense is in every sense the exception that proves the rule. It allows the court to treat every other defendant as someone who chose "between good and evil."

The basic problem in criminal law has been to keep the insanity defense an exception in the face of the determinist ideology which dominates the intellectual tradition of the 20th century. The sociology of crime and delinquency may be deterministic, the behaviorism which monopolizes the field of correction may be deterministic, but the criminal law is not. Those who have tried to expand the insanity defense forced the criminal law to confront its ideological isolation. Judge Weintraub recognized that fact in the decision quoted earlier. He wrote:

> The law's conception, resting as it does upon an undemonstrable view of man, is of course vulnerable. But those who attack it cannot offer a view which is demonstrably more authentic. They can tear down the edifice, but have nothing better to replace it (*51*).

The importance of the insanity defense is that it is an ideological battleground, but it takes some deciphering to identify which side the combatants are on. Former President Nixon and Professor Goldstein seem to be pointing in the same direction when they question the need for a separate insanity defense. But the former hopes to exclude determinist ideology by getting rid of the insanity defense where that offensive ideology intrudes, while the latter wants to free the determinist ideology from the limiting constraints of the insanity defense and allow it to wash over the entire criminal law.

It is important to consider what the goals of this ideological struggle are. Judge Bazelon is the jurist who comes closest to answering that question for the determinists. In *Brawner* he wrote that the jury should be instructed that: "A defendant is not responsible if at the time of his unlawful conduct his mental or emotional processes or behavior controls were impaired to such an extent that he cannot justly be held responsible for his act (*52*).

Here as elsewhere in Judge Bazelon's writings (*53*) it seems that the goal is to transform the trial into a morality play in which the community (the jury) rediscovers the meaning of justice. Justice Weintraub and others believe it would seem that justice resides in the existing system.

Psychiatric Participation in the Insanity Defense

The two sides of this argument are reflected in many opposing opinions written by Judge Bazelon and then Judge, now Chief Justice Burger of the Supreme Court. There is, however, an entirely different and practical problem which has led to confusion and led these worthies to argue about other problems of the insanity defense; namely, the medical model of illness and the role of the psychiatrist. The psychiatrist, or in his earlier incarnation, the alienist, was traditionally asked by the court to determine (a) whether the defendant was mentally ill and (b) whether that mental illness was such that the defendant lacked criminal responsibility.

Historically the answer to the first question was thought by the psychiatrists to be affirmative if the defendant was psychotic. Although witnesses are capable of disagreeing about whether a given defendant is or is not psychotic, those disagreements are not directly predicated on the degree of the experts' adherence to determinism. The answer to the second question, however, asks the psychiatrist to construct a relationship between a diagnosis and the thoughts and behavior which accompanied it. That relationship does touch on causal theories and therefore the psychiatrist knowingly or not will introduce his own version of determinism.

Many psychiatrists, however, compressed these two questions. Thus, if the answer to the first was psychotic, the answer to the second was not responsible and if not psychotic, then responsible. That compression again led to considerable dissatisfaction from both sides, the traditionalists arguing that someone could be psychotic, but criminally responsible, and the expansionists arguing that there were nonpsychotic defendants who should be found not guilty by reason of insanity. It is important to realize that both sides were asking the witness to embark on causal explanations which would inevitably rest on deterministic assumptions repugnant to criminal law.

Judge Bazelon's *Durham* decision was read by psychiatrists as they had read the earlier legal tests except that they felt they were no longer confined to an initial diagnosis of psychosis. *Durham* states: "An accused is not criminally responsible if this unlawful act was the product of mental disease or mental defect" (*54*).

Unfortunately, the *Durham* decision failed to define mental disease or defect, and in the current state of the psychiatric art it is rare that any criminal defendant examined by a psychiatrist will escape being labeled with some diagnosis.

The question immediately arose: Does any diagnosis mean the defendant has a mental disease or defect? Since most of the psychiatric testimony which comes to Judge Bazelon's court originates in Washington's St. Elizabeth's Hospital, it fell first to that psychiatric staff (or so they thought) to cope with this problem. Their first solution was apparently similar to the administrative practice utilized in the Armed Forces where the general policy was to consider psychoses and neuroses grounds for medical separation (mental disease or defect), and character and personality disorders grounds for nonmedical administrative separation (no mental disease or defect). This meant that the diagnosis of sociopath, listed under character disorder and a common result of psychiatric examination of accused criminals, would rule the defendant sane (*55*). This result equalled the irony of the *M'Naghten* case. The M'Naghten rule was formulated only after the trial when the judges were called on the carpet by the House of Lords. Most experts agree that M'Naghten himself did not meet the standards which bear his name. In *Durham's* case the diagnosis was sociopath, and given the subsequent interpretation, he, too, would have failed to meet the standard which bears his name.

The problem of the interpretation of the phrase mental disease or defect came to a head in the two *Blocker* cases. Blocker killed his common law wife, was tried, pleaded insanity, was diagnosed as a sociopath, found not insane, and was found guilty of murder. But less than 1 month later the St. Elizabeth's staff reversed their position and at another man's trial stated that sociopath was a mental disease or defect. Blocker's lawyer appealed on this basis and was granted a new trial. This sudden reversal of psychiatric opinion and its dramatic impact on the legal process provoked serious criticism. Judge Burger angrily stated: "These terms mean in any given case whatever the expert witnesses say they mean . . . . No rule of law can possibly be sound or workable which is dependent upon the terms of another discipline whose members are in profound disagreement about what those terms mean." Judge Burger concluded: "We tacitly conceded the power of St. Elizabeth's Hospital staff to alter drastically the scope of a rule of law by a 'week-end' change in nomenclature which was without any scientific basis." In a later decision he charged St. Elizabeth's staff with changing "its 'labels' for the purpose of bringing the maximum number of defendants under the protective umbrella" (*57*).

As I have said, Judge Bazelon hoped that at the very least *Durham's* broad definitions, if they accomplished nothing else, would allow psychiatrists latitude to tell the whole story of the patient rather than testify piecemeal within the stricter confines of the older tests.

This hope was dashed. Psychiatrists quickly responded to *Durham* by providing a conclusory diagnosis and attesting that this was in fact a mental disease or defect. The court responded to this tendency first in *Carter* v. *U.S.*, "Unexplained medical labels are not enough" (*58*). Then again, in *Lyles* v. *U.S.* (*59*), it said, "If psychiatrists are inclined to testify in medical conclusions, the lawyers should seek to elicit by examination testimony which is meaningful to the jury."

In 1962 Judge Burger warned that *Durham* was supposed "to open the inquiry to the widest possible scope of medical testimony, but in case after case we have tended to narrow the inquiry rigidly to the magic words 'disease' and 'product'" (*60*). Judge Bazelon, too, was worried and growing less and less enchanted with psychiatrists in the courtroom. In *Rollerson* v. *U.S.* he added his own warning: "The frequent failure to adequately explain and support expert psychiatric opinion threatens the administration of the insanity defense in the District of Columbia" (*61*). This warning failed to achieve what was desired, and perhaps in desperation Judge Bazelon wrote yet another decision on the subject. This time he himself composed an explanatory set of instructions to psychiatric witnesses which was to accompany all orders requiring mental examinations. These instructions were also to be read aloud in court before the first expert testified.

> As an expert witness, you may, if you wish and if you feel you can, give your opinion about whether the defendant suffered from a mental disease or defect. You may then explain how defendant's disease or defect relates to his alleged offense, that is, how the development, adaptation and functioning of defendant's behavioral processes may have influenced his conduct. This explanation should be so complete that the jury will have a basis for an informed judgment on whether the alleged crime was a "product" of his mental disease or defect. But it will not be necessary for you to express an opinion on whether the alleged crime was a "product" of a mental disease or defect and you will not be asked to do so.

> What is desired in the courtroom is the kind of opinion you would give to a family which brought one of its members to your clinic and asked for your diagnosis of his mental condition and a description of how his condition would be likely to influence his conduct. Insofar as counsel's questions permit you should testify in this manner.

Professor Goldstein suggests that nothing in fact was learned from the two decades of *Durham* because the court had never stated what it wanted to learn. Yet Judge Bazelon's decisions suggested he had hoped to learn whether psychiatry and social science could relate condition to conduct. That explanatory relationship is based not on the medical model of disease as Judge Bazelon seems to suggest, but on the deterministic causal theories of behavior current in psychiatry which have little to offer the moral decisionmaker. Jerome Hall recognized this aspect of *Durham* at the outset, he wrote . . . "the emphasis of the Durham test is on the question of causation . . . " (*63*). Psychiatry failed Judge Bazelon because like all of the social and behavioral sciences it lacks a concept of an evil-meaning mind as a cause, and I might add it also lacks a concept of what is good and right.

The legal test of insanity which replaced *Durham* was similar to that of the American Law Institute. That test and the other common tests are included as an appendix to this chapter. None of these tests solve any of the problems I have discussed; indeed, if Rita Simon, who studied jury deliberation is correct, the tests make little difference. The jury based on the human feelings Freud spoke of seems to come to its own conclusion (*63a*).

Coda

In the foregoing discussion, I have said that the insanity defense is the contradictory juncture between a deterministic modern theory of the causes of action, and an enduring free-will theory of the morality of action. I conclude that the contradiction is insoluble, because the epistemological structures rise on different foundations.

It is worth a moment, however, to examine the way some scholars have tried to seek an escape from the dilemma by another route than the insanity defense; namely, a notion of partial responsibility and a more general, more subtle mitigating defense.

Proposals to this end may be seen as occurring along a continuum. First, and least revolutionary, is what Goldstein has called the "trend toward subjective liability" (*64*). Under this notion, the defense's subjective state may mitigate both the offense charged and the sentence. For example, more than a dozen States now acknowledge partial responsibility for intoxication in murder cases; many permit proof of heat of passion, provocation, self-defense, and so on (*65*): The Model Penal Code generalizes this tendency, permitting a reduction in a homicide charge from murder to nonreckless manslaughter if "committed under the influence of extreme mental or emotional disturbance for which there is reasonable explanation or excuse" (*66*). The Code is doubly subjective in that it requires the excuse be evaluated "from the viewpoint of a person in the actor's situation under the circumstances as he believed them to be" (*67*).

But this is a situational and not a personal exculpation, and it is not a purely subjective standard in that it weighs not what the defendant did feel, but what a (normal) person in his position and his beliefs as to the facts would have felt. The effects of physical injury, drugs, or emotional grief are to be considered—but many other factors may not be. A second more radical standard along the continuum would also take into consideration the peculiar personal characteristics of the person: his intelligence, excitability, and capacity to control his acts. The so-called *Wells-Gorshen* doctrine developed in California but now embodied in a few States' statutes permits such factors to be considered and to result in a finding of partial responsibility—but only insofar as they negate the "capacity

227

of the accused to form the specific intent essential to constitute a crime (*68*). Or, as the Model Penal Code puts it, as "relevant to prove the defendant did or did not have a state of mind which is an essential element of the offense" (*69*).

If one examines these two formulas in the context of my dualistic analysis, it is as though they seek to balance deterministic data against free will in a special sense. Deterministic data are to be used not to explain why he did it but why his free will was compromised.

A third, still more radical model of partial responsibility could be posed. It would be extremely eclectic as to its factual triggers or sources and subtle or graded as to its results. That is to say, the jury could seek to mitigate punishments for persons on the basis of any number of factors which predisposed them to commit antisocial acts, reduced their capacity to conform their behavior, or made them less blameworthy. Mitigation might be appropriate not only for those with mental disorders, impaired behavior controls, but also for those who were reared in subgroups of different morals, or who had hostile or abusive parents, etc.

Whether or not it would be a moral achievement for the legal system to accommodate itself to a coherent doctrine of diminished responsibility based on all relevant grounds, it seems a distant possibility. So we are returned to the criterion of mental illness as one which, if not ethically or scientifically unique as a determinant of behavior, is at least one with a tradition of recognition and some popular sense of legitimacy.

Appendix: The Major Variants of the Insanity Defense

1. *The M'Naghten Test*

> (*Daniel M'Naghten's* Case, 10 C.&F. 200,210-211, 8 Eng. Rep. 718,722-723 [1843]).

> Every man is to be presumed to be sane, and ... to establish a defense on the ground of insanity, it must be clearly proved that, at the time of the committing of the act, the party accused was labouring under such a defect of reason, from disease of the mind, as not to know the nature and quality of the act he was doing; or if he did know it, that he did not know he was doing what was wrong.

This is now the sole test in fewer than half the States, but is one of the standards in most jurisdictions.

2. *The Irresistible Impulse Test*

> A. (*Parsons* v. *State*, 2 So. 854, 866-67 [Ala. 1887]).
>
> Did he know right from wrong, as applied to the particular act in question? . . . . If he did have such knowledge, he may nevertheless not be legally responsible if the two following conditions concur: (1) If, by reason of the duress of such mental disease, he had so far lost the power to choose between the right and wrong, and to avoid doing the act in question, as that his free agency was at the time destroyed; (2) and if, at the same time, the alleged crime was so connected with such mental disease, in the relation of cause and effect, as to have been the product of it solely. (Note: Most jurisdictions drop the key word "solely" from this formulation.)
>
> B. (*Davis* v. *United States*, 165 U.S. 373, 378 [1897] [The Federal Rule]).
>
> (The accused is to be classed as insane if) though conscious of (the nature of his act) and able to distinguish right from wrong, . . . yet his will, by which I mean the governing power of his mind, has been otherwise than voluntarily so completely destroyed that his actions are not subject to it, but are beyond his control.

The irresistible impulse test is nowhere relied on as the sole test, and has been rejected by 22 States, England, and Canada. However, it is used in conjunction with the M'Naghten test in an increasing number of jurisdictions, now about 15.

3. *The Durham Test*

> (*Durham* v. *United States*, 214 F. 2D862, 874-875. [D.C. Cir. 1954]).
>
> An accused is not criminally responsible if his unlawful act was the product of mental disease or mental defect . . . We use 'disease' in the sense of a condition which is considered capable of either improving or deteriorating. We use 'defect' in the sense of a condition which is not considered capable of either improving or deteriorating and which may be either congenital, or the result of injury, or the residual effect of a physical or mental disease.

The *Durham* rule, which originated in the Court of Appeals for the District of Columbia, has since been specifically rejected there. *United States* v. *Brawner*, 471 F. 2d 969 (D.C. Cir. 1972). It has, however, been adopted by statute in Maine and the Virgin Islands.

The New Hampshire test most resembles *Durham*, but its basic intent is to allow the jury to formulate the insanity standard.

4. *The American Law Institute (ALI) Test*

(American Law Institute, Model Penal Code, Proposed Official Draft sec.4.01 [1962] [First presented in 1955]).

1. A person is not responsible for criminal conduct if at the time of such conduct as a result of mental disease or defect he lacks substantial capacity either to appreciate the criminality of his conduct or to conform his conduct to the requirements of law.

2. As noted in the Article, the terms "mental disease or defect" do not include an abnormality manifested only by repeated criminal or otherwise antisocial conduct.

As of 1971, the ALI test has been adopted by statute in seven States, and by decision in three more. On the Federal level, six circuit courts of appeal have adopted the test as is, and two others have made minor modifications.

References

1. Cohen, Review of A. Goldstein, Insanity defense, 13 *Contemp. Psych.* 386 (1968).
2. N.Y.U. Colloquium, 1 *J. Psychiat. and Law* 297 (1973).
3. H.L.A. Hart, *The Morality Of The Criminal Law*, (Jerusalem: Magnes Press, 1964); T.S. Szasz, *Law, Liberty And Psychiatry* (New York: The Macmillan Co., 1963); S.L. Halleck, *Psychiatry And The Dilemmas Of Crime* (New York: Harper and Row, 1967).
4. Dershowitz, Abolishing the insanity defense: The most significant feature of the administrations proposed criminal code–an essay, 9 *Crim. L. Bull.* 435 (1973).
5. Hart, *supra* note 3.
6. *Durham* v. *U.S.*, 214 F.2d 862, 876 (D.C. Cir. 1954).
7. *Brawner* v. *U.S.*, 471 F.2d 969 (D.C. Cir. 1972).
8. Royal Commission on Capital Punishment 1949-53, report CMD No. 8932 at 98 (1953).
9. *The King* v. *Porter*, 55 *Commw. L. Rev.* 182, 186 (Austl. 1936).
10. P. Devlin, *The Enforcement Of Morals* (London: Oxford University Press, 1959), p. 17.
11. Dershowitz, *supra* note 4.
12. Criminal responsibility and psychiatric expert testimony, Group for the Advancement of Psychiatry, Report 5, 1954; Waelder, Psychiatry and the problem of criminal responsibility, 101 *U. Pa. L. Rev.* 378 (1952).
13. Halleck, *supra* note 3.
14. T. Szasz, *Psychiatric Justice* New York: Macmillan Co., 1965).
15. Dershowitz, *supra* note 4.
16. Katz and Goldstein, Abolish the insanity defense–why not? 72 *Yale L. J.* 853 (1963).
17. This is their fall-back position in their amicus brief in *Brawner*. Cited in: Stone, Law and Psychiatry, 1 *Psychiatric Annals* 22 (1971).
18. B. Wootton, *Crime And The Criminal Law* (London: Stevens and Sons, 1963).
19. Hart, *supra* note 3.
20. Morris, The dangerous criminal, 41 *So. Cal. L. Rev.* 514 (1968).
21. Szasz, *supra* note 3.
22. Dershowitz, *supra* note 4.
23. K. Menninger, *The Crime Of Punishment* (New York: Viking Compass, 1968).
24. Weintraub, *Annual Judicial Conference*, 37 F.R.D. 365 (1964).
25. Goldstein, The Brawner rule, 1973 *Washington U. L. Q. 126.*
26. *Morris, supra* note 20.
27. N. Walker, *Crime And Insanity In England*, Vol. I (Edinburgh: Edinburgh University Press, 1968).
28. *Cf.* Consultant's report on criminal responsibility, section 503, p. 251, Working papers of the national commission on reform of Federal criminal laws, 1970, U.S. Government Printing Office, Wash., D.C.
29. Walker, *supra* note 27.
30. *Id.*

31. *Durham* v. *U.S.*, 214 F2d 862 (D.C. Cir. 1954).
32. A. Goldstein, *The Insanity Defense* (New Haven: Yale University Press, 1967).
33. Stone, *supra* note 17.
34. J. Katz, J. Goldstein, and A. Dershowitz, *Psychoanalysis, Psychiatry And Law* (New York: Free Press, 1967), p. 362.
35. Consultant's report on criminal responsibility, *supra* note 28.
36. S. Freud, *Moral Responsibility For The Content Of Dreams* (1923) (London: Hogarth Press, 1961) Standard ed.
37. Goldstein, *supra* note 32 at 90.
38. Goldstein, *supra*, note 25.
39. *Brawner* v. *U.S.*, *supra*, note 7, at 986.
40. Goldstein, *supra*, note 25 at 127.
41. Wootton, *supra*, note 18.
42. Hart, *supra*, note 3.
43. Szasz, *supra*, note 3.
44. Dershowitz, *supra*, note 4.
45. Consultant's Report, *supra*, note 28.
46. Goldstein, *supra*, note 25.
47. Katz and Goldstein, *supra*, note 16.
48. *Brawner* v. *U.S.*, *supra*, note 7, at 985.
49. *Id.*, at 986.
50. Goldstein, *supra*, note 25.
51. Katz Et Al., *supra*, note 34 at 362.
52. *Brawner* v. *U.S.*, *supra*, note 7, at 1032.
53. Stone, *supra*, note 17.
54. *Durham* v. *U.S.*, *supra*, note 6 at 874, 875.
55. Cf., *Briscoe* v. *U.S.*, 248 F2d 640, 644 n.6 (D.C. Cir. 1957).
56. *Blocker* v. *U.S.*, 288 F2d 853, 859-861 (D.C. Cir. 1961).
57. *Campbell* v. *U.S.*, 307 F2d 597, 612 (D.C. Cir. 1962).
58. *Carter* v. *U.S.*, 252 F2d 608, 615 (D.C. Cir. 1957).
59. *Lyles* v. *U.S.*, 254 F2d 725 (D.C. Cir. 1957).
60. *Frigillana* v. *U.S.*, 302 F2d 670 (D.C. Cir. 1962).
61. *Rollerson* v. *U.S.*, 343 F2d 269, 272 (D.C. Cir. 1964).
62. Appendix to *Washington* v. *U.S.*, 390 F2d 457 (1967).
63. Hall, Psychiatry and criminal responsibility, 65 *Yale L. J.* 761, 780 (1956).
63a. R. Simon, *The Jury And The Defense Of Insanity* Boston: Little, Brown, 1967).
64. Goldstein, *supra*, note 32 at 191.
65. *Id.*, at 194-199.
66. American Law Institute Model Penal Code sec. 201.3, Tent. Draft No. 9 (1959).
67. *Id.*
68. *See, People* v. *Wells*, 202 P2d 53, 62-63 (Cal. 1949) *cert. denied* 337 U.S. 919; *People* v. *Gorshen*, 336 P2d 492, 503 (Cal. 1959).
69. ALI Model Penal Code, *supra*, note 66.

Chapter 14

Lawyers in the Mental Health System

The role of lawyers in the mental health system has long been an uneasy one. Those attorneys who have anything to do with the problems of the committed mentally ill are a small and lonely band at the poor periphery of the practice. The attorney is often uncomfortable in a context where the competing legal interest of his client and the opponent are not clearly defined. The State purports to be operating as parens patriae. If he accepts this simplified myth, the lawyer may do his client a disservice. If he rejects it outright and treats the proceedings as purely adversarial, he will likely antagonize the psychiatrists and perhaps the court, possibly upset his client, and even prevent the ministration of needed treatment. And in negotiating his way between the Scylla of abdication and the Charybdis of overreaction, the attorney has few professional bearings. Surely the analytic data of the law—rights, damages, agreement, case law, statutory wording, and legislative intent—are either irrelevant here or only weakly applicable. The typical statutes are open-ended, the legislative intent vague, and the case law, until quite recently, so limited, routinized, and unilluminating that even the Supreme Court has commented upon it (1). And the classic legal considerations are supplanted by notions of mental illness, competency, dangerousness, and treatability which are themselves formidably metaphysical and as to which the average attorney is unschooled.

The attorney's discomfort is augmented by the other participants—the client who may be strange, emotionally demanding, or uncommunicative, the family which may urge commitment but be ambivalent, the psychiatrist who is increasingly defensive and often obscure, the judge who is impatient and reinforces the feeling that this is not a proceedings worthy of much time or deliberation (2). And the attorney may come to agree, if the family does not want the person at home and the much lauded alternative treatment facilities simply are not available. One commentator who has studied the performance of counsel in such cases sums up their dilemma thus:

> The lawyer involved in a civil commitment case has no
> tradition to rely on, develops no expertise in this area

because of a limited number of appearances, has little in his professional training to prepare him for this role, and has no source to consult for guidance; . . . the attorney representing a proposed patient appears to sense the distinction between a civil commitment case and a criminal case, but seems unable to uncover the operational criteria based on the difference (3).

The sketch I have drawn is a composite collage of many of the difficulties of the system, and it may be extreme in the sense that a condensed bad dream is. And some of these problems may be less perplexing to the experienced legal aid worker or attorneys, what will hence be called the mental health bar. But in a sense the role-dilemmas facing the lawyer specializing in mental health are even more profound. I will discuss later in this chapter the vague and tortured application of the Code of Professional Responsibility to the emerging specialists in the mental health bar; but the basic conclusion one must reach is that such lawyers are performing functions as to which the traditional tenets of legal practice provide little guidance.

As I have seen it, the mental health lawyer can adopt two basic approaches to his work: that of the narrowly dedicated adversary for his client, or that of the committed ideologue crusading against inert megainstitutions (4). A third possibility, the neutral servant of the court, which has traditionally been the stance of sometime-appointed counsel (5), has increasingly been made untenable by awareness of the execrable conditions of most State mental institutions. Few if any regularly practicing members of the mental health bar believe it to be more than illusory. Each of the two plausible approaches for the mental health lawyer entails grave difficulties both as to the integrity of his role, and its systemic ramifications.

The basic problem with the concerted adversary stance is that the current mental health system provides neither the dense matrix of articulated policy principles and legal rule which adversarial resolution of disputes requires, nor a counterpart adversary for hospitalization. The record of careless, routinized commitment has largely been compiled without the participation of either experienced and skeptical defense counsel or hard-nosed prosecutors.

The few available studies and the reports of my former students indicate that both in commitment and after hospitalization, in habeas corpus proceedings for release, the presence of determined defense counsel has an overwhelming effect on the outcome (6). Indeed, it is my judgment that the psychiatric community, insofar as they are proponents of therapeutic hospitalization and see themselves as doing good with limited resources, are particularly apt simply to "cave in" when faced by hostile counsel.

It is just too damaging to the altruistic self-image of the psychiatrist to be cast as the coercive agent of the State and jailor of the helpless. Obviously his predictions of dangerousness cannot be validated, and if reforms of the commitment statutes move as they have been toward dangerousness as the central criterion, then the psychiatric witness will easily be discredited. The psychiatric profession will abandon the effort to confine patients involuntarily in the face of what they experience as harassment. Indeed, the talk is already of "patients who kill and die with their civil rights on."

The result of this, and whatever review procedures require psychiatrists to justify continued confinement, will gradually be to make involuntary confinement of the mentally ill almost impossible. Now, as is clear from my comments in other sections, this is a result I welcome to some degree. Indeed, if the dedicated adversary is operating in a jurisdiction where treatment is a myth, his role of advocacy will often be wholly proper. His dilemma arises only when he himself believes his client-patient is dangerous and he knows that there is no one to argue the other side. He is in fact the sole decisionmaker, and if he fulfills his traditional role he can be content as a "legalist," but surely not as a morally responsible human being.

These decisions become even more troubling when the concerted adversary knows that good treatment is available which would benefit a client he believes to be sick and dangerous. Some argue that even in this situation the lawyer should stick to his guns and fulfill the role of advocate for his client. I disagree. In my view there is an obligation in these situations to transcend the narrow role rather than to hide behind it.

But before that crunch has arrived, there is much that a lawyer can do to avoid it. He can investigate treatment alternatives and explore whether acceptable treatment will be provided in a timely fashion. If it will be, he should attempt to convince his client of the wisdom of accepting treatment voluntarily. A persuasive lawyer might be able to convince a person who cannot be convinced by a psychiatrist. In short, a lawyer should do all the things he normally does before he goes to court: investigate, inform, advise, and get to know his client and his client's interests. Some lawyers claim they lack the expertise to fulfill these functions, but given the medical expertise developed by the bar in the malpractice area, this is unconvincing.

If the lawyer has done all this and his client remains adamant in his demands, it is my view that he should withdraw from the case;

the role of adversary in the civil commitment context does not require a lawyer to behave irresponsibly. This situation should rarely occur; first, because few such clients will in fact be dangerous, and second, because most of the mentally ill will come to accept treatment voluntarily if they are treated decently.

The more common dilemma that faces the lawyer, though less fraught with peril, is no less poignant: namely, what should be his role with the harmless but sick client who refuses treatment for irrational reasons. I shall return to that later.

The second and broader role for the mental health lawyer is less problematic. It starts from the premise that megainstitutional treatment is bad, and it attacks the warehousing system not primarily through defense of a given individual (what we may call the micro level), but rather by bringing landmark individual or class action suits (the macro level). I welcome these battles, but it is doubtful the war can be won without the help of the legislature. Even if the procedural safeguards of the criminal process are extended to mental patients, if the criteria for commitment are made more strenuous, if the right to treatment upgrades care, and if periodic review expedites release, there will remain a paucity of family and community resources to help the mentally ill.

A recent suit against St. Elizabeth's Hospital in the District of Columbia attempts to forge a legal remedy for this growing problem. In effect, it is trying to force St. Elizabeth's and the officials of the District to deinstitutionalize those who do not need total care, and to provide less restrictive adequate alternatives. The lawyers bringing this suit feel it is justified both by the statute which includes a promise of less restrictive alternatives and by the Constitution (7).

If the spell and power of warehouse psychiatry are broken without adequate treatment alternatives, the criminal process may exercise its less genteel dominion over many of these people (8). Or there may simply be a painful void. Some would prefer that to what exists. But *the question is whether there are not vital new roles which lawyers are uniquely able to play, which may make that void a creative social space.* Ironically, if the quality of institutional treatment does markedly improve, the mental health bar will really face its dilemma. If alternative dispositions really do matter, the role of the attorney as decisionmaker-by-abdication will grow increasingly complex.

Later in this chapter I will discuss at greater length this impending dilemma, which has been referred to as an existential crisis for the mental health lawyer (9). By that characterization, I intend to indicate that it will call for a reevaluation not only of his professional acts or performances, but of his human relation to his clients and to the system. But before delving into that problem, it is worth taking a close look at two recent developments which have created expanded, if traditional, roles for attorneys: the ombudsman and New York's Mental Health Information Service.

The Ombudsman

During the past 6 or 7 years, the ombudsman concept has become the rage of bureaucratic decisionmaking theory. The interest in this Scandinavian invention is attributable to a number of factors, prime among them being the belief that the ombudsman is able to link individual citizens to an ever more distant and unfathomable array of government agencies. Such linkage is politically stabilizing and protective for the organs of government reduces inadvertent abuses and inefficiencies, and permits the feedback necessary to assure that the legislative will is being worked in the real world (10). Thus, ombudsmen have taken their places in business, schools, government organizations, and now hospitals. But in light of all three basic purposes of the ombudsman function cited, it seems especially necessary to the welfare-service providing agencies such as mental hospitals.

Prototypically, the ombudsman is an administrative critic who solicits and investigates grievances within an organization or system, and seeks to remedy the malfunctions which produce those grievances. It should be noted that a major American variation from the European model is that whereas the latter has been a life-tenured civil servant with. ties to all parts of government and roving authority as to all government acts (a "man for all issues"), the American ombudsman has generally been appointed for a limited tenure by, and for the purposes of serving one particular government agency.

The ombudsman's efficacy requires that he possess both persuasive power within the organization and access to external power sources (higher administrative channels, courts, the legislature, public opinion, etc.). Thus, he is both a mediator between power centers or interests and an independent source of power himself. He must be a skilled but forceful handler of the interplay of forces. His power within the organization requires that he be viewed as an insider who understands its problems, yet who has external power which makes him respected and enables him to get things done. Thus his personal prestige, manner of appointment (whether by legislature, executive, etc.), and tenure are vital. Conversely, his ability to invoke external government aid or force will depend to some degree on whether he is sufficiently an insider that his information on organizational performance can be relied on and his mandate obeyed. In a real sense, however, the true raison d'etre and duty of the ombudsman relates to a third constituency—the public— which must view him as accessible, independent, honest, and prestigious enough to encourage their bringing their grievance to him.

In light of these conceptual propositions, what then could be the constructive role of an ombudsman within the mental health system? Given the mediating, negotiating, quasi-governmental nature of the ombudsman role, it has been natural to assume that lawyers would often fill it. Is this a proper conclusion, and is there, thus, a powerful new role of the lawyer in the system?

A suggestive response (if not quite an answer) to these questions is posed by a unique ombudsman project conducted by the Catholic University Law and Psychiatry group in St. Elizabeth's Hospital during 1969-70 (11). The study, which was sponsored by the National Insitute of Mental Health and reported by Professor Broderick, concentrated on John Howard Pavilion, the maximum security section of the hospital. A previous 2½ year study by the same group had first identified the primary grievances of the patients. Not surprisingly, although the stated purpose of the project was to provide legal or other assistance to patients on matters not relating to the validity or duration of their confinement, release from the hospital came to dominate both the patients' grievances, and hence the project's concern (12).

The project installed itself as an ombudsman office manned by attorneys (and aided by others) right on the ward. First, it conducted a thorough review of the hospital's operating regulations, intake, and outgo procedures. It later sought to uncover patient grievances by studying hospital records and interviewing patients, and it investigated complaints which were brought to it. The ombudsman office always attempted to solve grievances within the hospital framework by negotiating with staff, patients, family, etc. Only when this failed did the project refer the matter to outside counsel. The ombudsman-project attorneys then played no part whatsoever in the conduct of any ensuing litigation.

The reported results of the project are as follows:

1. *Litigation.* The project staff summarized their conclusions thus:

> Although we later compiled extensive statistics from the hosptial records, engaged in large scale interviewing of patients and staff, and maintained contact with outside

agencies concerning patients' problems, the project's
chief fruits were derived from the progress of the court
cases (13).

Thus, as put by that commentator, in a narrow, direct sense the
ombudsman was a failure. But that is true only if its purpose
is conceived to be that of avoiding the resort to coercive power to
reform hospital practices. However, this is, in my view, too limited
a view of the ombudsman's role. His purpose is not to avoid
friction, but to minimize it while assuring patient rights and the
regularity of hospital actions; and litigation, though possibly coercive, is not war but government at work.

In one of the ombudsman-referred cases, *Dixon v. Jacobs* (14),
the District of Columbia Circuit Court criticized the sloppy recordkeeping at St. Elizabeth's, as well as the hospital's routine defense
of "failure to exhaust hospital remedies" in suits brought by
patients—when it knew that there was no really effective inhospital
grievance procedure. In other cases (15) the ombudsman team used
its influence to the fullest so as to assure due process in the transfer
of patients believed but not known to have committed antisocial
acts. The court declared that until the hospital begins to keep
adequate records of its administrative hearings, the courts will have
to conduct de novo review and ordered the hospital to institute due
process procedures for transfers. Thus, the ombudsman team may
have bequeathed processes which will avoid future grievances and
frictions. Broderick called the ombudsman one-legged, but he chose
to consider legal action a separate organic entity. I consider it the
other leg.

2. *Information.* The ombudsman study concluded that

one major contribution that an ombudsman can make is
the compiling of data that the administrator may use as a
basis for decisionmaking in place of the uneducated guess
(16).

In this light, it catalogued patient grievances and compiled statistics.

3. *Liaison with agencies.* The ombudsman project apparently
formed useful and hitherto undeveloped contacts with many government agencies which directly affect the welfare of patients.
These include: (a) NIMH — which was in effective charge of
policymaking for St. Elizabeth's; (b) the Social Security Administration — which had been erratic in disposing of patients' benefit
claims; the study also found that fewer than half of the eligible
patients had even applied to SSA; (c) the juvenile courts — which
resulted in the transfer of juveniles out of the maximum security

adult ward in which they had been illegally held, (d) the Administrative Conference of the United States — which then conducted a comprehensive study of hospital practices in a number of States; (e) the Senate Judiciary Committee — which then held hearings which will help to inform its later actions; (f) the Veterans Administration; (g) the Parole Board, and (h) the D.C. Jail.

More important even than the direct results of the study, however, is what it suggests about the potential role of the ombudsman in a large public mental hospital system. And that, in turn, is indicative of the potential roles for lawyers in this system. Among the questions which the ombudsman study helps to answer are the following:

Is the hospital ombudsman administratively feasible? The experience of the study seems to be an only slightly qualified yes. Two basic sources for administrators' initial abhorrence of the ombudsman concept were said to be (a) a misperception of his role as that of a superadministrator with plenary authority over all aspects of hospital affairs, and (b) prior bad experience with attorneys in their adversary roles.

Whether or not these criticisms arise from good faith or not, from fear, selfish institutional or professional interests, or sound administrative experience, the point is that the ombudsman, even though a lawyer, can overcome these objections. As the study progressed, it found fine cooperation from upper-level administrators, and even decreasing resistance from the lower staff who had originally felt particularly threatened. It is possible that knowing that NIMH sponsored the project, or that it would cease in a few months, encouraged cooperation. But there is also evidence that some of the staff welcomed the ombudsman as a sounding board for their own grievances as to hospital operations (*17*).

What is the ombudsman's scope of activity? The study found that there was a great tendency to become involved in litigation because of its dramatic results. This would, however, betray the ombudsman's neutral role and deprive him of any unique good he may do apart from his role as another attorney. The ombudsman should have at least investigative authority with regard to any patient complaints—whether they relate to the hospital, other government organizations (welfare benefits, etc.), the courts, or personal or family problems. Thus, the ombudsman will save other agencies time and facilitate remedies by being a first channeling agent of complaints and by alerting the responsible officers to the problem. Among his specific functions the ombudsman may: receive and investigate complaints, refer inhospital complaints to any appropriate body within the hospital, evaluate the decisions of that body and take other action if advisable, arrange for referral of matters to outside counsel where necessary, oversee and report on responses of the hospital and patients to orders or recommendations of courts or other bodies, develop and analyze data, develop and ameliorate patient contacts with family, civic groups, educational services, or any other interested and beneficial people, foster interdisciplinary exchange on matters relevant to patients, and encourage a regularized inquiry into the alternatives to hospitalization.

Who, then, should appoint the ombudsman, and what is his real constituency? A prerequisite of his successful performance in this mediating role is that the ombudsman be perceived as having personal prestige, independence, and honesty. In the study discussed here, part of the ombudsman project was supported by NIMH, then the hospital's parent governing-body. The project staff concluded that this aura of authority was of enormous help, and that in the normal case, if the ombudsman is directly appointed by the executive or legislature, he should be given a guarantee of relative personal independence and a guaranteed tenure. The staff should not view him as subject to political pressure except as a responsible official would consider such opinion.

What characteristics should be sought in designating the person to serve as ombudsman? Aside from the personal prestige and integrity already mentioned, the project concludes that there are no specific personal characteristics absolutely necessary. They believe that some lawyers, psychiatrists, and others could well serve the role. Though there is often acrimonious opposition by psychiatrists to appointment of lawyers and vice versa, the project found that both professions could agree to have some neutral officer (e.g., the Chairman of the District of Columbia Administrative Conference) choose the ombudsman.

Based on the project's analysis, I would go somewhat further. Some of the cited functions of the ombudsman (such as investigating alternatives to commitment and compiling data) could be performed as well or better by professionals other than lawyers, such as social workers, psychologists, or public health nurses. Other functions, however, (such as arranging for referral of cases, monitoring response to court decrees, and devising grievance procedures) are likely best performed by attorneys. It might be suggested that the ombudsman office encompass a number of different professionals; but the touchy position of the ombudsman requires that there be one final responsible official. So the most that can be said is that in many cases the ombudsman concept is likely to pose a valuable new role for attorneys, but one in which their traditional professional skills will be of much use.

Mental Health Information Service (MHIS)

The MHIS developed from a 2 year study of commitment laws and procedures by a special committee of the Association of the Bar of New York, composed of judges, attorneys, and psychiatrists. The New York State legislature responded in 1964 with a revision of the law. The amended law sought to establish, as one commentator put it:

> procedures . . . which could satisfy both legal and psychiatric interests—procedures which could accommodate the conflicting claims of individual liberty and protection of society, as well as insure prompt care for the sick (18).

Prior to the new law, New York had what was ostensibly a judicial commitment procedure, but what through abdication and lack of information, turned out in practice to be an unregulated process of commitment through medical certification (19). Hearings were held in less than 10 percent of the commitment cases, and even these were abridged; after commitment, the duration of confinement was almost exclusively at the discretion of the institutions. The 60-day limit on original commitment was usually extended indefinitely by certification to county clerks, usually without notice to the patient or his relatives (20).

The MHIS was intended to do more than bring some due process to the commitment area; it was intended to improve the human condition of patients and aid the courts as well (21). And while embracing the medical certification model of commitment, it did so openly and with safeguards rather than covertly, as before. Embracing the principle that prompt therapy is good therapy, the legislature enacted a medical admission procedure, but set up the MHIS to assure "organized and continuing safeguards of (the patients') rights" (22). Basically, the MHIS is required to monitor the admission and retention of involuntary patients, inform them of their rights, advise them when they seek aid on legal or institutional matters, and collect information for use by the courts in future proceedings.

Under the new law, upon the application for his commitment signed by two physicians, the proposed patient has the right to have notice sent to him, his nearest relative, up to three other persons, and the MHIS. Any of these parties may request a hearing. The hospital director then sends the patient's record to MHIS, and the court must hold a hearing within 5 days. MHIS may interview the patients' family, or others, and submits a report to the court; indeed, as to later continuations of confinement, MHIS must submit a report even if no hearing is requested. The reports must contain personal, social, and medical background, as well as any possible alternatives to hospitalization. And apart from the MHIS, New York law gives the patient a right to be represented by counsel (23), and to secure independent medical opinions. In postponing judicial review until after admission, therefore, the law merely attempts to save the courts the trouble of hearing cases which will never be contested. This, at least, is the charitable interpretation of the law (24). As one commentator has said:

> The new judicial review provision was, then, not so much an abandonment of traditional belief in the adversary process as it was a recognition . . . that due process is not always best served by providing remedies for the contentious and litigious alone (25).

The organization of the MHIS offices reflects its dual functions vis-à-vis patients and the courts: each headquarters is located at or near the courthouse of the appellate division, but branch offices are maintained in hospitals. The presiding judge of each department of the appellate division appoints the MHIS staff. Significantly, the first and second departments (primarily New York City) MHIS offices are manned almost exclusively by attorneys, while the third and fourth departments (upstate New York) are staffed by social workers. This, as I shall point out, produces interesting and different outcomes.

Given this rough sketch of the rationale and structure of the MHIS, it is worth examining the effects it has had at each stage of the commitment process, particularly with attention to the role of lawyer-functions in its performance.

Admission, initial contacts, and the hearing. The MHIS performs the vital function of personally relating to the patient his legal rights, thus minimizing the effect of illiteracy, mental state, or medication which had negated the impact of mere written notice. MHIS staff also explain the nature of proceedings where hearings and so on are to be held. They investigate alternatives to hospitalization, and compile personal histories for use by the courts.

On a purely numerical basis, the most dramatic effect of MHIS has been to reduce markedly the number of cases decided by judges on hearings as to hospitalization (26). However, this may be due to the deterrent to hearings posed by the longer potential duration of judicial commitment over certification. And there is some evidence that a negotiation process involving MHIS has resulted in a far higher rate of releases ordered by psychiatrists than court mandated releases (27). Finally, there is a widespread impression that the MHIS reports to the court have often had a dispositive effect, and have made the process better informed. And the MHIS staff has apparently resisted successfully becoming advocates (28).

Continued confinement and periodic review. A hospital must, under the new law, seek a renewed authorization for confinement at intervals of 60 days, 6 months, 1 year, and 2 years. Before the MHIS this would have been both onerous and largely illusory; the courts simply did not have enough information on the progress of the patient or the changing availability of alternatives. Now, MHIS submits relevant reports for each of these review hearings. In addition, however, MHIS attorneys represent patients in some of these hearings. Examination of their performance reveals a number of significant points.

First, the MHIS attorneys, conscious of their role as servants of the court, are not true adversary advocates of release of the patient-client. They varied in their recommendations to the court— and their posture appears to have been given great weight in the disposition (29).

Second, this incourt power has enabled the MHIS attorneys to negotiate with mental health staff so as to achieve a high rate of consented to release of patients. Alternately, they may focus the attention of the treatment staff on particular patients so that therapy is stepped-up (30).

Habeas corpus and release. The results here are quite simple: in those departments where MHIS is staffed by lawyers there are hundreds of petitions submitted, and tens of releases ordered, while in the departments staffed by social workers, there are only a very few petitions and no releases (31). And the habeas petitions have a tidal wave effect on psychiatric discharges: of petitioners who withdrew their requests before disposition, 30-40 percent were discharged.

It is extremely difficult to separate the effects of the MHIS from those of New York's new law generally. What is known is that during the first year of the new scheme discharges from State hospitals rose more than 35 percent, and are now about twice the discharge rate in 1965 (32). What we are to conclude about the role of the attorney is equally paradoxical. The MHIS lawyer has been much lauded for his functions in informing patients and negotiating matters of care and release without resort to litigation; in this sense he has been likened to an ombudsman. At the same time, he has been given the role, via abdication, by both physicians and courts of actually determining the disposition of many patients, but this conflicts with his neutral ombudsman role, as well as challenges his dedicated advocate role. Moreover, the utility of the lawyer's new roles is questioned by the fact that his traditional weapons of litigation and the threat of it seem to have been the primary motivating force in much of the change that the MHIS has effected.

The answer may simply be that MHIS must remain a troubling paradox. Its dual personal v. legal roles may best be served if each department has social workers and lawyers on the staff. The traditional legal services should be expanded to cover voluntary patients and the tangential legal problems (property, marriage, driver's license) of all patients. Those who believe in a strict adversary role are troubled that a patient is deprived of unilaterally loyal counsel by being represented by an MHIS lawyer who may be unprepared to pursue his desires. On the other hand, the mediating role of the MHIS attorney can be of use in securing treatment, arranging transfer, evaluating alternatives to confinement, and in arranging for release.

Thus, the ombudsman concept and, to an even greater degree, the MHIS brings the lawyer to the brink of a crisis of role. To the degree the lawyer accepts the position of deciding what is best for the client, he may betray his traditional legal duty to the client. And whatever the allures and special powers of that role, he is also, as emphasized in the beginning of this chapter, in peril of being made the involuntary decisionmaker.

The mental health professionals, on the other hand, are growing increasingly weary of fighting what they see as time consuming pyrrhic battles with the civil law and criminal systems. They may become increasingly willing to forego responsibility for locking up patients, be they dangerous or not, particularly if it means that they must press criminal charges themselves, as seems to be the case in New York (33). This might signal a great victory for the lawyers' traditional role of gadfly to commitment; but in his capacity as a morally responsible decisionmaker, he may remain troubled. The vast job of coordinator of the systems of mental health (hospitals and the many forms of alternative care), welfare, and the criminal law will remain. Guiding his client through this complex web of services to those that are truly helpful may be the new role for the lawyer. He will also emerge as a super-ombudsman—the only person in a position to mediate between the various systems.

The lawyers' Canons of Professional Ethics and Code of Professional Responsibility reflect the difficulties attorneys will face in these new roles. These codes are intended to be practical guides to professional life; but they are inapplicable or deficient as applied to lawyers who view themselves as neutral agents of the system, as decisionmakers, as coordinators, or even as social change agents. They provide that:

> The lawyer owes . . . entire devotion to the interest of the client . . . (*34*).
> The obligation of a lawyer to exercise professional judgment solely on behalf of his client requires that he disregard the desires of others that might impair his free judgment. The desires of a third person will seldom adversely affect a lawyer unless that person is in a position to exert strong economic, political, or social pressures . . . . These influences are often subtle and a lawyer must be alert to their existence (*35*).

> A lawyer must decline to accept direction of his professional judgment from any layman. Various types of legal aid offices are administered by boards of directors composed of lawyers and laymen. A lawyer should not accept employment from such an organization unless the board sets only broad policies and there is no interference in the relationship of the lawyer and the individual client he serves . . . . Although other innovations in the means of supplying legal counsel may develop, the responsibility of the lawyer to maintain his professional independence remains constant . . . (*36*).

These guidelines envisage a profit relation between one lawyer and one client and no competing systemic role for the lawyer (except insofar as he owes respect to the court). The attorney who would venture to perform system-mediating roles must, therefore, develop his own standards of moral and political accountability.

Even beyond this crisis of role, the future mental health attorney must face an existential crisis. That is to say two things: at the same time he is stripped free of guidelines for his conduct, he is burdened by the duty of formulating new social roles for himself; and the existence of these new professional roles depends upon a reformulation of his personal relation to the objects of his work. As Sartre has said of Proust in *Being and Nothingness:*

> (His accomplishment) is neither the work considered in isolation nor the subjective ability to produce it; it is the work considered as the totality of the manifestations of the person (*37*).

The lawyer's role is particularly an existential dilemma to the degree that he seeks to mediate between systems so as to produce a more total appreciation of and response to the problems of the mentally ill. As Sartre has said in his most recent, most socially conscious work:

> If he is to be totalized by history, what is important here is to relive his affiliations with human groups of different structures and to determine the reality of these groups, through the links that constitute them . . . . And to the extent that he personally is the living mediation between these heterogeneous groups . . . his critical experience must discover if this mediating bond is itself an expression of totalization (*38*).

Thus, the emerging roles of the mental health lawyer will require that he be willing at times to establish a closer relation with the patient—as a person and not just as a client. The lawyer may no longer be merely the aloof and secretive court-performer; he will explain to the patient, allay his fears, provide a continuing sense that someone is following his daily life in the institution, interview the family, compile information, investigate alternatives, negotiate with staff, and so on. These roles will require a complex of personal qualities and attitudes which lawyers have generally not striven to cultivate. In addition, these represent lower status roles than the lawyer may be accustomed to; this, too, may be a difficult adjustment. The existential crisis fundamentally means that the attorney must foresake the comfortable, structured hierarchy of the attorney-client relation in favor of a far more complex and shifting array of relations. There will, of course, be strong temptations to revert to traditional behavior; thus the tendency of the ombudsman project to gain most through litigation. But gradually new relations can be forged, as those who work in poverty law well know.

What, then, are the inducements for attorneys to embrace these new roles? If not money or prestige, it must be the same currency which has funded all of the other burgeoning public interest law movements thus far—a sense of purpose in mediating between society and those it extrudes. As one commentator has said:

> If the attorney fails to perform these functions, in all likelihood they will not be performed by anyone else (*39*).

The mental health bar has labored hard to halt the reign of coercive and warehouse psychiatry. It now faces the equally disheartening prospect of benevolent abandonment. Its challenge is to place itself squarely in the vacuum and to help the mental health profession fashion a mediated flexible system of care for the mentally ill. The new system must use law, but it ought not succumb to a purely legal model just when it has broken with a purely medical model. The personal-caring model must remain a vital albeit distant ideal. Thus, the emerging mental health system may need the law, but it will need enlightened lawyers even more.

References

1. *Jackson* v. *Indiana*, 406 U.S. 715, 738 (1972).
2. *Cf.* Kay *et al.*, Legal planning for the mentally retarded: The California experience, *60 Cal. L. Rev.* 438, 460-461 (1972).
3. Cohen, The function of the attorney and commitment of the mentally ill, 44 *Tex. L. Rev.* 424, 441 (1966).
4. B. Ennis, *Prisoners Of Psychiatry* (New York: Harcourt Brace, Jovanovich, Inc., 1973).
5. See, e.g., D. Martindale and E. Martindale, *Psychiatry And The Law: The Crusade Against Involuntary Hospitalization* (Chicago: Adams Press, 1973).
6. See, e.g., Cohen, supra note 3; Gupta, New York's Mental Health Information Service, 25 *Rutgers L. Rev.* 405, 426-435 (1971); Goldstein, The role of defense counsel in the criminal commitment process, 1972 *Am. Crim. L. Rev.* 409.
7. *Robinson, et al.* v. *Weinberger, et al.*, C.A. No. _____ D.D.C., filed Feb. 14, 1974.
8. *See* Abramson, The criminalization of mentally disordered behavior, 23 J. *Hosp. Comm. Psych.* 101 (1972).
9. *See* Schaffer, Introduction, symposium: Mental illness, the law and civil liberties, 13 *Santa Clara Lawyer* 369, 376 (1973).
10. *See generally*, W. Gellhorn, *Ombudsmen and Others* (Cambridge: Harvard University Press, 1966); *When Americans Complain* (Cambridge: Harvard University Press, 1966); D.C. Rowat, *The Ombudsman* (London: G. Allen and Unsin, 1968); The ombudsman or citizen's defender: A modern institution, 377 *Annals* (1969); Foegen, Ombudsman as complement to the grievance procedure, 2 *Labor L. J.* 289 (1972).
11. *See* Broderick, An institutional approach to involuntary hospitalization for mental illness, 20 *Cath. U. L. Rev.* 547 (1971); One-legged ombudsman in a mental hospital: An over the shoulder glance at an experiment, 22 *Cath. U. L. Rev.* 517 (1973) [Hereinafter cited as Broderick].
12. Broderick, *id.* at 584-85.
13. *Id.* at 534.
14. *Dixon* v. *Jacobs*, 427 F.2d 589 (D.C. Cir. 1970).
15. *See Williams* v. *Robinson*, 432 F.2d 637 (D.C. Cir. 1970); *Jones* v. *Robinson*, 440 F.2d 249 (D.C. Cir. 1971).
16. Broderick, *supra* note 11, at 558.
17. *Id.*, at 548-551.
18. Gupta, *supra*, note 6 at 409.
19. *See* Special committee to study commitment procedures of the Association of the Bar of New York, *Mental Illness And Due Process* 123 (1962).
20. *Id.*, at 170-171.
21. *See* N.Y. *Mental Hygiene Law* sec. 88 (McKinney Supp. 1966).
22. *Supra*, note 19 at 17, 22.
23. Though New York statutes merely permit appointment of counsel, *see* N.Y. *Mental Hyg. Law* sec. 88(b), N.Y. *Judiciary Law* sec. 35(1)a and (2),

court decisions have made appointment for indigents mandatory, *see People ex rel.* v. *Stanley,* 217 N.E. 2d 636 (1966); *Woodall* v. *Bigelow, 235 N.E.2d 777 (1967).*

24. The constitutionality of this aspect of the law has been upheld, *see Fhagen* v. *Miller,* 36 App. Div. 2d 926, 321 N.Y.S. 2d 61 (1st Dept. 1971). Nevertheless, there is a worthy constitutional question here, and one which was not fully confronted by the court. *See generally,* Note, The New York MHIS: A new approach to hospitalization of the mentally ill, 67 *Col. L. Rev.* 672, 682-696 (1967). However, since my primary purpose here is to consider the role of attorneys in the system rather than to criticize the prevailing law, I will not deal with this constitutional issue.

25. Gupta, *supra,* note 6 at 416.

26. *Id.* at 421.

27. *Id* at 423-425.

28. Note, *supra,* note 24 at 680.

29. Gupta, *supra,* note 6 at 437-439.

30. Rosensweig, Compulsory hospitalization of the mentally ill, 21 *Am. J. Pub. Health* 121, 123-124 (1971).

31. Gupta, *supra,* note 6 at 430.

32. *Id.* at 449.

33. See, e.g., Meyerson, Panel report: When is dangerous, dangerous, 1 *J. Psychiat. And Law* 427, 456 (1973).

34. *Canons Of Professional Ethics* No. 16.

35. *Code Of Professional Responsibility* EC-521.

36. *Id.* EC-524.

37. J. P. Sartre, *Being And Nothingness* (Barnes, trans.) (New York: The Citadel Press, 1966), XLV.

38. J.P. Sartre, *Critique De La Raison Dialectique* (Paris: Gallimard, 1960), 143.

39. Cohen, *supra,* note 3 at 455.

Chapter 15

New Liability for the Mental Health Practitioner

During the past two decades psychiatry has been a low risk profession from the perspective of legal liability. Malpractice suits, excepting those attendant to the administration of EST, were few and far between. When Dawidoff published his slender but comprehensive monograph on *The Malpractice of Psychiatrists (1)* at the beginning of the seventies he had to scrape around to find appellate cases *(2)*. Liability of psychiatrists for violating their patients' civil rights was the libertarian dream of Dr. Szasz *(3)* and was touched on only in passing by Dawidoff *(4)*. Liability of psychiatrists for monetary damages under a Section 1983 *(5)* action was not even discussed. Psychologists and social workers were almost immune from professional liability and many were uninsured.

All that has changed, and in the decade of the seventies, it seems reasonable to predict that there will be more than enough appellate cases on the liability of psychiatrists and other mental health professionals to produce a major monograph *(6)*. Central to that monograph will be the various Section 1983 actions both for money damages and for court ordered reform. These cases have become everyday grist for the mills of the federal courts. This chapter is an outline for the weighty monograph that someday will have to be written. It will attempt to describe and to some extent predict the growth of mental health liability in the decade of the seventies. That growth must be understood, of course, as part of the general pattern in medical malpractice. Thus, for example, the increasing willingness of all patients to sue their physicians and of juries to award ever larger damages means that all the conventional forms of psychiatric malpractice have increased and, as I will suggest, new forms of liability have been and are being developed. First, let me give you a sense of the old forms of psychiatric malpractice. The range of cases described by Dawidoff includes the following: psychiatric liability for negligently diagnosing medical illness as hysteria *(7)*, psychiatric liability for not properly informing a patient as to the possible side effects of EST *(8)*, psychiatric liability for leaving a suicidal patient unattended *(9)*.

These were and are the typical kinds of malpractice attributed to the psychiatric profession. Based on my own review of recent cases,

251

it would seem that patients and their families are increasingly willing to bring such law suits *(10).* For example, there seem to be more law suits claiming psychiatric negligence as a proximate cause of suicide, and here the damage awards can be quite substantial. All of the mental health professions and the institutions that employ them are also potential defendants in these cases.

Although it falls within the traditional scope of medical malpractice, psychiatrists have until recently rarely been sued for the negligent prescription of medication. It is my expectation that now enormous malpractice liability will begin to accrue over the next decade because of cases of tardive dyskinesia secondary to neuroleptic drugs. I believe that major tort suits might be possible both against the pharmaceutical houses *(11)* and against that segment of physicians who have prescribed and continue to prescribe neuroleptics without adequate consideration of deleterious side effects such as tardive dyskinesia *(12).* Based on existing law the following practices of psychiatrists might be considered negligent:

1. Prescription of neuroleptic drugs for purposes of behavioral control in institutions where the primary diagnosis of the patient is not such as to suggest that the drugs were being given for therapeutic purposes *(13).* Good examples are: the wholesale administration of neuroleptic drugs to mentally retarded patients in institutions, or to patients with character disorders in hospitals, jails, and prisons. Given the rather high incidence of tardive dyskinesia reported in the literature *(14),* these populations will generate a large number of potential law suits. Somewhat more dubious, but still a possible instance of negligence, is the prescription of neuroleptics for neurotic anxiety where the risks of tardive dyskinesia may outweight the value of the treatment *(15).* A review of the pharmaceutical houses' own literature makes it clear that they have advertised neuroleptics as a panacea, effective for every condition from masturbation to enuresis to schizophrenia, and they have over the years, it seems to me, only reluctantly limited their claims *(16).*

2. Even where the drug had been prescribed for a patient whose diagnosis would suggest it was the treatment of choice, there has been no real attempt, in the vast majority of cases, to inform patients of side effects and to obtain informed consent. Where patients are administered drugs without being informed of their possible and significant side effects, courts have found doctors negligent *(17).* Courts have also held that doctors can choose not to mention the side effects if they believe that to be deleterious to the

patient *(18)*. But it is unclear how far this excuse will stretch and whether the psychiatrist is also excused from obtaining the informed consent of the next of kin under these circumstances.

3. For some years the existence of tardive dyskinesia has been known and described in the literature *(19)*. Yet it is clear that systematic efforts have not been made to review the large chronic populations who are maintained on neuroleptics. Good practice arguably would require that all of these patients be provided drug holidays, given neurological examinations, and attempts be made to ascertain whether early and potentially reversible signs of tardive dyskinesia exist. Thus, psychiatrists may be liable for negligently failing to detect the onset of tardive dyskinesia while maintaining their patients on medication, and thus contributing to an irreversible condition. Pharmaceutic houses may also be liable for failure to notify physicians of the masking of tardive dyskinesia by large dosages, and of other dangerous aspects of neuroleptics. Patients with tardive dyskinesia are sufficiently disabled and grotesque so as to suggest to me that juries will be most sympathetic when they consider the amount of damages.

It would seem that at the very least a major and systematic campaign must be undertaken throughout the profession to educate psychiatrists to the importance of obtaining the informed consent of the patient as to the side effects of the major tranquillizers. Without some assumption of risk on the part of the patient or a responsible relative, the psychiatrist may in the future be risking liability. Psychiatrists may have already accrued such liability for their failure to do so in the past.

Another expansion of liability arises from the major changes in mental health practice and the legal regulation of involuntary hospitalization. Many more patients remain in hospitals for short periods of time and therefore more patients dangerous to themselves and others are circulating in the community. Psychiatrists and hospitals, as a consequence, are increasingly charged with liability for patients who assault, murder, and commit suicide after discharge *(20)*, or while on leave from hospitals *(21)*, or having eloped from nonsecure facilities *(22)*. As other mental health professionals assume primary care responsibility, they, too, assume this liability.

The specific responsibilities of psychotherapists as to dangerous patients was given considerable legal attention as a result of the Tarasoff case *(23)* in California. There the Supreme Court of California held that a psychotherapist had a duty to protect the public when, in the course of a therapeutic contact, the therapist became aware of risk to some third person. Previously, in

California and other states, there had been no such duty to warn third parties, although the psychiatrist did have the right to do so to protect the public (24). If the psychiatrist has a right but not a duty to warn, then the victim may not have a cause of action to sue the psychiatrist for negligence. For example, if a psychiatrist decides a patient is dangerous and attempts to confine the patient rather than tell the third person who is endangered, then presumably he has used his judgment and performed in a nonnegligent manner. The problem with the duty to warn, as many legal and psychiatric commentators have pointed out, is that it pushes the therapist to reveal confidences in order to protect himself. In effect, it creates a conflict of interests; a situation which the law generally avoids.

In a brief submitted by a consortium of mental health professionals a number of other points were made (25). The most important was that the problems of overprediction and false positives would cause psychotherapists to reveal patient confidences to third parties with great damage done to the confidentiality of psychotherapy and to the detriment of patients who, when viewed statistically, rarely commit violent acts. Indeed, the duty to warn might be a counterproductive social policy because if therapists have a duty to warn third persons, then they probably also have a duty to tell their patients in advance of this requirement (26), and this would make potentially dangerous persons unwilling to explore and examine their violent impulses in psychotherapy.

There is a crucial empirical question involved in all of this kind of civil liability that psychiatrists may have for violent activities of their patients. Based on my own review of the relevant literature (27), I am convinced that therapists are unable to predict dangerousness with a degree of accuracy sufficient to impose on them a duty to warn third parties; most authorities agree with that conclusion. However, a few psychiatrists are convinced that they can and do accurately predict dangerousness (28). If they are correct, then a court can sensibly impose a duty and hold therapists liable for failing to predict and prevent violence.

Liability for Sexual Activity

Dr. William Masters, the noted sex researcher, has suggested that any therapist who exploits the power and position of his professional status to have sexual intercourse with a patient should be charged with rape:

We feel that when sexual seduction of patients can be firmly established by due legal process, regardless of whether the seduction was initiated by the patient or the therapist, the therapist should initially be sued for rape rather than for malpractice; i.e., the legal process should be criminal rather than civil. Few psychotherapists would be willing to appear in court on behalf of a colleague and testify that the sexually dysfunctional patient's facility for decision making could be considered normally objective when he or she accepts sexual submission after developing extreme emotional dependence on the therapist (29).

There are in fact three possible legal sanctions against sex between therapist and patient. First, there are the various statutes of the criminal law, including rape and rape by fraud or coercion; the latter at least theoretically might be applicable to the situations Dr. Masters has in mind. Second, there are tort actions, including malpractice, in the civil courts. Third, there is revocation of license to practice by the medical board of licensure. Beyond these legal approaches the effect of ethical sanctions by professional associations, societies, and institutions could limit career opportunities, patient referrals, and staff privileges at various institutional facilities.

For the purpose of this discussion, I shall assume that the problem is one of male therapists being involved with female patients. However, the legal ramifications are by no means confined to that area; indeed, one of the most well known criminal cases involves homosexual activities between a male physician and his male adolescent patients (30). Second, I have omitted the legal problems of utilizing sexual surrogates other than the psychotherapist in sexual treatment. Third, I have elected as a matter of personal judgment not to use the names of psychotherapists or patients despite the fact that the records are in most instances in the public domain. The references provide adequate citations for the interested reader to track down the cases.

My review of the legal literature suggests that the criminal courts have been extremely reluctant to adopt Dr. Masters' policy. Rape charges apparently are rarely brought and rarely do they stick. The few reported cases involve some element of physical coercion or force rather than the kind of psychological coercion Dr. Masters reported as typical. In fact, where psychiatrists have been

255

convicted of rape, sexual assault, etc., their behavior has been egregious by almost any moral or legal standard.

Thus an East Coast psychiatrist who gave his patients electric shock treatment and/or injections of hypnotic drugs and then had intercourse with them was convicted and served time in prison. Similarly, a West Coast psychiatrist who had intercourse with a sixteen year old girl referred to therapy for promiscuity was prosecuted for and convicted of statutory rape (32).

In contrast to these cases, when a legally competent patient is told that sexual intercourse is to be administered as therapy, and the patient consents, the prevailing judicial opinions are that there is no rape for there has been neither force nor fraud (33). However, a few states have passed statutes which specifically encompass Dr. Masters' moral judgment. The clearest example is Michigan which has adopted the following statutory language defining coercion in rape:

> When the actor engages in the medical treatment or examination of the victim in a manner or for purposes which are medically recognized as unethical or unacceptable (34).

Under this statute sex as therapy might be construed as rape. Ohio has adopted even broader statutory language that would inculpate psychotherapists for the lesser offense of sexual battery. The Ohio statute reads:

> The offender knowingly coerces the other person to submit by any means that would prevent resistance by a person of ordinary resolution (35).

Although the criminal law has been invoked almost not at all when a psychotherapist exploits the transference for sexual gratification but does not claim that the sexual activity is treatment, this Ohio statute might be applicable if prosecutors and juries believed that transference creates a coercive relationship.

Summing up, without new criminal statutes, criminal charges of rape or related sexual offenses against psychotherapists who exploit their patients are a remote possibility at best.

Let me then turn to the civil area, which involves suits for damages and particularly malpractice. Although it may be an unimportant professional distinction, it is as we have already noted significant to the legal cases whether the sexual activity is designated as therapy or not. If a therapist induces a patient to engage in sexual activity on the basis that it is treatment, it will be more readily considered under the rubric of malpractice. If the therapist has an affair with a patient separate from the treatment, no legal cause of action may be available. This legal distinction becomes apparent when suits are brought by husbands whose wives have been seduced by their therapists. The courts in this context seem unwilling to allow the husband's claim of malpractice; indeed most suits of this sort have failed *(36)*.

However, this legal distinction is somewhat muddied since there are cases in which judges have held that misuse of the transference is a basis for psychiatric malpractice. One Southern psychotherapist who told his patient that he was going to divorce his wife and wanted to marry her was said by the court to have engaged in "conduct below acceptable psychiatric and medical standards" *(37)*. The husband was allowed to recover the cost of his wife's hospitalization and treatment. All of the experts in that case agreed that the psychiatrist had acted out his countertransference and that his profession of love was inappropriate. Presumably, all of the experts would *a fortiori* agree with the testimony given in a recent case by Dr. Willard Gaylin that "there are absolutely no circumstances which permit a psychiatrist to engage in sex with his patient" *(38)*. All such instances constitute misuse of the transference.

Unfortunately, there are more legal complications to a civil suit of this sort than one might imagine. Many states have passed so-called heart balm statutes which bar civil liability for sexual activity—e.g., seduction, alienation of affections, or criminal conversation. It is the heart balm act which keeps the husbands from collecting. In a recent case an East Coast psychotherapist claimed that this heart balm act meant there could be no basis for a malpractice suit by the patient. The court held to the contrary that the relationship of a psychotherapist to a patient was a "fiduciary relationship" analogous to that between a guardian and his ward. Further, that "there is a public policy to protect a patient from the deliberate and malicious abuse of power and breach of trust by a psychiatrist when that patient entrusts to him her body and mind."

The judicial decision that analogized the therapist-patient relationship to the guardian-ward relationship not only undercuts the heart balm act, but also does away with the difficult problem of consent.

The facts alleged in this case were that a patient with homosexual predispositions and heterosexual anxiety was induced to have repeated sex with her psychiatrist as a form of therapy *(39)*. There is in this case, as in all sexual situations that take place in private, the problem of corroborating evidence for the patient's testimony. Ordinarily in such cases testimony as to similar conduct by the psychiatrist could be excluded, but here the psychiatrist claimed to be impotent. Therefore the patient was able to offer the testimony of three other women patients, two of whom reported similar sexual experiences with the psychiatrist and one who described blatant and inappropriate sexual behavior and attempted seduction by him. Some of this testimony was stricken from the record as not relevant to the time period during which the psychiatrist claimed impotence, and the psychiatrist claimed the other two patients were both suffering from erotomania *(40)*. The jury, after a lengthy trial, awarded the patient $250,000 compensatory damages and $100,000 punitive damages. But these huge awards did not remain in effect.

The reasons are quite complex and I will summarize and highlight what I take to be important. First, the therapist's malpractice insuror refused to defend him, leaving the therapist to support three years of litigation on his own. However, once the damage judgment was awarded, the patient sued the insurance company for part of the damages and settled for $50,000. The therapist pursued his own legal appeals, and in a subsequent decision, a higher court dismissed the punitive damages of $100,000 and reduced the compensation award to no more than $25,000. At most, therefore, the patient will receive $75,000 less legal fees. Furthermore, despite the significant holdings in this case, the decision does not clarify the malpractice implications of sex between therapist and patient for the following reasons.

There were two lines of defense that this therapist did not assert. First, that the patient had freely consented to an affair and had known it was not therapy. Second, that he believed sex between doctor and patient was therapeutic, and that the patient had been told in advance that sexual activity would be part of the therapy—that is, she had been given full disclosure before the transference developed. Instead, the therapist insisted that the patient had a psychotic transference. Both of the defenses I enumerated, though unacceptable to the mental health profession, may still be appropriate defenses in a court of law.

Nonetheless, insurors have responded as if sex between therapist and patient is a clear instance of malpractice. Insurors have been quick to settle claims. The result is that malpractice rates for all will escalate while the offending therapists are protected from the adversities concomitant to a trial.

The American Psychological Association has pursued an alternate avenue—they have obtained insurance that excludes liability for sexual activity. Whether the adverse effects of sex between therapist and patient should be compensable by an insurance policy is, I think, a debatable question.

The problem of estimating the damages suffered in these malpractice suits was reflected in the appellate decision in the case I have been discussing. The court reduced the $350,000 award to $25,000. There was one dissenting judge who was prepared to argue that there was no malpractice and no damages. He argued that the civil courts were not the place for dealing with the problems of sex therapy or sex between doctor and patient. As he put it:

> Although the plaintiff was suffering from a number of emotional problems, her competency was never placed in issue.

Thus he rejected the fiduciary theory, insisting that she was legally competent to consent to have intercourse. He went on:

> Is it not fair to infer therefore that she was capable of giving a knowing and meaningful consent? For almost one and a half years while this "meaningful relationship" continued the plaintiff was not heard to complain. Upon the defendant terminating the relationship this law suit evolves.

Although the judge made it clear that he believed the jury finding that the psychiatrist had had intercourse with his patient, and that the psychiatrist "obviously did not help his cause by denying what the jury found to be the fact; . . . nevertheless, however ill-advised or ill-conceived was the choice of his defense, in my view this did not constitute malpractice."

> I neither condone the defendant's reprehensible conduct, nor maintain that it was not violative of his professional ethics and Hippocratic oath. . . . For violation of his Hippocratic oath, if there be any, let him suffer the sanctions of the medical ethics board or other appropriate medical authority (41).

In this disposition of turning the case over to the medical licensing board and the profession for appropriate action, the dissent was in fact joined by the majority. Said the majority:

> Sex under cloak of treatment is an acceptable and established ground for disciplinary measures taken against physicians either by licensing authorities or professional organizations (42).

Interestingly enough, the court did not foreclose the matter of whether the psychiatrist should be deprived of his license or sanctioned by his professional organization:

> Whether defendant acted in such manner as to seriously affect his performance as a practitioner in the psychiatric field should be left to these more competent fora. The only thing that the record herein supports is that his prescribed treatment was in negligent disregard of the consequences. For that and that alone he must be held liable (43).

Now, as one looks at the capability of licensing boards and professional associations that are considered the appropriate fora by this court, there is, based on my research, an almost total lack of capacity to act. Let us first consider the professional associations. They have no subpoena power, they have no expertise in criminal or other evidentiary investigation. They have neither formulated necessary procedures nor have they employed sufficient legal staff to protect the due process rights of either a therapist charged with some such act, or to protect themselves if the charged therapist sues them. Indeed, it often happens that when a therapist is charged with any ethical complaint, since his whole career is at stake, he hires a lawyer who immediately threatens to sue the society, the association, and its ethics committee who have no indemnification. Lawyers expert in private association law tell me that none of the associations have the proper machinery, and many of them behave as do the mental health professions by postponing any and all action until all legal appeals are exhausted in the criminal and/or civil area.

So, finally, we turn to the licensing boards in hope that there something can be done. The fact that a number of cases exist where licensing boards have in fact revoked licensure for sexual activity of doctors with patients suggests that there some power actually resides and is being utilized. However, the licensing board of each of the states is organized quite differently. Some have a close relationship to the medical society, others do not. Some are impotent bureaucracies reluctant to do anything, and therefore one cannot expect real consistency across the different jurisdictions. Each jurisdiction has enabling statutes that limit the scope of authority. In one Western state a doctor guilty of the grossest sexual impropriety could not have his license revoked because the only ground was grossly negligent or ignorant malpractice, while the board had found he was guilty of grossly negligent or immoral malpractice *(44)*. Licensure for the other mental health professions is so recent in its development that no pattern has yet emerged.

I have briefly described four possible avenues for punishing, disciplining, or deterring sexual activity between therapist and patient. None of these avenues seem to provide an effective system of control. In the end, in this, as in most other things, patients must depend on the decent moral character of those entrusted to treat them.

Civil Rights Liability

The most significant increases in liability arise from constitutional litigation around the civil rights of the mentally ill. The applicable law is Section 1 of the Civil Rights Act of 1871, passed in the years immediately following the Civil War. It is now known as USC Section 1983. A Section 1983 action has teeth in it as far as psychiatric liability for monetary damages is concerned. The statute reads:

> Every person who, under color of any statute, ordinance, regulation, custom or usage of any state or territory, subjects or causes to be subjected any citizen of the United States to the deprivation of any rights, privileges, or immunities secured by the Constitution and laws shall be liable to the party injured in an action at law, suit in equity, or other proper proceeding for redress.

It is under this provision of the Civil Rights Code that suits are brought for illegal arrest and detention, wire tap invasions of privacy, etc. The scope of the Section 1983 action has in the last five years been widened to include the area of mental health law. Section 1983 actions can include injunctive and declaratory relief that asks the judge to declare the civil commitment statutes unconstitutional or to order the state to stop certain practices or change them. Section 1983 actions have also, however, been pursued in the form of a personal damage action against mental health administrators and individual psychiatrists attached to state and private hospitals. The trend toward pressing for damages in civil rights litigation under Section 1983 arrived with the landmark case of *O'Connor v. Donaldson (45)*. The success of that case at the federal court level led litigating attorneys all over the country to crank out Section 1983 actions against psychiatrists. Some, but not all of these law suits ask for monetary damages.

The kinds of actions by a psychiatrist that might produce Section 1983 liability can be catagorized in the following ways: First, there are the obvious examples of psychiatrists taking the law into their own hands and detaining an individual in a mental health facility in contravention of the explicit dictates of the state's commitment statutes. Thus, in *Johnson v. Greer (46)* the administrator of a psychiatric diagnostic clinic knowingly detained a patient on his own decision for five consecutive days beyond the time of the specific commitment procedure. The Fifth Circuit Court of Appeals held that "good intentions which do not give rise to a reasonable belief that detention is lawfully required cannot justify false imprisonment" *(47)*.

But the bulk of the Section 1983 civil rights litigation for damages deals with the scope of the psychiatrists' lawful discretion to administer treatment, to order their patients' daily lives and living conditions, and to make decisions relative to the release of patients from a lawful commitment. Here it may not be obvious to psychiatrists that their actions are violating the rights of their patients. Every psychiatrist working in the public sector should know the *O'Connor v. Donaldson* standard articulated by the Supreme Court. A psychiatrist cannot continue to confine a patient who is not dangerous to himself or others and who can survive outside the hospital if he is not getting treatment *(48)*. Unfortunately, the Supreme Court did not define treatment or survival outside the hospital in any clearcut way, but I think at the very least that they were saying that a psychiatrist who retains in involuntary custodial care a nondangerous patient who can survive outside the hospital is liable for violating that patient's civil rights. Again, as psychologists and social workers assume primary care roles, they will become similarly liable.

Other cases decided at lower courts hold that a patient is entitled to protection from assaults by fellow patients *(49)*. Whether that protection can be afforded if patients also have a constitutional right to refuse treatment is problematic.

Although there is as yet no federal court which has recognized an absolute right of involuntarily committed mental patients to refuse treatment, suits are now being litigated in that area. In one Massachuetts hospital a federal court issued a temporary restraining order that requires the hospital to allow patients to refuse treatment and limits the use of seclusion. That order has apparently led to an increase in assaults. Although the right to refuse treatment is not yet clarified, courts have made it clear that the use of medication and seclusion for other than treatment reasons is a violation of patient's civil rights (50).

In *Negron v. Preiser (51)* the court threatened contempt citations against doctors who, it was alleged, were using isolation cells for punitive rather than for treatment purposes at a state hospital for the criminally insane.

Psychiatrists may also be liable for transferring inmates to seclusion or to maximum security units if it can be shown that such actions were solely because the patients were exercising their right of free speech, or because they were pursuing legal redress against the hospital or its doctors (52).

The courts have also suggested that when medication is imposed on a Christian Scientist, whose religious beliefs are protected by the free exercise clause of the First Amendment, liability under a Section 1983 action will result. *Winters v. Miller (53)* is such a case. However, despite the appellate decision, as of this writing the case had not resulted in any damages being awarded, although Ms. Winters' lawyers intend to appeal still further.

Despite all of these examples of newly defined areas of civil rights liability, very little money has changed hands as of this point in time. For example, Dr. O'Connor, who has recently died, was ordered to pay only $28,500 in compensatory damages and $10,000 in punitive damages by the jury that found that he had improperly confined Mr. Donaldson for fifteen years. Three years after that original decision, no money has changed hands, and it is possible that none will. The Supreme Court subsequently held that Dr. O'Connor's liability for damages must be construed in light of their decision in *Woods v. Strickland (54);* i.e., did Dr. O'Connor know or should he have known that his actions violated the plaintiff's constitutional rights, or did he take the action with the malicious intention to cause a deprivation of constitutional rights? The Court stressed that an official has, of course, no duty to anticipate unforeseeable constitutional developments. It is my view that Dr. O'Connor had no reason to anticipate the Supreme Court decision and therefore should not be held liable. Mr. Donaldson's lawyer claims, on the other hand, that the jury award of punitive damages makes it clear that they felt Dr. O'Connor had acted maliciously. This dispute is yet to be resolved.

However, the mental health professions cannot continue to claim ignorance of the constitutional rights I have outlined in the cases above. Future violations of rights could lead to substantial monetary damages. But there are real costs to the professions even if in the end no legal liability rests on them. Those costs relate to the very practical problems of legal representation, separate from any damage award.

Recently a rather extensive Section 1983 action was brought against psychiatrists at a hospital in Massachusetts (55). As that litigation developed, several interesting problems of legal representation arose. Psychiatric residents in the state hospital system are for tax purposes defined as students rather than employees in state statutes. The Attorney General interpreted that statute to mean that they are therefore not entitled to the benefits of legal protection from his office. He has, therefore, indicated that in all future law suits he will not provide a legal defense for psychiatric residents.

The Attorney General's withdrawal of legal representation of course creates major problems if in the next suit residents are forced to pay their own lawyers in an extended civil liberties litigation. Some residents will have malpractice insurance, but some insurors have claimed that civil rights actions under Section 1983 are not covered by medical liability insurance; thus they will provide neither legal defense nor monetary damages, if any are awarded. It is important to all mental health professionals that liability insurance includes provisions for payment of legal fees whatever provision of law the damage action is brought under.

Certain problems remain for mental health professionals working in the public sector who obtain their legal defense from the state. First, the quality of legal representation afforded to the mental health professions by attorneys general in various law suits over the past few years has often been worth what was paid for it. Second, there is an inherent conflict of interests at times between the state and the mental health professional; the attorney general is not likely to resolve such conflicts in favor of the professional. During the oral arguments before the Supreme Court in *Donaldson v. O'Connor* one of the Justices pointedly asked the State Attorney General whether he was defending the state or the psychiatrist.

Third, many states as a matter of public policy do not, in certain kinds of damages, assume the liability of a state official who violates a person's rights. In damage actions whose reimbursement is not against public policy, some states have a maximum cash amount of $10,000 beyond which they are unwilling to assume responsibility. Thus if a psychiatrist or psychologist at a state hospital is sued in a Section 1983 action, or even in a simple malpractice suit, he might really be well advised to hire his own lawyer to defend him for the surplusage. Given the flood of litigation and the vulnerability to suit of state hospital employees, the state legislatures should consider providing them with some greater financial protection; perhaps private liability coverage should become a perquisite.

It is obvious that the mental health professionals, and particularly those working in the public sector, are moving into a mine field of liability and many seem unaware of the risks. The purpose of this chapter is simply to alert the profession to these increased risks. We can only cope if we familiarize ourselves with the strange legal terrain, and those in the public sector must insist that they be provided with adequate liability coverage and with expert legal advice to guide them through this dangerous terrain with the least possible cost to patient care and professional integrity.

References

1. D.J. Dawidoff, *The Malpractice of Psychiatrists* (Springfield: Thomas, 1973).
2. The Foreword to Dawidoff's book acknowledges the relative paucity of appellate cases at pages vii and viii. In accord is the Introduction at page xi. Finally, a quick review of the author's "Index to Cases" reveals the same lack of appellate cases.
3. T.A. Szasz, *Law, Liberty, and Psychiatry* (New York: Macmillan, 1973).
4. *See* pages 100, 106, and 127 in Dawidoff, *supra,* note 1.
5. Title 43, Sec. 1983, of the *U.S. Code,* text cited herein will apparently form the basis for more and more law suits in the psychiatric malpractice area because of the increasing state involvement in the administration of mental health facilities and programs.
6. Even conceding that psychiatry is not exactly the prototype of medical science, it is not necessarily true that psychiatry may not be examined by conventional malpractice techniques. Malpractice itself and the tort propositions that underlie its scope are elastic enough to be applied to psychiatry.
7. *For a general discussion,* see Dawidoff, *supra,* note 1, pp. 109-126, and cases cited therein; *See also, Weinshenk v. Kaiser Foundation Hospital,* No. 40027 (Cal. Super. Ct., Alameda Cty., 1971).
8. *For a general discussion,* see Dawidoff, *supra,* note 1, pp. 135-141, and cases cited therein; *See also, Lester v. Aetna Casualty and Surety Co.,* 240 F.2d 676 (5th Cir. 1957).
9. *For a general discussion,* see Dawidoff, *supra,* note 1, pp. 129-134, and cases cited therein; *See also, Kent v. Whitaker,* 58 Wash. 2d 569, 364 p.2d 556 (1961).
10. As a basis for liability, *see* Restatement Torts (2d) Sec. 402A and the commentary therein; *See also, Tinnerholm v. Parke Davis and Co.,* 285 F. Supp. 432 (1968); *Reyes v. Wyeth Lab.,* 498 F. 2d 1264 (1974).
11. *See Generally* Physician liability for drug reactions, 213 *JAMA* 2143 (1970), and W.L. Prosser, *Law of Torts* (St. Paul: West Publishing, 1971), Sec. 32; *See also, Mitchell v. Robinson,* 334 SW 2d 11 (1960) and *Marchese v. Monaco,* 145 A 2d 809 (1958).
12. *See* Prosser, *supra,* note 11, Sec. 9 and 32, for battery and negligence basis for liability.
13. L.S. Goodman, and A. Gilman, *The Pharmacological Basis of Therapeutics* (New York: Macmillan, 1970), p. 169; *See also,* Side effects of phenothiazine drugs, 5422 Brit. Med. Jour., 1412 (5/12/64).

14. Goodman and Gilman, *supra,* note 13, pp. 168-169 and Freedman, Kaplan, and Sadock (eds.), *Comprehensive Textbook of Psychiatry* (Baltimore: Williams and Wilkins, 1974), p. 1932.
15. *Physicians' Desk Reference* is a compilation of materials furnished by drug companies concerning their products. It is in essence a manual for physicians to consult when wishing to obtain information on a drug. It permits us to assess exactly what drug companies were telling physicians about their products.
16. *Koury v. Follo,* 158 S.E. 2d 548 (N.C. 1968); *Sharpe v. Pugh,* 155 S.E. 2d 108 (N.C. 1967).
17. *Canterbury v. Spence,* 464 F. 2d 772 (D.C. Cir. 1972), at 789; *Salgo v. Stanford University Board of Trustees,* 154 Cal. App. 2d 560, 317 A 2d 170 at 181, (1957).
18. C. Fried, *Medical Experimentation* (New York: North-Holland, 1974), p. 22.
19. Faurby viewed the symptoms of TD as constituting a separate disorder that he proceeded to name tardive dyskinesia. *See G.E. Crane,* Tardive dyskinesia in patients treated with major neuroleptics, 124 *Am. J. Psych.* 8 (February 1968) Supp. 40-47, note 12.
20. *Kendrick v. United States,* 82 F Supp. 430 (D.C. Ala.).
21. *Austin W. Jones Co. v. State,* 122 Me. 214, 119 A 577 (1923). *Merchants National Bank and Trust Co., v. U.S.,* 272 F. Supp. 409 (D.ND. 1967).
22. *Benjamin v. Havens,* 60 Wash. 2d 1962, 373 P. 2d 109 (1962). *Wood v. Samaritan Institution,* Inc., 26 Cal. 2d 847, 161 p. 2d 556 (1945).
23. *Tarasoff v. Regents of University of California,* 13 Cal. 3d 177, 529 p. 2d 553, 118 Cal. Reptr. 129 (1974), rehearing granted, March 12, 1975, reconsidered July 1, 1976.
24. American Psychiatric Association, *The Principles of Medical Ethics* (1973), Sec. 9.
25. Brief of Amicus Curiae, The American Psychiatric Association, *Tarasoff v. Regents of the University of California,* Supreme Court of California, No. 23042, rehearing from 13 Cal. 3d 177, 529 p. 2d 553.
26. J.G. Fleming, and B. Maximov, The patient or his victim: The therapist's dilemma, 60 *Cal. L. Rev.* 1025, at 1066 (1974).
27. A.A. Stone, chapter 2, Dangerousness, pp. 25-40.
28. See letter to the Editor by Augustus Kinzel, 132 *Am. J. Psych.* 1331 (1975).
29. W. Masters and V. Johnson, Principles of sex therapy. 133 *Am. J. Psych.* 548-554 (1976).
30. J. Goldstein, R. Schwartz, and A. Dershowitz, *Criminal Law: Theory and Process* (New York: Free Press, 1974), pp. 3-23.
31. Reference omitted.
32. 340 P 2nd, 299 (1959).
33. Note; Recent Statutory Developments in the Definition of Forcible Rape. 61 *Va. L. Rev.* 1500 (1975).
34. Michigan General Law A. Sec. 750. 520b (f). This places definition of rape in the hands of expert witnesses.
35. Ohio General L.A. Sec. 2907. 03.
36. 162 NW 2nd 313 (1968).
37. 263 S 2nd 256 (1972).
38. Plaintiff's brief in case cited in note 39.
39. 366 N.Y.S. 2nd 297, 300-301 (1975).
40. *Id.,* Slip Opinion No. 458, dissenting memorandum of Judge Riccobono, pp. 1 and 2.

41. *Id.,* Concurring memorandum, Judge Markowitz, p. 4.
42. *Id.*
43. There have been at least eight reported appeals from license revocation that were grounded on sexual impropriety by a physician. Several are by psychiatrists. 22 Cal. Rep. 419 (1962); 116 NW 2nd, 797 and 402 p. 2nd 606.
44. 15 ALR 3, 1173.
45. *O'Connor v. Donaldson,* 422 U.S. 563 (1975).
46. *Johnson v. Greer,* 477 F. 2d 101 (5th Cir. 1973).
47. *Id.,* at 106.
48. *Supra,* note 45, at 576.
49. *Blair v. Anderson,* 325 A. 2d 94 (Del., 1974). *Muniz v. U.S.,* 280 F. Supp. 542 (N.D. N.Y. 1968). *University of Louisville v. Hammock,* 127 Ky. 564, 106 S.W. 219 (1907).
50. *Nelson v. Heyne,* 491 F. 2d 352 (7th Cir. 1974). *NYARC v. Rockefeller,* 357 F. Supp. 752 (E.D.N.Y. 1973).
51. *Negron v. Preiser,* 382 F. Supp. 535 (S.D.N.Y. 1974).
52. *Brown v. Schubert,* 389 F. Supp. 281 (E.D. Wisc. 1975). *Cruz v. Beto,* 405 U.S. 319 (1972). *Johnson v. Avery,* 393 U.S. 483, 485.
53. *Winters v. Miller,* 446 F. 2d 65 (2d Cir.), cert. denied, 404 U.S. 985 (1971).
54. *Woods v. Strickland,* 420 U.S. 328 (1975).
55. *Rogers v. Macht,* CA 75-1610, hearing slated on preliminary injunction motion (Mass.).

Appendix

In the 12 months that have passed since the text was submitted for publication, the burgeoning mental health area has brought forth a mass of new materials. There have been new legislative enactments, hundreds of reported cases, thousands of publications, and innumerable changes in administration and policy. At this stage, it is not possible to review all of the developments which have come to my attention or to evaluate their impact on what has been said. However, since they can be easily cited and their essential innovations drawn to the reader's attention, I have cataloged at least some of the new legal cases which bear on the issues discussed in the preceding chapters. At the very least this catalog should bring home to the reader the ongoing ferment in the law-mental health system.

Civil Commitment

In the text I dealt at some length with *Lessard* v. *Schmidt*, which challenged many of the procedures and some of the substance of current civil commitment statutes. The impact of *Lessard* should be augmented by the similar holdings in the recent case of *Bell* v. *Wayne County General Hospital at Eloise (1)*. There a three-judge Federal court struck down the Michigan temporary commitment law for being unconstitutional on a handful of grounds. The court indicated that in order to meet constitutional standards, the commitment statute would have to be changed in the following ways: (a) It must provide for service of the commitment petition itself on the respondent himself and sufficiently in advance to permit him to evaluate the allegations and prepare his response.

(b) The respondent must be notified that he has a "right to legal counsel, and, if indigent, to appointed counsel, to assist him at every step of the commitment proceedings." The court also noted its agreement with the *Lessard* court that a guardian ad litem is not a substitute for adversary defense counsel:

> Even where an attorney is appointed guardian ad litem, his representation of the prospective patient may be inadequate since in these circumstances he usually sees his

role not as defense counsel but as a traditional guardian who determines for himself what is in the best interests of his ward and proceeds on that basis, virtually disregarding the latter's will.

(c) The statute may not provide for a prehearing determination that the respondent's condition is such that he ought not be present at the commitment hearing. He must be permitted to attend, and may be excluded only where alternatives, such as conducting the hearing at the mental health facility, have failed.

(d) The statute must provide for notice to the respondent of his right to a jury trial.

(e) The court found that under the present statute, "a person whose affliction, in the view of a given court, falls anywhere within a vast, uncontoured description of mental ills, is subject to both temporary and indefinite commitment, whether (or not) his particular ill presents a realistic threat of harm to himself or others. In our opinion, the standard of commitment for mental illness is fatally vague and overbroad." The court then cited recent Supreme Court cases implying that commitment statutes ought to require that danger to self or others and need for and amenability to treatment be balanced against the curtailment of liberty commitment represents.

(f) The law may not permit involuntary detention without a hearing for more than a short period, probably 5 days. The preliminary hearing should establish whether there is probable cause to believe that further confinement is necessary, and though it need not be as formal as a final commitment hearing, it should nevertheless provide notice of allegations, and an opportunity for the respondent to respond, with the aid of counsel. Moreover, the court rejected the possibility of even temporary commitment on any standard of mental illness lower than that required for a final adjudication.

(g) The statute may not permit "involuntary treatment of a physically intrusive nature" prior to a final adjudication of mental illness, except where "the patient is presently dangerous to himself or others ... provided such treatment is necessary to maintain physical health."

Since temporary commitment is in fact the most common legal vehicle for involuntary confinement and most often utilized in emergency situations, these procedural requirements may well create serious practical problems for psychiatric management. Many psychiatrists may be deterred from initiating commitment proceedings on appropriate patients not only because of these legally created procedural obstacles, but also because of the legal constraint on treatment. Perhaps the U.S. Supreme Court will deal with these problems; *Lessard* has now been appealed to that tribunal.

Perhaps the most significant reform in civil commitment involves its decreasing use, i.e., the move toward deinstitutionalization. As noted in the text, however, this raises new problems of community care, or of community neglect. One interesting recent case may be an omen for what is to come. In an open attempt to maintain its "desirable" atmosphere, and to prevent the influx of elderly and mentally ill persons extruded from institutions, the City of Long Beach, N.Y., enacted an ordinance prohibiting the registration in hotels and boarding homes of any person who required more or less continuous medical or psychiatric treatment. In *Stoner* v. *Miller (2)*, the court declared this ordinance unconstitutional, saying:

> It is apparent that this ordinance can effectively frustrate the movement towards deinstitutionalization in the treatment of the mentally ill, also the issues herein bear directly on the rights of citizens who are mentally ill to be treated in the least restrictive setting appropriate to their needs, and upon the right of such persons to choose their own places of residence, without unreasonable governmental interference. The State of New York . . . has begun to discharge non-violent patients from state hospitals. The social workers are attempting to place these patients in hotels best suited to their needs . . . . A reading of the ordinance indicates clearly that it is exclusionary in nature, and, therefore, a restriction on a citizen's right to travel.

The Right to Treatment

The legal "cutting edge" of mental health reform has been the concept of the right to treatment. But as recently as a year ago, there existed but one case (*Wyatt* v. *Stickney*) holding unequivocally that there was such a constitutional right, a few cases implying it (see chapter 3), one case rejecting the right (*Burnham*), and one case gainsaying it, while apparently enforcing it under the rubric "right to protection from harm" (*NYARC* v. *Rockefeller*). It can now be said that absent a definitive contrary ruling by the Supreme Court in the case of *Donaldson* v. *O'Connor (3)* now before it, the constitutional right to treatment will have become, this year, an accepted part of our legal order. Even more remarkable is the speed with which courts have extended the right beyond the civilly committed mentally ill, to apply as well to other classes of persons.

a. *Involuntarily Committed Mentally Ill* — In the *Donaldson* case, the Fifth Circuit Court of Appeals upheld a jury verdict of $38,500 in damages against attending psychiatrists and hospital officials for denial of the mentally ill plaintiff's right to treatment. In a strongly worded opinion, the Court held that "where a nondangerous patient is involuntarily civilly committed to a State mental hospital, the only constitutionally permissible purpose of confinement is to provide treatment, and that such a patient has a constitutional right to such treatment as will help him to be cured or to improve his mental condition."

Yet *Donaldson* is in many ways atypical of the right-to-treatment cases. First and most significant is the fact that it was not a class action seeking to upgrade conditions, but an individual suit for money damages for past denial of the right. The plaintiff was a Christian Scientist who had refused medication and electroshock. These complexities make *Donaldson* a unique case. Perhaps partly for this reason the American Psychiatric Association in its amicus curiae brief in *Donaldson* urged that the Supreme Court affirm the concept of the right to treatment, while setting aside the monetary verdict against the individual physicians.

Given the peculiarities of the *Donaldson* case, it may be that even after the Supreme Court's decision the most persuasive law on the general right to treatment will remain the Fifth Circuit's forceful opinion in *Wyatt* v. *Aderholt* (4). The court affirmed each and every ruling of the lower court in *Wyatt* and correspondingly reversed the holdings of *Burnham* v. *Department of Public Health* (5)—that there is a right to treatment for civilly committed mentally ill and retarded persons, that courts are competent to evaluate the adequacy of treatment, that a class action seeking a mandatory injunction is a proper method of enforcing the right because of the absence of other adequate legal remedies, and that the court has the power to order specific changes requiring the expenditure of funds by the State. And in one important respect, the Court of Appeals went beyond the District Court. Whereas the lower court had provided little analysis of why there is a right to treatment, and had implicitly relied primarily on a theory that treatment is the quid pro quo for society's right to confine those it seeks to be protected from, the Court of Appeals said that the right to treatment would adhere even when the motive for commitment is the benevolent parens patriae function. It said:

> We find it impossible to accept the Governor's underlying premise that the "need to care" for the mentally ill—and to relieve their families, friends, or guardians of the

271

burdens of doing so—can supply a constitutional justification for civil commitment . . . . The state interest thus asserted may be, strictly speaking, a "rational" state interest. But we find it so trivial beside the major personal interests against which it is to be weighed, that we cannot possibly accept it as a justification for the deprivations of liberty involved.

b. *The Mentally Retarded*—Perhaps the most important case is the continuing litigation concerning the Willowbrook State School in New York, the nation's largest institution for the mentally impaired. In the first trial of *New York State Association for Retarded Children* v. *Rockefeller (6)*, the court refused to hold that there was a constitutional right to treatment for the mentally retarded placed there by their families, since "a large part of the residents of Willowbrook entered because they had no alternative, and none have been denied a right to release." This rationale is impaired by the portions of *Wyatt* previously cited, and in any case, Judge Judd merely held that he did not need to decide the issue of the right to treatment. He did find that there was a right to protection from harm and proceeded to enforce it in detail.

In the second Willowbrook trial, just concluded, the plaintiffs sought to bring within the "protection from harm" rubric additional relief in the form of improved conditions and procedures. Their basic point was that a positively therapeutic environment is necessary to prevent harm—harm in the sense of deterioration and loss of potential for physical, intellectual, emotional, and social development. Discussions concerning the possibility of a consent decree in the Willowbrook case took place between plaintiffs' attorneys and the staffs of then Governor Wilson and present Governor Carey, though the trial was concluded and submitted to Judge Judd for decision. Prominent both in the settlement negotiations and the judge's consideration was a Joint Request for Relief Submitted by Plaintiffs and by the United States. This was an 80 page document covering some 30 categories of reforms in staffing, services, conditions, and procedures. Whatever the outcome of the Willowbrook case, this type of broad-gauged demand for change will likely characterize future right-to-treatment litigation, as plaintiffs seek to convince both courts and administrators that the right can be specifically enforced and monitored.

In *Welsch* v. *Likins (7)*, another class action case brought by mentally retarded residents of State institutions, a Minnesota Federal court reviewed virtually all the right-to-treatment cases and concluded that there was an enforceable constitutional right to treatment. It found the "quid pro quo" theory inapplicable because of the unusually ample procedural safeguards of the new Minnesota civil commitment law, but it went on to say:

> But the second major rationale does strike a responsive chord in this case. Simply put, it is that because plaintiffs have not been guilty of any criminal offense against society, treatment is the only constitutionally permissible purpose of their confinement, regardless of procedural protections under the governing civil commitment statute.

The court in *Welsch* indicated that a right-to-treatment claim can validly be grounded on the eighth amendment and *Robinson* v. *California*, on the due process clause and *Jackson* v. *Indiana*, or on the least restrictive alternative doctrine.

In *Renelli* v. *Department of Mental Hygiene* (*8*), a suit brought by a retarded child, the court said that when "someone in the Willowbrook bureaucracy decided twelve years ago that Adrienne was, in effect, a hopeless case, and no meaningful attempt was ever made to improve her condition . . . (the State violated) the duties imposed on it by both the Constitution and the Mental Hygiene Law."

There are a number of other cases involving the mentally ill or mentally retarded which have also recognized and begun to define the contours of the right to treatment. *See, e.g., Ricci* v. *Greenblatt* (*9*), *Davis* v. *Watkins* (*10*), and *Kesselbrenner* v. *Anonymous* (*11*).

c. *Juveniles*—Recent cases have also found that juvenile delinquents, "persons in need of supervision," State school residents, and other juveniles have a right to rehabilitative treatment. Many of these cases quote, and all subscribe to the basic view of *Martarella* v. *Kelley* (*12*), that:

> However benign the purposes for which members of the plaintiff class are held in custody, and whatever the sad necessities which prompt their detention, they are held in penal condition. Where the state, as parens patriae, imposes such detention, it can meet the Constitution's requirement of due process and prohibition of cruel and unusual punishment, if, and only if, it furnishes adequate treatment to the detainee . . . . Effective treatment must be the quid pro quo for society's right to exercise its parens patriae controls. Whether specifically recognized by statutory enactment or implicitly derived from the constitutional requirement of due process, the right to treatment exists.

In his thorough and learned opinion in *Martarella*, Judge Lasker affirmed the right to treatment for all nontemporary juvenile detainees, and in a supplemental order he set out specific mandatory standards including numbers and qualifications of staff, a definition of adequate treatment, and provisions for education, individual treatment plans, periodic review, recordkeeping, and appointment of an ombudsman.

In *Nelson* v. *Heyne* (*13*), the court recognized the right to treatment, established strict procedures for corporal punishment, solitary confinement, and administration of drugs, and required the development of individual treatment plans.

In *Morales* v. *Turman* (*14*), the court found that the brutal practices and degrading conditions in Texas juvenile facilities violated both the eighth amendment and the juveniles' "statutory and . . . federal constitutional 'right to treatment.'" The court entered a detailed order regulating the challenged practices and appointed an ombudsman.

Other cases which, though they do not deal with the theory of a right to treatment, reflect courts' increasing concern with placements likely to be nontherapeutic, are mentioned below in the comments on the chapter dealing with the juvenile system. However, the right-to-treatment litigation in the juvenile area seems aimed at ameliorating abuse rather than formulating treatment. I take it that this omission in some part reflects the difficulty I discussed in the text of defining treatment for juveniles whose deviance is not readily conceptualized within the "medical model."

d. *Mentally ill criminal offenders*—Similarly, there are a number of cases dealing with special offenders (and discussed below under the heading Quasi-criminal Commitment) which have at least acknowledged the duty to provide treatment. *See, e.g., Davy* v. *Sullivan*(*15*), *Gomes* v. *Gaughan* (*16*), and *Stachulak* v. *Coughlin* (*17*).

United States v. *Pardue* (*18*) is a case revealing the frustration of a judge in attempting to find a place for a dangerously mentally ill offender, without sacrificing either the right to treatment or society's safety. The court said: "The plain fact of the matter is that there are no federal facilities which offer appropriate psychiatric services and adequate security for the treatment of the defendant with a mental disorder, not temporary in nature . . . ." Refusing to abandon the right to treatment, the court gave the State 30 days to find a place for the defendant, failing which he would be released.

Reynolds v. *Neill* (*19*) held that criminally committed patients have a right to treatment—and, indeed, that the Texas scheme whereby those mentally ill who are civilly committed are entitled to the highest and best medical treatment, while those criminally committed are entitled to a far lower standard, violated equal protection.

The Right to Refuse Treatment

The right to refuse treatment has received increasing judicial protection, at least where extreme procedures are involved. In a recent order in *Wyatt* v. *Aderholt* (20) the court cut short the "increasing rate" of sterilizations of mentally defective persons in Alabama's institutions by imposing a "last resort" requirement and comparatively strict procedural protections. In *Wade* v. *Bethesda Hospital* (21) it was held that liability for an involuntary sterilization may fall to the judge who ordered it without proper legal justification, and to the hospital which performed the operation. In *Mackay* v. *Procunier* (22) the court recognized as substantial the plaintiff prisoner's claim that his consent to undergo electroshock did not also authorize submitting him to experimental aversive therapy.

Perhaps most significantly, in *Winters* v. *Miller* (23), the Second Circuit Court of Appeals reversed the dismissal of a damages suit by a mental patient who was a Christian Scientist and who was subjected to medication against her wishes. It stressed that the plaintiff, though mentally ill, had never been found incompetent to decide matters such as whether to accept medication, and that with respect to a nondangerous patient, the State has no parens patriae interest in forced treatment. This case has been remanded for a new trial before Judge Judd, the same judge who is deciding the Willowbrook case.

In *Bell* v. *Wayne County General Hospital at Eloise* (24) the court declared unconstitutional various aspects of Michigan's civil commitment scheme, including involuntary treatment of persons not yet adjudicated mentally ill. It said that both due process and the right-to-privacy bar the administration of "physically intrusive forms of treatment designed to alter or modify a person's behavior"—among which the court included surgery, electroshock, and chemotherapy—before there has been a final commitment order. The only exception was where the patient was "in immediate need of treatment in order to prevent him from physically harming himself or others, provided such treatment is necessary to maintain physical health." The court did not deal with right to refuse treatment after final commitment.

Both physicians and courts may be even more influenced in the future by laws which are being enacted in an increasing number of States, granting patients at least a limited right to refuse certain treatments—usually including psychosurgery, electroshock, and experimental drugs or procedures (25). The ways in which these rights may be supervened, or adjusted to varying exigencies, remain problems for the future. The tendency of legislator and judges to lump together electroshock therapy with experimental procedures and psychosurgery has caused great consternation among psychiatrists.

Institutional Peonage

In at least one new reported case, *Weidenfeller* v. *Kidulis* (26), a Federal court has unambiguously recognized as substantial each of the arguments for the patient's right to compensation for non-therapeutic labor which were advanced in the text of chapter 7. The court found that the Fair Labor Standards Act, the 13th amendment (barring "involuntary servitude") and the due process clause all provide good claims for the mental patient's right to be paid for labor performed for the benefit of the institution. Although this case involved mentally retarded patients at a privately owned for profit institution, the county welfare department paid for plaintiffs' maintenance cost; there was no mention in the opinion of any right of recoupment for wages which might be paid.

In the text it was noted that compensation suits by patients in State institutions might be hindered by the ruling of the Supreme Court in *Employees* v. *Missouri Public Health Department* (27) that States could raise the defense of sovereign immunity, and that the 11th amendment might bar any recovery against the stay in Federal court. However, in 1974, the Fair Labor Standards Act was amended, and one of the amendments purports to overrule the Missouri case so as to permit suits against the State by patients (28). At least two recent cases have proceeded with this in mind. In *Carey* v. *White* (29), a peonage suit by patients of a Delaware mental institution, the court found that plaintiffs had forceful constitutional claims for damages and injunctive relief. At first it dismissed the Fair Labor Standards Act claim but later granted reargument in light of the 1974 changes. And in *Townsend* v. *Treadway* (30), a peonage suit seeking, among other relief, damages of more than $9 million for wages due, the court recently affirmed class action status, and proceeded to conduct hearings.

In the text I warned that peonage suits might lead to the abolition of patient work rather than to the advent of compensated labor. A survey (*31*) reveals that abolition has in fact occurred in many States. Where compensation has been instituted, the number of patients working has been greatly reduced.

The Juvenile System

In discussing developments in the right to treatment, I mentioned suits to upgrade conditions in juvenile institutions in Texas (*Morales* v. *Turman*), and in Indiana (*Nelson* v. *Heyne*). I have also cited the remarkable opinions in *Martarella* v. *Kelley*, in which Judge Lasker declared unconstitutional New York's practice of detaining young Persons in Need of Supervision (PINS) in execrable, nontherapeutic facilities, ordered that some be closed and other improved.

In another case, *Sero* v. *Preiser* (*32*), Judge Lasker held that the "sole constitutional justification for imposing a longer sentence on a youthful offender than an adult for the same crime is the assurance of the 'quid pro quo' of rehabilitative treatment." He then made the interesting distinction that a separate dispositional hearing is not required when the court decides between an extended youthful offender sentence and a shorter adult one, while a separate hearing is required, under recent court rulings, when the court chooses between normal adult sentences and special sentences for sexually dangerous persons, because the special sentence involves factfinding as to a separate issue (i.e., is he a sexual deviate?) while the regular sentencing evaluation, of whether the defendant shows rehabilitative potential, is traditionally within the sentencing function. However, the court was influenced by the recent holding of the Court of Appeals for the Second Circuit that in sentencing a person eligible for treatment under the Federal Youth Corrections Act the court must make explicit findings as to whether the defendant will benefit from treatment, and must state the reasons for its findings (*33*). Thus, while some might quarrel with his conclusion that a separate hearing is not necessary, it is clear that Judge Lasker wrestled with the basic paradox of juvenile dispostions and sought by the requirement of stated reasons and a guarantee of effective treatment, to mitigate the harms of the system. As he said, "To guard against the irony of the indeterminate sentence—intended to be beneficent—becoming more burdensome than the sentence it was intended to supplant, the Constitution requires procedures which will prevent the imposition of an extended sentence for the purpose of punishment rather than rehabilitation."

Given the description in the text of the awful state of most New York juvenile institutions, it is interesting that at least a few judges have, over the past few years, refused to simply agree to placements and ignore the practical consequences. Whether these reported cases are insignificant as against the mass of routine, unreported dispositions, or whether on the contrary they represent just the tip of an iceberg of resistance by judges to commitments which betray their purpose, is not easily discerned. In either instance, these cases are worth mentioning.

In *In re I.* (*34*) the court had committed a 15-year-old girl to a State training school as a PINS. However, upon being informed that no psychotherapy was being provided, the court terminated the placement.

In *M* v. *M.* (*35*) the court found that the respondent had become too old to be treated as a PINS. However, the court took the occasion to note that "if a society confines an infant in the name of treatment and fails to provide the treatment, then the cause of detention becomes illusory and a sham." The court had suggested that the legislature might want to extend PINS dispositions to young persons up to 18 years of age. As to this suggestion, however, it has one reservation:

> In view of the inadequacy of facilities now serving the Family Court system for the jurisdiction it already has, would any useful purpose be served in extending the jurisdiction of this Court when no funds are available to match its new responsibilities? If litigants are to put their lives and expectations in the hands of this Court, would it not be incongruous to raise their hopes preparatory to a rude awakening that Society's priorities put other matters first in the allocation of available funds.

In *In re Lavette M.* (*36*) the court expressly recognized a juvenile's right to treatment, saying:

> Where the State, as *parens patriae*, involuntarily places a PINS child in a training school, it is for the purpose of individualized treatment and not mere custodial care.

Though the court denied relief on the ground that the two schools specifically in issue were being improved, it did say:

> Our decision is without prejudice to an application to the Family Court for appropriate relief should it appear at any time that adequate treatment and supervision is not being provided.

Quasi-criminal Confinement, and Rights of Mentally Ill Offenders

Each passing month brings a score of reported cases dealing with various aspects of special offender laws. A few cases are, however, of special significance.

In *Davy* v. *Sullivan* (*37*), a three-judge district court declared unconstitutional Alabama's Sexual Psychopath Law for failing to provide full due process rights for a defendant when commitment under the law can lead to a sentence longer than that for the underlying criminal offense. The court said that in Alabama's institutions there was no credible promise of treatment for such offenders, that "full and permanent recovery" was an impermissibly high standard for release which could not be required merely because commitment was by "noncriminal" procedures, and that in order to retain an offender beyond the normal criminal sentence, there must be a likelihood of conduct which is truly dangerous not just "repulsive or repugnant."

In *Stachulak* v. *Coughlin* (*38*) it was held that in order to confine a person as a sexually dangerous person, the State must prove all necessary facts beyond a reasonable doubt. These are changes compatible with recommendations made in the text.

There have also been a number of significant cases concerning the rights of mentally ill offenders in general. Increasingly, courts are acknowledging that "treatment" facilities for the mentally impaired offender may not be an unmitigated boon, and that the circumstances of confinement must be more closely scrutinized than in the past.

In *Reynolds* v. *Neill* (*39*) the court made careful judgments on three important issues. First, it ruled that equal protection was not violated by the difference between Texas' criminal commitment proceeding where the defendant bears the burden of proving his mental illness, where this issue may be raised only by the defendant or the court, and where the defendant has the right to a jury trial of his mental condition, and Texas' civil commitment process, where the State must prove that the person is mentally ill and in need of protective custody, where any "interested" person may initiate the inquiry, and where the right to a jury determination may be waived by the family. Second, it held that mentally ill offenders committed after an acquittal by reason of insanity have a right to treatment equal to those civilly committed. It said that:

Striking differences in treatment provided for criminally and civilly committed persons create a denial of due process and equal protection in that treatment is unreasonably withheld from one group of persons whose treatment goals are the same as another group . . . . There is no aspect of punishment in either commitment, and it hardly seems possible that the state can justify failing to help the criminally committed reach release goals.

Third, it found that the difference between the standard for civil release (at the discretion of the hospital) and that for criminal release (the person must convince a jury that he no longer needs protective confinement, and he may apply only once yearly) did violate equal protection. It said:

Although the state may have an interest at the time of commitment in assuring that one who has recently plead and proved his insanity is not still insane and dangerous, and thereby committing him on different standards than those used for civil commitment, this state interest dissolves once it may be determined that such patient is not dangerous. The state interest becomes even more tenuous when it becomes evident that the confined person cannot benefit from further treatment.

Chesney v. *Adams* (40) held, after *U.S. ex rel Schuster* v. *Herold*, that a prison inmate transferred to a mental institution is entitled to the full panoply of procedural rights due a free person about to be committed. The court explained:

The premise of the Second and D.C. Circuits is that commitment of a prisoner is not merely an administrative matter, within the broad and largely unreviewable discretion accorded prison officials. Rather, commitment compels prisoners to suffer additional "deprivations, hardships and indignities," . . . that make incarceration in a mental hospital significantly different from confinement in a prison. The stigma attached to the mentally ill, the restrictions and routines in a mental hospital, the possibility of emotional and psychic harm, and the increased difficulty of parole—combine to make the prisoner "twice cursed".

McAuliffe v. *Carlson* (41) declared unconstitutional as a violation of equal protection various aspects of the Connecticut scheme for commitment of offenders, including the practice of charging inmates for care and treatment if they are sent to a facility for the mentally ill.

In *Negron* v. *Preiser* (*42*) the court specifically held unconstitutional the use of seclusion cells at Matteawan, a New York institution for mentally ill offenders. The court went on to say:

> The instant case presents especially difficult problems because Matteawan is both a correctional facility and a hospital. The same behavior which in an ordinary institution would simply be a violation of stated rules, incurring defined sanctions imposed only after some fair procedure, in Matteawan is called a symptom or expression of mental illness, which is not a violation of the rules, for there are no stated rules, but which warrants a treatment on the surface resembling in every respect serious punishment in a prison.

In *Clonce* v. *Richardson* (*43*) a number of challenges to the Federal Detention Center's involuntary behavior modification program for obdurate inmates were mooted by the government's agreement to terminate the program. But the court did hold that transfer from a usual seclusion cell to the behavior modification program did constitute a major change in the conditions of confinement such as to invoke due process, and under recent court rulings, to require a prior hearing at which the inmate may be heard. The court said:

> The fact that the Bureau of Prisons may view or label a transfer to a behavioral modification program . . . as a "treatment program" for the prisoner's benefit rather than as a sanction or as some form of punishment is not a relevant factor in the determination of the due process question involved.

References

1. 384 F. Supp. 1085 (E.D. Mich. 1974).
2. 377 F. Supp. 177 (E.D.N.Y. 1974).
3. 493 F.2d 507 (5th Cir. 1974), argued and awaiting decision in the Supreme Court (see 43 U.S. Law Week 3397-3399).
4. *Wyatt* v. *Stickney*, 325 F. Supp. 781 (M.D. Ala. 1971), enforced 344 F. Supp. 373 and 344 F. Supp. 387 (M.D. Ala. 1972), aff'd sub nom. *Wyatt* v. *Aderholt*, 503 F.2d 1305 (5th Cir. 1974).
5. 349 F. Supp. 1335 (N.D. Ga. 1972), rev'd and rem. 503 F. 2d 1319 (5th Cir. 1974).
6. 357 F. Supp. 752 (E.D.N.Y. 1973).
7. 373 F. Supp. 487 (D. Minn. 1974).
8. 340 N.Y.S. 2d 498 (Sup. Ct. Richmond Co. 1973).
9. Civ. Action No. 72-469 (D. Mass. 1973) (consent judgment).
10. No. C 73-205 (N.D. Ohio, September 1974) (interim order).
11. 33 N.Y. 2d 161, 305 N.E.2d 903 (1973).
12. 349 F. Supp. 575, 585, 600 (S.D.N.Y. 1972), enforced 359 F. Supp. 478 (S.D.N.Y. 1973).
13. 355 F. Supp. 451 (N.D. Inc. 1972), aff'd 491 F. 2d 352 (7th Cir. 1974), cert. den. U.S. See also *Collins* v. *Bensinger*, 374 F. Supp. 273 (N.D. Ill. 1974).
14. 364 F. Supp. 166 (E.D. Texas 1973).
15. 354 F. Supp. 1320 (M.D. Ala. 1973) (three-judge court).
16. 471 F.2d 794 (1st Cir. 1973).
17. 364 F. Supp. 686 (N.D. Ill. 1973).
18. 354 F. Supp. 1377 (D. Ct. 1973).
19. 381 F. Supp. 1374 (N.D. Texas 1974) (three-judge court).
20. 368 F. Supp. 1282 (M.D. Ala. 1973), Supp. order, 368 F. Supp. 1283 (J.D. Ala. 1974).
21. 356 F. Supp. 380 (S.D. Ohio 1973).
22. 477 F. 2d 877 (9th Cir. 1973).
23. 446 F. 2d 65 (2d Cir. 1971), cert, den. 404 U.S. 985.
24. 384 F. Supp. 1085 (E.D. Mich. 1974).
25. See, e.g., *Cal. Welf. and Inst'ns Code* sec. 5325 (f)-(g) (West Supp. 1974) (shock treatment and lobotomy); *Ga. Code Ann.* sec. 88-502.3 (a) (1971) (written consent required for therapy which is not recognized as standard); *Idaho Laws* 379 (right to "refuse specific modes of treatment"); *N.Y. Mental Hygiene Law* sec. 15.03 (b) (4) (McKinney Supp. 1973) (surgery, electroshock, major medical treatment, or experimental drugs or procedures); *N.C. Gen. Stat.* sec. 122-55.6 (1974) (nonemergency surgery, electroshock, or experimental drugs, or procedures); *Wash. Rev. Code Ann.* sec. 71.05.370 (7), (9) (Supp. 1974) (surgery or electroshock).
26. 380 F. Supp. 445 (E.D. Wis. 1974).
27. 411 U.S. 279, 93 S. Ct. 1614 (1973).
28. See 29 U.S.C. sec 216, as amended by public law 93-259 sec. 6 (d) (1), 25 (c), 26.
29. 375 F. Supp. 1327 (D. Del. 1974).

30. CCH Labor Cases (75LC) No. 33, 187 (M.D. Tenn. 1975).
31. 5 *Behavior Today* 344 (1974).
32. 372 F. Supp. 663 (S.D.N.Y. 1974).
33. See *United States* v. *Kaylor*, 491 F.2d 1133 (2d Cir. 1974).
34. 316 N.Y.S. 2d 356 (Family Ct. Queens Co. 1970).
35. 336 N.Y.S. 2d 304 (Family Ct. Bronx Co. 1972).
36. 35 N.Y. 2d 136, 359 N.Y.S. 2d 20 (Ct. of Appeals 1974).
37. 354 F. Supp. 1320 (M.D. Ala 1973).
38. 369 F. Supp. 628 (N.D. Ill. 1973).
39. 381 F. Supp. 1374 (N.D. Texas 1974).
40. 377 F. Supp. 887 (D. Ct. 1974).
41. 377 F. Supp. 996 (D. Ct. 1974).
42. 382 F. Supp. 535 (S.D.N.Y. 1974).
43. 379 F. Supp. 338 (W.D. Mo. 1974).

Index